NO LONGER HER(E)

A WOMAN'S JOURNEY THROUGH BREAKUPS, REINVENTION AND THE SEARCH FOR HOME

A MEMOIR

CONNIE KULCZYCKI

BOSS
Being of Sacred Service
BOOKS

BOSS
Being of Sacred Service
BOOKS
Published worldwide by:
BOSS (Being of Sacred Service) Books
www.bossbookspublishing.com
Toronto ✦ Tulum

Text © CONNIE KULCZYCKI 2026

The moral rights of the author have been asserted.

A catalogue record for this book is available from the Library Archives Canada.

Paperback ISBN: 978-1-997765-02-8
Ebook ISBN: 978-1-997765-01-1
Audio ISBN: 978-1-997765-03-5

For McDreamy — you were the one I thought I'd spend forever with, but instead, you gave me forever with *myself*. Thank you for teaching me presence, for showing me how to savor the moments we're given and for being a part of the journey that led me back to me.

TABLE OF CONTENTS

FOREWORD

I HAVE BEEN TO many funerals lately, and they have all been for myself.

Not in the literal sense, of course. But in the quiet, soul-deep moments where old versions of me took their final breath. Where I stood at the edge of who I once was, threw flowers on the grave and whispered a soft goodbye.

This is a story of heartbreak and grief — not just the grief of losing others, but of losing parts of myself. Of releasing identities, expectations and dreams that no longer fit. It's not a traditional grief saga. It's an unspooling, a remembering, a reclamation.

Though the roots of this reckoning reach all the way back to childhood in Chicago, Illinois, United States, the real transformation began in my mid-twenties — when the picture-perfect life I had built cracked open. The Man in Finance cheated. Everything I thought I knew about love and security collapsed. Then came the whirlwind: marriage to GI Joe, moves across the globe, a divorce and what felt like a hundred reinventions of self.

But the true breaking — and the true becoming — happened in my early thirties, when the pieces I had so carefully put back together shattered once more. The career, the heart homes, the hard-won healing, the partnership with Mc-Dreamy, the identity I thought I'd finally arrived at, all of it came undone.

And yet, that destruction made space. For divine truth and grace and growth.

This is not a story about having it all figured out. This is a story about learning to live through the mess. About choosing yourself, again and again, even when it breaks your heart to do so.

Welcome on in.

WHO THIS IS FOR

There are a lot of reasons why I feel called to share my story — but at the heart of it, the act of writing has always been my most powerful therapy. It's how I make sense of my emotions. It's how I untangle the chaos and find the meaning beneath the mess. Whether through blog posts, long-winded Instagram captions or scribbled journal entries, writing has been my most trusted companion.

I dreamed of being a published author since early childhood. One of my favorite memories is of "Publishing House" — a program run by the Parent Teacher Association (PTA) moms at my grade school. Every other week, they'd come in and help us edit our stories and laminate the pages to create a bound "book." While most kids were casually participating, I treated it like my personal publishing deal. I wrote as many stories as my little brain and cramping hand could manage — collecting discarded postcards, old computer paper and junk mail from around the house to fuel my next "release." Ultimately, my mini masterpieces suffered the same fate as many indie authors — they sat on a shelf only appreciated by my parents and the dust bunnies. But a seed had been planted, nonetheless.

Now I've finally written my first adult "release" and I've realized something essential about the process: this book isn't just for me.

It's for the one still sitting in the thick of it — feeling unsure, ungrounded, unrecognizable to themselves. It's for the person quietly questioning the life they were told they're supposed to want and not knowing who to talk to about their itch for different, for other. It's for the ones who don't quite know where they belong, but know in their bones they're meant for more.

I've found, again and again, that when I allow myself to be fully seen, it gives others permission to do the same. Vulnerability is a bridge and my hope is that these words and pages help someone feel a little less alone and a little more seen as they cross their own threshold.

This is something I care deeply about — not just the writing, but the *why* behind it. In a world where we're subtly and overtly asked to shrink, silence ourselves and conform, I offer this book as a quiet rebellion. A reminder that your voice matters. That your truth matters. That playing small is not the medicine this world needs.

Let these pages be a hand on your back when things get hard. Let them be a reminder that you're not alone. I'll be here — not only as a voice of support but as a friend. Because it took me far too long to trust myself on this journey, to trust those surrounding me. And while I know that was part of the path I had to walk, *I'd love to help you collapse time, to be a catalyst for your own self-trust to rise faster, steadier and stronger.*

BUT WHO WANTS TO TALK ABOUT HEARTACHE?

Wandering the colorful streets of Mexico City, I first described this book to a friend and I called it — a journey to self-trust through breakups and grief. Confused, she quietly asked, "Why grief? Doesn't that carry a negative connotation? Unless you're telling some kind of hero's journey where it all works out in the end?"

That question stopped me. Because we're so conditioned to seek resolution, to tie everything up with a bow. We're taught to only dip into pain if there's a happy ending waiting for us on the other side. "Otherwise, what's the point of the story?"

As street vendors with carts full of churros and cigarettes pushed past us and dogs barked their greeting across the tree-lined path of Avenida Amsterdam, I slowed my steps and turned to her. "Have you ever read When Things Fall Apart by Pema Chödrön?"

"No, I don't think so." she replied, still dubious about my breakup and heartache theme.

"In it, she says *"Hopelessness means that we no longer have the spirit for holding our trip together. We no longer have to keep the pieces together. We just let them fall apart."* My life has fallen apart in slow, relentless ways and every time I grasped for the structure I used to rely on — relationships, jobs, familiar friend groups — it was gone. And I know what it's like to melt into a pool of hopelessness and broken heartedness. But there's power in being there. And there's power in what comes next. So while grief may not be sexy, the shattering and the aftermath is so damn beautiful."

My friend was silent and I chewed on the quote, remembering how I'd felt when I first read it, like no amount of yellow highlighter could do it justice. It was like Pema had reached into my ribcage and held my heart. And that's what I had been doing, unknowingly — gripping, clinging, forcing things to stay intact that were already trying to dissolve. The version of myself I worked so hard to become. The life I swore was the right one. The identity I crafted from perfection, productivity and performance.

And I was so, so tired. My young body felt like it was hit by a bus every morning when I got out of bed and no amount of medical grade skincare could hide the circles of doubt under my eyes.

I was so caught up in the chaos of the breakdown that I couldn't see — maybe I wasn't failing, maybe I was finally getting it right.

Maybe letting it all fall apart wasn't the end. Maybe it was the beginning.

Maybe it was the beginning of a chapter where I didn't act and actually just existed as myself. In middle school, high school and college, I played the part. I talked in other people's words, mimicked their actions, borrowed their opinions. I silently studied the way they dressed and styled their hair so I could mirror it and blend in. Belonging felt like something I had to earn by erasing the parts of me that didn't match. So when I began my travel chapter in 2017, I didn't realize that I'd have to part with and grieve those old selves in order to make space for the real me — the one I'd spent so long repressing.

THE EMOTIONAL SCORPIO

Grieving has always come easily to me. I wasn't someone who cried in public as a child — even though I've always had a flair for the dramatic — but once I was alone in my room, I'd fling myself onto my purple satin comforter and let it all pour

out. Full-body sobs, performed for an imaginary camera, capturing the depths of my despair. And when it wasn't sadness,
it was performance — dancing around with a hairbrush mic,
screaming the latest S Club 7 lyrics, or reenacting conversations with friends, parents, soccer coaches, testing new scripts
to see how I could shift the outcome. I've long attributed my
emotional depth to my Scorpio moon, but what I've had to
learn is how to hold that intensity without letting it drown me
— how to honor the release without letting the sadness become who I am.

And now, in this moment, as I grieve a partnership that
once felt like my future — the final piece of the life I thought
I had figured out — it only feels right that this book walks the
same path I'm walking. Not a retrospective memoir with tidy
answers and perfect hindsight. But a real-time, in-process story
of unbecoming and becoming. Of loss, yes. But more than that
— of return.

HOUSEKEEPING

And now, a bit of housekeeping — because I imagine
some of you fancy yourselves amateur sleuths. I've changed the
names of the people in this book. Not because I'm hiding, but
because I'm honoring boundaries — theirs and mine. This is
my story to tell. And while I know I have every right to share
it as it unfolded through my eyes, I want to be clear: I hold
no animosity towards the people I've crossed paths with, even
those who may be perceived to have hurt me. I was an active
participant in every chapter of my life — even when I forgot I
had the pen in my hand. And because of that, I take full own-
ership of my actions.

You may very well be able to piece together who's who, but

I ask that you don't get stuck there. Instead, follow my lead — hold love, compassion and gratitude in your heart for each of them. They were my mirrors, my teachers. And the lessons they brought were exactly the ones I needed.

That said, some of what I share may be surprising and uncomfortable. But please know this: I've already done the heavy lifting — the shame, the guilt, the anger. I've carried it, sat with it, worked through it and let most of it go. I've forgiven myself, even when I tried to convince myself I didn't deserve it. That doesn't mean I'm perfect or finished — only that I'm choosing to walk forward with intention and integrity.

Now, if you're still with me — let's take a trip.

One that spans years, countries, heartbreaks and rebirths. One where the destination isn't a place, but a homecoming. Let's begin.

ONE

BETWEEN A STEAK AND
A HARD PLACE

O UR FIRST DEPARTURE gate isn't a gleaming terminal in a far-off city, but a cornfield-flanked university in the American Midwest. A school of 2,500 students. It was here, late in my sophomore year, that I met the Man in Finance.

At 20, I had barely cracked 100 pounds, but that didn't mean I wasn't strong — I had played elite-level soccer through high school before burning out at 18. In college, I threw myself into CrossFit, yoga and running instead. My highlighted blonde hair swept the tips of my shoulder blades and hung stick-straight, though I was always fluffing it for volume. I paired every bodycon skirt with four-inch heels, trying to look older, more put together, more experienced — trying to belong. I filled my closet with all of the hottest trends, inviting others to "Borrow whatever they liked!" I'd been loosely raised Catholic, and while I had started to question the rules and rigidity of religion, some ideas still held a quiet grip on me — especially the ones about sex, shame and what made a girl "good."

Back in high school, I was always reaching for something

else to make me seem older, more experienced than I really was. I lost my virginity to a soccer player a year older, then dated one a year younger — a relationship that ended just before I left for university, when he told me he didn't love me anymore. That loss hollowed me. And when he ended up at a college near mine, we slipped back into old patterns. When I started my sophomore year, we were tangled in a cycle of crisis and codependency — and one night, there was a suicide scare. I was the one who talked him down. I stayed calm. I made the calls.

But being so young, I didn't know how to carry the weight of that moment. So I pushed it down. Pretended I was fine. A few weeks later, after too many shots and too little sleep, I landed in the hospital with an IV strapped to my arm — my body was keeping score, even when my mind refused to.

So by the time I met the Man in Finance, I wasn't just a girl looking for connection. I was trying to prove she could be chosen. That she was worth stability. Worth staying for. That not saving myself for marriage wouldn't come back and bite me in the ass. I was a girl looking for the fairytale relationship I grew up being told would complete my life.

The Man in Finance was two years older. On the surface, he looked the part — clean-shaven face, collared polos and a calm, curated demeanor that suggested direction and dependability. He had the kind of body you'd expect from someone clinging to the glory days of college football — bulked up, a little too rigid, striving to hold onto something. He lived off-campus in a house that, by college standards, was considered "nice" — scuffed linoleum floors, hand-me-down furniture from former athletes and a basement bar that had absorbed more spilled beer and secrets than light.

He was charming. Polished. Confident in a way that made you think he had a five-year plan — and that I might be lucky enough to be part of it. The finance major, the wardrobe, the self-assured smile — it was all part of the persona. A quiet insecurity, carefully masked. I didn't see it then. I only saw certainty. I saw stability. I saw someone who made the next step feel clear.

And that felt adult.

We had the kind of college relationship that looked polished from the outside — matching formal wear, tagged photos, carefully crafted captions, post-grad plans. But behind closed doors, it was a different story: sloppy drunk nights, next-morning amnesia, apologies that came too late or not at all. Fights swept under the rug. Feelings buried beneath performative affection. From a distance, we sparkled. But up close, we had begun to tarnish.

The summer going into my senior year, I was working as a marketing intern for the local minor league baseball team. I was living in a house just off-campus while the Man in Finance had moved into an apartment in the neighboring town. One afternoon, as I organized the day's promotional giveaway, my phone buzzed in the back pocket of my jean shorts.

"Hey girl…"

My stomach dropped. My eyes blurred. That phrase was never followed by anything good.

I stepped away from the table, heart pounding, as a flurry of texts flooded in. Friends asking if we were still together. Saying they thought I should know — he'd been out the night before and had tried to take one of my sorority sisters home, that they'd seen his profile on Tinder recently. I stood there frozen, gripping my phone with trembling hands, blinking hard to keep the tears from falling. The sun was beating down, the crowd was gathering and I was stuck in place.

I fired off a quick text: "Did this happen? Tell me the

truth." Then I shoved my phone back into my pocket and made it through the game on autopilot. Afterward, I drove straight to his apartment, rage bubbling just beneath the surface. We exploded the moment I walked through the door — yelling, blaming, crying. And then, as always, we collapsed into each other. Sex as apology. Silence as resolution. By the next morning, we were dressed and smiling for brunch with friends — playing the part, pretending everything was fine.

We kept smiling through the cracks until he moved back to Chicago midway through my senior year. While visiting over the holiday break, I noticed him angling his phone away from me at the club — subtle, but not subtle enough. My gut told me something was off.

When we got home and he quickly passed out, reeking of vodka, I crept out of the bedroom with his iPad in hand. I curled up on the too-big sectional that barely fit in his living space, a quiet certainty guiding me. I opened the Photos app. There they were: screenshots of messages, saved images from Snapchat — conversations he clearly didn't intend for me to see, images of half-naked girls.

I forgot — or maybe didn't care — that he was still drunk and sleeping it off. I stormed back into the bedroom, heart pounding.

"What the hell are these? Are you cheating on me?" I shouted, hurling a pillow at his face.

Startled awake, he rubbed his eyes and slurred, "You're crazy. Why would you think that?"

"These," I snapped, throwing the iPad at his chest. "These are why."

He glanced at the screen and shrugged as he deleted the photos. "Oh... those? That's nothing. I was just messing around, babe."

Time slowed. Every moment I'd ever second-guessed myself, every lie I'd convinced myself wasn't a red flag — they all
rushed in at once. For two years, I had been trying to prove we
were worth it. That we could make it. That I could be chosen.
I had once believed I would marry my high school sweetheart.
When that dream fell apart, I clung to the next best story —
the college one. The shiny, polished, publicly validated version
of love. But he didn't deserve the loyalty I had given him.

We broke up that night. He didn't fight for me. Just admitted he was worried he'd "actually" cheat if we stayed together. It
shattered me in a way I hadn't felt since losing my grandpa in
eighth grade. For weeks, I cried myself to sleep face down on
my bed, not taking off my makeup, then scrubbing away the
evidence each morning so my friends wouldn't see the damage
he'd wrought.

But when I graduated and moved to the city myself, he saw
it on socials and reached out. A few flirty texts later and we
found our way back to an old familiar routine of going to bars,
bed, brunch and barely mentioning the past. We moved in together shortly after. He said he missed me. That he'd changed.
That this time could be different.

And I wanted to believe him. We were finally in the same
city, both graduated, both adults. I hoped the story could end
differently than the last chapter had.

"Connie, are you sure he's good for you?" my college best
friend, Jacqueline, asked one Saturday as we shopped for wedding guest outfits for the Man in Finance's cousin's wedding.
Witty and direct, she was an Italian firecracker who always
masked her serious side with well-timed jokes — but I knew
when she dropped the humor, she meant business.

"Oh yes, he's completely turned around. We're looking at
condos to buy and he planned an entire trip around this wed-

ding. I think I might be the next one in the family to be getting married! I mentioned Tiffany's to him." I said with a squeal. "Do you think this dress is too much or just enough?" Holding up a floor length sequin gown.

That's how it went. I told everyone we were perfect, because to say anything else would've meant confronting my own gnawing uncertainty. And I didn't know how to sit with that kind of discomfort. To do so would've meant asking myself hard questions — questions that might lead to decisions I wasn't ready to make. Decisions that would mean starting over. And starting over was something I was deeply terrified of, because I had always believed I was already behind. So I smiled wider. I played the part. I clung harder.

But the Universe doesn't reward performances. And it definitely doesn't let you ignore yourself for too long.

The Man in Finance brought out parts of me I didn't like — or maybe just exposed the parts I hadn't made peace with. He fed my materialism, sharpened my edges, redirected my focus to the way things looked instead of how they felt. Slowly, I forgot my softness. Or maybe I offered it up in hopes that if I made myself small and polished enough, he'd choose me.

And he did, until he didn't.

While we stood outside of yet another Chicago club, he was going on about something, only focused on getting more. I was ready to go home and get out of my heels, get out of my skirt and out of the numbness wrapped around my mind like medical gauze. I had tried to get his attention three times until, screaming internally for emotional intimacy, rather than say it out loud, I slapped him across the face. Loud enough for the girls behind us to gasp. My need for drama fueled by my inability to confront my own needs, had been unhinged.

"Fuck you!" I screamed, the only words I was able to muster through my frustration in the moment.

I adjusted my skirt, spun on my heels and stormed home. He followed. We screamed. I cried on the balcony while he passed out in our bed, unwilling to bother. I sobbed harder at his indifference, asking the city and then the sky why love — or at least whatever this was — had to feel like war. Somewhere deep down, I had internalized that struggle meant value. My parents had modeled that everything worth fighting for was hard — that life was supposed to hurt and love was supposed to require endurance. And so I stayed, thinking the pain was proof I was doing it right.

It should've been my wake-up call. But it wasn't. Neither were the nights when he started to disappear, ignoring his phone, sometimes not coming home at all. Neither were the bags of drugs that began littering our apartment — small, scattered threats that transformed him into someone I didn't recognize and quietly dared me to test my own limits. Neither were the DMs from strangers or the friends who pulled me aside, hesitating before telling me they'd seen him on dating apps again. If I didn't look too closely, if I didn't say it out loud, maybe it wouldn't be real.

Two years post-grad, I was already onto my second job — a move that made those closest to me raise their eyebrows and question my inability to "sit in discomfort." But they didn't get it. I wasn't uncomfortable, I was restless. The job was the one thing I could bear to change — the safest way to rearrange the pieces without touching the one that scared me most: the relationship.

I was working as a social coordinator at a paid media agency, pulling in $40,000 a year — just enough to skip brunch,

stalk the clearance racks at TJ Maxx and squeeze in a long
weekend trip every month if I stretched it. From the outside, I
was a young professional with a decent job in a big city. On the
inside, I was suffocating.

February 16, 2017

CHICAGO, ILLINOIS, UNITED STATES

*I want out — out of Chicago. Out of this hellish loop. I
am done pretending this life is enough, done pretending
HE is enough. We haven't even had sex in weeks — nor
do I want to.*

*He's chasing all the wrong things — designer watches,
luxury vehicles, tables at the club with a bag of cocaine in
his back pocket. It's such a turn-off. I want something real.
Something trustworthy. Something that feels like home.
What if I gave it all up and went to Rome or London
or Sydney for the summer? When did I stop dreaming of
travel?*

Travel was the hum beneath my skin, always present
and calling attention to itself. My grandparents had come to
America through Venezuela and Greece and I'd grown up on a
steady diet of Passport to Paris and The Lizzie McGuire Movie. While my peers studied abroad, I stayed back — for money reasons, then later for the Man in Finance. I told myself it
wasn't the right time. But it was always the dream. And now I
had a paycheck and autonomy, but no courage. I didn't have the
language for it then, but something in me already knew I was
shrinking to fit.

Until one night, tucked into yet another dimly lit steakhouse, I looked across the table at the Man in Finance and finally let the dream bubble to the surface:

"What would you do if I said I wanted to quit my job and go to Europe for a few months?"

He looked at me in between mouthfuls of filet mignon and replied, "I'd break up with you."

I didn't flinch or look him in the eye, I just kept cutting my steak.

That should've been the moment. A neon sign blinking: "This is not your person." But I wasn't ready to let go of the college sweetheart fantasy. I didn't hear "Red flag!" I heard "Protect the relationship." I still thought love meant shrinking and I thought that sacrifice was noble. I still believed staying small would make me feel safe.

Until the charade wasn't enough.

Five years into our tumultuous relationship, while the Man in Finance was on a guys' trip to Nashville, I had a dream that he cheated on me. I sat up in bed, heart pounding, spine straight and murmured to myself, "It's over," then fell right back to sleep. A few days later, he confirmed it.

That night, I barely slept. By morning, I had a therapist appointment booked and a prescription for Lorazepam in hand — just enough to keep me steady while I dismantled the life I had built with him. I executed my plan as It Ain't Me by Kygo and Selena Gomez looped through my mind and earbuds like a prophecy. Over and over I sang along in a low mumble as I packed my life up with robotic precision:

"I had a dream, we were sippin' whiskey neat,
Highest floor, The Bowery, and I was high enough,
Somewhere along the lines, we stopped seein' eye to
    eye,

You were stayin' out all night, and I had enough,
No, I don't wanna know where you been or where
     you're goin',
But I know I won't be home, and you'll be on your
     own."

I didn't scream or sob. I didn't dance or shake. I left the walls of our apartment bare, stripped of every print and photo I had once hung to make our space feel like home, forcing him to sit with the emptiness once he returned.

Jacqueline, feral with rage, wanted to break his TV and pee on his pillow. I wouldn't let her — not because he didn't deserve it, but because I refused to let my exit be anything but sovereign. "You're letting him off too easily." she said.

Maybe. But I had already picked up his pieces too many times. I wasn't going to do it again. Not while the drinking escalated, not while the drugs whispered louder than I did, not while I kept hoping he'd come home — only to realize he already lived in a world I could no longer reach.

I grabbed the last houseplant — a large, bushy ficus, almost too heavy to lift, but I was determined to get it to the elevator.

And then I took one last look around and walked out of our perfectly curated city apartment — the one with the matching mugs and monogrammed towels, the one I had thought would hold a forever. I didn't want to know where he'd go next, I just knew it wouldn't be with me.

One month later, I landed a remote marketing job that doubled my salary. A year after that, I bought a one-way ticket to London.

Just like that, my life split into a before and after.

The girl I had been — obedient, performative, half-asleep — stayed behind in the steakhouse.

Some initiations don't come in ceremony. They come in the form of dreams that shake you awake and plane tickets that rip you from who you thought you were.

The woman who boarded that plane? She was ready to begin.

Thank you to the Man in Finance for unknowingly initiating me. You were the first chapter. But this is where the story really begins.

TWO
THE GI JIG

A s expected, life didn't follow the itinerary I had imagined. After breaking up with the Man in Finance and before I boarded that liberating flight to London, I moved back in with my parents — finding solace in a new floppy-eared puppy, Lulubelle, whose unconditional love kept me sane in that in-between space. Lu was tiny enough to nearly fit in the palm of my hand, with fur as soft as a baby blanket and a body that never grew beyond eight pounds. She was all warmth and affection, always curling into my side like she couldn't bear not to touch me. Her big, soulful brown eyes seemed to understand things I couldn't yet say out loud — like she was seeing straight into the ache I was trying to hide.

As my mom helped carry my boxes into my childhood bedroom, she offered gently, "We can redecorate you know, it's no problem."

I flopped onto the purple satin bedspread, shut my eyes against the matching purple walls and fuzzy pillows, and mumbled, "No need. I won't be here long enough."

My mom stood just a few inches shorter than me, with cropped brown hair streaked with gold and warm chocolate eyes to match. She was strong — the kind of woman who could run a marathon in the morning and show three houses in the afternoon, juggling life as a realtor with the same intensity she later brought to CrossFit in her fifties. She was caring in a way that made you second-guess yourself — the kind of care that asked questions instead of offering answers. She walked like she wasn't quite sure of her place in the world, but every so often her laugh would crack through the tension and set her shoulders free.

What I thought would be a brief stopover became a year-and-a-half layover in limbo. Every morning, I woke up surrounded by purple and groaned. Leaning over the bathroom vanity, I'd stare into my eyes — constantly shifting between green and blue, like they couldn't decide who they wanted to be, wondering what came next. It had been seven years since I'd lived under my parents' roof and returning as a full-grown adult felt like a regression I couldn't swallow. I was supposed to be married by now, wasn't I? Pinterest-perfect life in full bloom. Instead, I was undoing everything I'd carefully tried to stitch together.

And yet, that pause became a lifeline. Without the noise of city life or the distraction of a relationship, I began to slow down. I went on long, meandering evening runs, I played with Lu in the front yard, I listened to my heartbeat and let my soul speak during the hour-long drives between my parents' and the city to see friends. With no distractions, the questions got louder: "What do I really want — from my career, from love, from myself? Who am I when I stop performing?" I journaled for hours like a woman possessed, words spilling out like wildfire. And slowly, the scattered pieces of my heart began stitching themselves together, forming something I hadn't heard in a long time: my own voice.

But just as I began to lean into the stillness, enter GI Joe.

He was kind. Steady. Military — Navy, to be exact. Standing nearly a foot taller than me, he carried a quiet strength that matched his towering presence. His hair was cropped close to his scalp, his face always clean-shaven — both in strict alignment with military standards. His hazel eyes were kind and the way he enunciated his t's — crisp and deliberate — often made me giggle. He was originally from a few towns over, but felt like a world away from the polarity of the life I left behind in Chicago. Where the Man in Finance had been polished but volatile, GI Joe felt solid, dependable — like a life I could trust. He represented both the picket-fence partner and the promise of a new adventure. He was transitioning from Florida to Virginia, but with deployments always looming, he could be stationed anywhere. To me, he was the fantasy: the relationship *and* the freedom. The security *and* the passport stamps. I could have my cake and eat it too — or so I thought.

From September 2017 to April 2018, I flew to Virginia once a month to see him. I'd book us an Airbnb to escape the cramped bunk bed he slept in aboard the aircraft carrier and each reunion began the same way — with him scooping me into his arms and spinning me around, my laughter echoing through the parking lot, our whirlwind romance quite literally sweeping me off my feet. GI Joe was all warm shoulders and open smiles. At night, I'd curl into him under scratchy rental sheets, my head pressed to his chest, listening to his steady breath and feeling, just for a moment, like I'd found something solid.

He was consistent. Supportive. The kind of man who

would quietly bring me a bottle of water when I was hungover and rub my back when I fell quiet, asking gently, "You good, babe?" But beneath the steadiness was something harder to name — a kind of ungroundedness. Whenever I asked what he wanted for his future — what city, what kind of job, what kind of life — he'd shrug, offer a different answer each time, then laugh if I tried to hold him to it. The military gave him structure, but without it, I wasn't sure what anchored him.

Still, it was easy to overlook in the thrill of it all. With every new boarding pass and each deep, stirring kiss at the arrivals gate, I reminded myself: "This is so much better than what I just escaped. He's got his flaws — but don't we all?"

As my relationship with GI Joe accelerated at breakneck speed, I was still living at my parents' — which, as humbling as it was, came with one silver lining: I was saving money. A lot. Enough that the dream I'd shelved — quitting my job and traveling through Europe — suddenly felt within reach. So I bought a one-way ticket to London for July.

And then eight months into our relationship, fate handed me the perfect plot twist: GI Joe's deployment was on the horizon. The timing felt cinematic — he'd be abroad, I could be roaming Europe and with a little luck and strategic planning, we could meet up somewhere on the other side of the world. It was the most romantic scenario my inner teenage dreamer could imagine — one that trumped the high school or college sweetheart.

There were a lot of tears before he left — silent ones at night and sudden ones in the middle of the day at inopportune moments. I had loved the idea of it all but his imminent departure had set me on a mood swing to despair. I kept asking the Universe why — why if I've finally found someone who feels safe, why does he have to be taken away?

And just like that, the Navy took him away.

"Few thousand miles, and an ocean away
But I see the sunrise, oh, just like the other day
Picture your eyes as I fall asleep
Tell myself it's alright, oh-oh, as the tears roll by"

— OCEANS AWAY, BY ARIZONA

Our only form of communication was email. So we wrote to each other — words that felt both intimate and distant at once. And while I waited for his replies, the thing keeping me steady was the ticket to London tucked inside my inbox. It wasn't just a vacation, it was a reclamation. A chance to stick it to the Man in Finance, to finally choose myself, to live the dream I had pressed pause on for far too long.

Since all of my emails with GI Joe were monitored by the military, we developed a secret code so he could discreetly let me know when he'd be headed to land. If I managed to crack it — a subtle breadcrumb in a sea of generic sentences — I could plan a spontaneous trip to meet him wherever he docked.

In June 2018, the stars aligned. I deciphered the code, got a flight alert for a cheap ticket and five days, seven hours, thirteen minutes and forty-one seconds later, I was on a plane from Chicago to France. We spent three sun-soaked days in Marseille, walking slow circles through narrow streets, plunging into the cold sea, then warming ourselves in the sun only to cool off again with a beer. Every moment felt touched by magic — the kind you know can't last, which only makes it sweeter. We couldn't stop touching — his hand on my thigh, fingers laced in mine, lips pressed to my forehead while we waited for a dinner table. At night, we held each other tightly in our tiny bed, whispering sweet nothings into each other's necks like we could slow down time if we tried hard enough.

The morning light filtered through the gauzy curtains, painting his bare chest in gold. The air smelled like sea salt and croissants. His kisses tasted like espresso and sun, slightly bitter, entirely addictive. Waking up beside him felt like slipping into a life I didn't know I'd been waiting for.

It was just long enough to make my heart ache for more. The taste of what could be, made me hungry for the future. I flew back to the States, ready for my solo adventure in four weeks. I was feeling both giddy and grieving — the fantasy had finally touched earth, but it couldn't hold.

I had planned my European escape knowing GI Joe would be deployed, with the fantasy of crossing paths again somewhere abroad if I decoded another message correctly. But, as I quickly learned, the military has a special talent for upending even the best-laid plans. GI Joe's deployment ended early. He returned to the States and my dreams of an exotic meet up were crushed, so I booked a last-minute flight to Virginia before I officially took off for Europe.

In the week leading up to that trip, a wild idea lodged itself in my brain: we should get married.

Maybe it was the offhand comment from a friend trying to lift my spirits — that the next man I met would be the one I'd marry. Maybe it was my grandma saying GI Joe deserved someone waiting for him when he returned. Maybe it was the fact that I had just quit my job, had no health insurance and had recently stood up in Jacqueline's wedding. Maybe I just wanted to anchor something that felt so fleeting.

So I floated it — casually, impulsively — over text. "What if we just did it? Got married before I left?"

He replied with a string of exclamation points and "Calling you my wife? I can't wait!"

We went back and forth like school kids planning a field trip, feeling euphoric about the idea without once stopping to ask what marriage actually meant. There was no ring. No formal proposal. Just two people swept up in the adrenaline of a ticking clock and the fantasy of locking something down before it could disappear.

I cancelled all other plans and went dress shopping with my mom.

"This is so cute! Is it the one?" she asked.

"Yeah... it'll do," I replied.

It was anticlimactic. I didn't cry. I didn't feel like a princess. Standing in that dressing room, staring at my reflection in a short white dress that felt "just fine," I ignored the quiet tug in my gut. It was the same sinking feeling you get on a roller coaster, just as it starts to drop. I should've stopped right then. Should've asked, "Is this really what I dream of?" But I bought it anyway — not because I found *the one*, but because I felt like I needed *a* one.

No one except my parents knew we planned to elope. I paid for the dress myself and tucked it into my suitcase bound for Virginia, ready for our big moment. I already had the Instagram caption drafted — something cheeky involving a Ring Pop — a playful way to announce our surprise after we stepped out of the courthouse. But I never got the chance to post it.

"Send pictures!!!" My mom's text came in as GI Joe and I ate pizza on the Airbnb couch.

I replied with a picture of my empty ring finger and a slice in hand, "It didn't happen."

"What do you mean?" she answered immediately.

"His mother won't give her blessing. No mama approval, no wedding."

"Why???" I could practically hear her slamming her fingers into the phone.

I put the phone down, pretending I wanted to be present with GI Joe and soak in every moment together. In reality, my mind was spinning. Why didn't his mom approve? I hadn't been brave enough to ask. Maybe I was scared that if I heard her reasoning, I'd agree with it. Instead of sitting with that possibility, I turned to anger — told GI Joe he needed to grow a backbone, to do something for himself for once. Over the past year, I had started to notice just how much his mother stepped in for him — how she softened the blow when he didn't graduate college, how she smoothed things over when he bounced from job to job before landing in the military, how she still handled so many of his administrative tasks behind the scenes. I wanted him to step up. I wanted him to choose me without needing her permission slip.

But the outburst didn't bring clarity. It didn't make me feel stronger or more certain. It just left me hollow. I left that trip feeling defeated — like I had lost my one chance at the kind of spontaneous, rebellious love story I had always dreamed of. Only Lu's big brown eyes begging for a walk could make me smile and feel any kind of warmth inside.

As we wandered the quiet suburban streets, the sun dipped low behind rows of identical rooftops, golden light softening the edges of everything. Lawns were manicured. Driveways empty. The world felt hushed and tidy — like everyone had already settled for a version of life I wasn't sure I wanted. I looked down at Lu, then up at the fading sky and asked aloud, "Is this what I want? Or do I want the kind of love that's messy and passionate and a little taboo. I want to feel alive. Why can't I live a love story like the ones they write about in books?"

I was still in the story, but GI Joe and I didn't know what the next chapter would look like — especially with the military always looming, ready to throw a wrench in any dream we dared to build.

So July came. I flew to Europe and began my grand adventure — but the emotional weight of what had almost happened followed me. I was trying to reconcile the whiplash: one minute imagining an elopement, the next boarding a plane alone. I was so used to getting what I wanted that being shut down during what I thought was going to be a big romantic moment felt like a punch to the gut.

But instead of pausing to process, I barreled ahead with a packed itinerary blazing through cities, yet still obsessing over finding a way to marry him. It was present even when we both tried to talk about something else.

A few weeks into my trip, GI Joe FaceTimed me with an update — he'd picked out a ring with his dad. After talking it over with his mom, he agreed to compromise: we'd wait until after his next deployment and have a "real" wedding back home. I had once said I'd love to celebrate on New Year's Eve — now, we were making it happen. I squealed on the call, shaping my face into the right expression — big smile, glistening eyes, just like I'd practiced in middle school mirror sessions. I had won, but then why did it all feel so fake? Why was I so conflicted? It didn't matter though, because from the outside looking in, it was a fairytale. So I went along with it — unwilling to meet those questions head-on.

From that moment on, the adventure I had planned — the freedom I had long fantasized about — began to blur. I couldn't stay present. My mind was already months ahead. What was the point of wandering cobblestone streets of Italy solo when there was a wedding to plan? A new identity to step into? A picture-perfect life to execute?

I returned to the States in September 2018 and got to work — my Pinterest boards were so detailed they could've been submitted to an interior design firm for full approval. I was a woman on a mission: planning and paying for a 150-person wedding in under four months. GI Joe was again deployed, so while I flooded his inbox with far too many emails, the actual planning fell entirely on me. It was a sprint. Each day at my desk, I'd pull up my wedding spreadsheet and think, "Let's get it, girl — time to plan your dream wedding!" only to slowly sink deeper into my chair, my head lolling to the side as the dissonance set in.

I kept pushing anyway. Checked every box. Ordered every detail. I told myself this was just wedding stress — that the heaviness would lift once he was home. That seeing his face would make everything click into place.

For once, the military didn't interfere — he was scheduled to return two weeks before the wedding and he did.

I bought a new outfit, flew down to Virginia, made a "Welcome Home!" sign, and found myself nervously shaking in a crowd of thousands gathered to greet their sailors as they returned home. The energy was electric — posters waving, children crying, spouses clutching flowers, a brass band playing a patriotic tune that made everything feel like the set of a 1950's movie. Luckily, GI Joe was tall so it didn't take long to spot him moving through the sea of uniforms. Without thinking, I dropped my sign and ran toward him, launching myself into his arms. Cameras flashed, American flags waved exuberant, people clapped and hooted their approval. And then, just like that, he dropped to one knee. Right there, in front of the crowd and the cameras, he asked me to marry him. The crowd went wild.

It was broadcast on Good Morning America the next day. Strangers online called it "The perfect love story." I scrolled through the comments, nodding in agreement. On the surface, it was. And yet — I woke up with a flutter of panic in my chest and a sour stomach that refused most food. I splashed water on my face at the bathroom sink and stared at my reflection — pale, hollow. I'd lost at least seven pounds from the pre-wedding stress but didn't think much of it.

"It's okay," I told myself. "It's just pre-wedding jitters. This is normal. Everything is going to look gorgeous. The balloon drop at midnight is epic. We are great together. We're in love. This is solid. The Man in Finance is a stupid idiot and I'm finally getting my happy ending. Everyone will see how well it turned out. And then we'll get moved to Italy or Japan or Australia! Life abroad. The best of all the worlds!"

I clung to the narrative — the girl scorned by the Man in Finance who found healing in a military love story. I thought this relationship was the reward for all the pain I'd endured. The happy ending tied up in a red, white and blue bow. I told myself that the friction — the rushed timeline, the unanswered questions, the tension I felt deep in my gut — was normal. I reminded myself that this was just what adult relationships looked like.

I had doubts in those two weeks leading up to the wedding. Real, heavy, gnawing doubts. I wasn't sleeping, I was barely eating and I was pushing myself to exhaustion in my workouts, hoping the sweat would drown out the noise in my head. I drove from the seamstress to the print shop in silence, gripping the steering wheel with clammy hands, whispering to myself,

"It's okay, Connie. If you just walk down the aisle, everything will settle into place."

I didn't know myself well enough — or trust myself deeply enough — to listen to the part of me that was screaming. I believed certainty would come after ceremony. That love would bloom from commitment. That doubt was just part of growing up.

So I buried my truth. I stuffed it down beneath the dress fittings, the seating charts, the performance.

On the last day of 2018, I walked myself down the aisle — not alone, but with my dad by my side, beaming with quiet pride. My mom was elated, glowing as she watched my dad's speech during dinner. GI Joe's mom kissed my cheek just before the dancing began and whispered, "Welcome to the family." The room glittered with candlelight and gold accents. We danced the night away, ringing in 2019 under a shower of sparklers and champagne. By all accounts, it was perfect.

And still — deep beneath the sequins and toasts, the doubts remained. I had hoped the ceremony would silence them. That the weight of the ring would anchor me in certainty.

But of course, they came back.

THREE
MARRIED FOR BENEFITS

A MONTH AFTER GI Joe and I got married, I moved to Virginia. My mom and aunt had driven a U-Haul down two weeks earlier, unloading boxes into our new apartment off-base so that by the time I arrived, everything looked ready. By all appearances, it was a fresh start. But beneath the polish, a quiet tension pulsed — the same one I had swallowed on my wedding day and carried with me across state lines.

We had never actually lived together. Despite all of our weekend getaways, the spontaneous adventures, the FaceTime calls across time zones, we had never shared space. Never fought over dishes or what to watch on a Tuesday night. And now, we were married. The reality of that hung in the air like humidity.

Still, I did what I'd always done — I curated the version of life I could live with. My Instagram feed told a beautiful story: dreamy photos of our new apartment, sunset walks with Lu, snapshots of military life that made it all seem romantic and brave. I posted polished moments as if they could anchor me in certainty. As if the right caption could quiet the storm I felt building inside.

I told myself it was different than the years I spent living with the Man in Finance, and therefore, this would work. Because it had to. I had chosen it. I had *committed*.

That word, so heavy on my tongue, became something I repeated like a spell — proof that I was doing the right thing, even as my body kept bracing for the fallout.

The first few months of 2019 — of marriage, of living in a new state, of adjusting to military life — hit me harder than I expected. It was my first time living outside of Illinois. I didn't have close friends nearby. No one to grab a spontaneous glass of wine with. No deep belly-laugh conversations to ground me in this unfamiliar place. Just Lu's warm body to snuggle with after evening walks.

I was trying to keep up with a military schedule that made no sense to me — sometimes GI Joe came home earlier than expected, throwing off my routine. Other times, he was late or gone for days without warning. It felt impossible to find a rhythm, to plan anything. So I threw myself into the only kind of structure I could control: performing the role of the good military wife. I baked cookies from scratch. I broke out the KitchenAid pasta attachments — a wedding gift paired with Jacqueline's grandma's recipe — and spent entire afternoons coaxing flour and eggs into ribbons of tagliatelle. I told myself I was nesting. Creating comfort. But beneath it all, I knew it was borrowed time. The underways were coming — short deployments that could last anywhere from two weeks to two months. They were meant to prepare us for the longer deployments, but they only added to my sense of instability.

Everything felt off and I was terrified to say it out loud. I'd lay in bed, listening to GI Joe's breath deepening on the brink of sleep and wonder, "Should I say something?" But I just rolled over and went to sleep. Because if I said I was struggling, it might mean I had made a mistake.

So I threw myself into fitness. I joined a CrossFit gym. I tried a run club. But I just didn't fit in. I was a military spouse without kids, which made me an anomaly. At 30 and 27, we were considered "old" by military standards, and babies were the expected next step.

"No children?" the young moms would ask with concern and a slight forehead frown. "Oh you're newly wed. Don't worry hun, they'll come soon!" I smiled, as if that was the best news ever.

But I didn't want children. I didn't fantasize about strollers and nursery colors. I didn't ache for tiny hands in mine. That dream had never lived in my body the way it seemed to for others.

GI Joe had never questioned that path before he met me. Marriage, kids, stability — it was the blueprint he had always seen for his life. When I made it clear that path wasn't mine, he shifted. He stopped bringing it up. He mirrored my doubts instead, parroted my hesitations. And somewhere deep down, I wondered if that was his truth, or just his way of trying to hold onto me.

Still, something between us had started to sour. The cuddles on the couch became opposite corners. Conversations turned into updates. Most nights, he sat across the room glued to the TV while I scrolled my phone, pretending not to notice the silence stretching between us. We were sharing space, but not a life.

And then my period was late.

"Babe, it's only a few days," he said, when I told him I was worried. He didn't look away from the TV screen.

"I know, but it's late," I said, pacing from the bathroom to the kitchen and back again. "Like, actually late. What if I am...?" Too scared to even say the word.

He shrugged. "We'll deal with it if we have to."

I stared at him, waiting for something more — concern, comfort, a plan — but he just went back to the game. I kept checking, every hour, every cramp that felt like a false alarm.

By that night, I was sweating through my shirt, a fever burning in my chest. I curled up on the couch, shivering and overheating at the same time, while he scrolled silently beside me.

"I can't have a baby right now," I whispered, not sure if I was talking to him or myself. "I can't even figure out if I want to be here." I confessed.

He didn't respond.

The next morning, I got my period. All was well — physically, at least. But the emotional spiral had already left a mark. The panic, the fever, the silence between us — it all pointed to something I hadn't wanted to admit: I didn't like what I had gotten myself into. The fairytale I had sold myself was curdling into something brittle and bitter. And instead of naming the fear, I projected it.

I judged. I judged the young military wives with their messy buns and minivans, their lack of degrees and wild children running amuck on base. I told myself I was different, better — more educated, more evolved, more intentional. But the truth was, I was just scared. Lonely. Untethered in a life that looked nothing like the one I thought I'd signed up for.

And when GI Joe left for those underways, I ran. Not metaphorically — literally. Every chance I got, I packed up Lu and drove the fifteen hours back to Chicago, because it was easier to escape than it was to root. But in doing so, I was closing myself off from the very thing I craved most: community.

Our finances quickly became a source of tension — despite what the national ads would have you believe, the military didn't offer much in the way of financial support. Less than two weeks before the wedding, I discovered that GI Joe had a significant amount of credit card debt he hadn't fully disclosed — not because he was hiding it, but because he didn't understand it. He thought making the minimum payments meant he was managing it responsibly. I was stunned. The day after our wedding, I paid off the five-figure balance in full — not out of generosity, but because I couldn't fathom starting our marriage with that kind of burden hanging over us. Meanwhile, I was in the early stages of building my freelance marketing business, and somehow, most of our expenses still fell on me. My income wasn't where I needed it to be and the pressure of trying to keep us afloat unleashed the most insecure, uptight version of myself — the one who pinched pennies by limiting the number of Aldi eggs GI Joe could eat per day. I dictated and silently seethed.

So I turned to what I knew: margaritas, wine, IPAs and journal entries filled with bitterness.

Weeknights were reserved for FaceTime calls with friends back in Chicago. I'd show up with dark circles under my glazed eyes and a bottle of wine in hand, a hollow smile stretched across my face. I'm not sure who I was trying harder to convince — them or myself — that I was okay. On weekends, GI Joe and I would visit yet another brewery. The vibe was always the same: two pints too many, me blinking back tears by closing time, waking up in a haze the next morning.

I was too busy numbing to see that I had slipped back into the same old patterns — letting a relationship define me, shape my days, blur my desires. Was it him? Was it me? Or was it the system I kept unconsciously agreeing to?

The only thing that had changed was the aesthetic. Gone were the luxury cars and steakhouse dinners — replaced now with craft breweries and loosely imagined travel plans for his next deployment. Nothing was set in stone, of course — it never was with the military. But because it looked different on the outside, I convinced myself it was.

But it wasn't, not really.

As military life goes, another deployment was scheduled for late 2019. Thankfully, we were able to squeeze in our belated honeymoon before he left. GI Joe was relatively sheltered and hadn't ventured far from home before we met but he eagerly embraced my passion. I narrowed down my extensive wish list to realistic options, and together we settled on Brazil.

After a long red-eye, we landed in Rio de Janeiro just as the cafés were opening for breakfast. Exhausted and jet-lagged, GI Joe struggled to communicate with the waiter — slipping into a Spanish accent instead of Portuguese. Frustration quickly bubbled up in him, while I sank a little deeper into my chair, thinking: "This is why Americans get a bad reputation abroad."

Despite GI Joe's ignorance, that trip was a brief, mostly beautiful escape from the realities waiting for us back home. Because when we returned, the looming question could no longer be ignored: Where would I stay during GI Joe's deployment? Having just emerged from an extended stay at my parents', the thought of moving back in with them felt like another regression I couldn't stomach. But staying in Virginia wasn't an option either — not in a place that never truly felt like mine and not alone where solo military wives were often targeted and vandalized.

That's when Remote Year appeared, like divine timing disguised as an Instagram ad.

FOUR
DON'T WRITE IT DOWN

FOUNDED IN 2015, Remote Year was a splashy and well-known company that catered to digital nomads by curating programs that blended travel, community and remote work. While they originally ran year-long itineraries across twelve countries, in 2018 they launched shorter-term options. I signed up for a four-month program through South and Central America, set to begin in November — it perfectly aligned with GI Joe's deployment. I told others that "If I had to be alone, I might as well do it in beautiful places." Along with a group of others, I'd spend a month each in Colombia, Peru, Chile and Mexico.

Right before I left, a friend who guessed at how much was unsaid in my life, gifted me a leather-bound journal — rich, soft and full of empty pages waiting to be filled. Waiting to be filled with my truths, to be my safe container, to provide clarity. It had been some years since I regularly journaled so I was excited to start the practice again, especially on such an epic adventure.

On the inside cover, I taped the quote: "You need look nowhere but where you are right now." I wanted this journey to be
different. I didn't want to miss it. After racing through Europe
the year before, always thinking about what was next, I was
determined to stay present for every messy, magical, uncomfortable moment.

On November 3, 2019, I stepped up to the gate for my
flight from Chicago to Medellín. I sent my Chicago friends a
group text: "This will be my last big trip and then I'll settle
down. Promise. Wish me luck!" and then switched my phone
to airplane mode.

Upon landing in Medellín, I did what I always did when
faced with uncertainty — I tried to control it. I attempted to
recreate the version of my life I had known in Virginia. I made
a strict budget, kept conversations light with no chance of deep
bonding or friendship and signed up at a CrossFit gym where
I could sweat out my feelings instead of speak them. It felt like
I was sealing myself inside a pressurized container — holding
everything in with a tight lid, fully aware that the second it
popped off, nothing would be the same. That just couldn't happen. Until it did.

That moment came on our last full weekend in Colombia.
We were on a group day trip to Guatapé, weaving through the
lush countryside in a colorful bus, when we stopped at a rickety
bridge that stretched forty feet above the Peñol-Guatapé Reservoir. It was the kind of bridge that creaked when the wind
shifted and dared you to let go. And we were gearing up for a
jump off the bridge into the aqua water far below.

After much hesitation, I climbed over the guardrail along
with seven others, lowering myself onto the ledge, my hands
gripping wood, legs dangling above the water below. My heart

thudded. The fear wasn't just about the insane height — it was everything that jump represented.

We counted down: three, two, one.

And I leapt.

The shriek that left my throat was part terror, part release. Watching the video later, I realized I'd gone first. Without waiting. Without thinking. Without needing permission.

That jump didn't just break the seal on a literal plunge — it was the beginning of a metaphorical one.

The next week, we landed in Peru, and with that shift in scenery came a shift in me. GI Joe had officially deployed and in his absence, I found something I didn't know I'd been missing: permission. Permission to make myself the main character again. To loosen the grip on my budget, on my schedule, on the version of me I thought I had to be in order to be loved. I was the one being deployed. Launching myself out of the carefully constructed role I had stepped into — the military wife, the dutiful partner, the woman who kept quiet and played safe.

And so I climbed into new terrain. Grand hikes in the Peruvian Andes became a sacred ritual. Each summit I reached brought a different kind of clarity. At higher altitudes, in the mirrors of crisp lakes and open skies, I could finally see myself — there she was. Cheeks flushed not from CrossFit and run club, but from sunshine and wind and wonder. A genuine smile gleaming from her eyes. The dark circles under them had begun to fade. I stood a little taller. I danced — arms flailing, feet skipping over gravel, laughter echoing down the trail. Worn hiking boots adorned my feet and salt-dried shorts hung from my hips, and still I felt more radiant than I had all year. I was making friends with strangers. Making jokes. Making space for joy. The girl who used to play soccer barefoot in the backyard, who laughed without a filter and dreamed without limits — she had come back. I hadn't seen her in years. Not since I started trying so hard to make the "thing" work. But here, finally, she had room to breathe.

Each mountain showed me another version of what my life could look like: "What if… what if, I wonder what if…"

I asked and asked, giving myself permission to wonder and re-imagine. "What did *I* like? What was *I* settling for and why?" As we climbed up, out of breath yet exhilarated, each new view of the majestic mountains asked me a harder question.

I could imagine it, how it would all feel. Was I willing to choose it? Even if it meant letting go of everything I'd built so far?

I silently battled these questions throughout the month and into our next country, Chile.

GI Joe and I were days away from our one-year wedding anniversary. With him deployed, our communication was limited to email and the occasional Facebook message. The messages came at odd hours — short, delayed bursts that never quite allowed for a live exchange. So we relied on email to keep our marriage alive, to stitch some semblance of intimacy through screens.

Since my arrival in Chile, I hadn't heard a word from him.

Then, on December 30, headlines broke around the world: the U.S. had launched airstrikes against Iranian-backed forces in Iraq and Syria the day before. My stomach dropped. I knew, thanks to our secret location code, that GI Joe's ship was in the area. I pieced the dots together — I was convinced his crew had executed the strike and that something had gone terribly wrong.

By New Year's Eve, our one-year anniversary, still nothing.

My mind spun into catastrophic what-ifs: I imagined the start of World War III. His ship, captured or sunk. GI Joe, gone. Just like that.

So I did what I knew. I drank gin and tonics like water. I danced myself numb. Then I cried myself to sleep.

On the first morning of 2020, I woke to an email from GI Joe's best friend: the ship was on lockdown due to the air-strikes, but he was safe. He loved me. "Happy first anniversary," the message said. It was not the love letter I'd hoped for, but it was a lifeline.

And yet, that email left me emptier than I'd felt the night before.

On New Year's Eve, I was a widow in my mind — untethered and undone, grieving a life that had ended before it could even begin. I mourned the version of our marriage we'd never gotten to live out. I hadn't even fallen fully in love with him yet, not truly, and yet I had already started to grieve what could've been. There was a sense of release in that heartbreak, like the Universe was offering me a chance at a do-over — something that felt honest, something that didn't require me to contort myself to make it work.

But then morning came and with it the truth: I was not a widow. I was still married. To a man I barely heard from. To a relationship that felt increasingly distant, not just by geography, but by energy. I was growing, expanding — not just from the places I visited but from the pieces of myself I was finally meeting and acknowledging. And that growth was beginning to make our marriage feel like a cage. Like a vow made by a version of me that no longer existed.

I had carried my journal through five countries in four months, but I'd only written in it sixteen times. Every time I sat down to write, the truth would start to emerge — and I wasn't ready to face it. So instead, I wrote gratitude lists. They were bulleted points that tried to convince me of my happiness. I'd put GI Joe at the top, like an anchor meant to keep me grounded in a commitment I no longer felt rooted in.

January 13, 2020
SANTIAGO, CHILE

There have been some weird situations lately but rather than focus on that, I'm choosing to put good out into the Universe.

What I am grateful for:

- *GI Joe and his strength + love.*
- *Guidance, support, centering, ambition and leadership from each of my friends.*
- *Remote Year and the lessons + job potential.*
- *My parents and their love.*
- *Jacqueline's baby.*

Later that day, I tried to give shape to the ache, writing:

Lots of feels today. Mainly relief though. Thinking of things that I want and some of the broad thoughts are:

- *Financial freedom.*
- *Loving home.*
- *Experiencing new cultures & places.*
- *Love.*
- *Respectful employers.*

Now to get them.
Me.
I always come first.

And even later, in a quiet moment of truth, I asked myself
when I'd last felt alive:

Moments I have felt most alive:

- *Jumping from the bridge in Colombia.*
- *Hiking Rainbow Mountain.*
- *Sunsets.*
- *Patagonia.*

And then scribbled on the bottom of the page as if it were
an afterthought — "Our wedding."

As the month progressed, I found myself drifting even further from GI Joe. He couldn't keep up with the momentum
of my unfolding days — while I was scaling mountains and
chasing sunrises, he was stuck in a dark room on a ship in the
middle of the ocean. He wasn't able to track the dreams I kept
tossing into the air, one after another, as my mind bounced like
an arcade pinball machine with possibilities — wild, beautiful
and bursting with energy he simply couldn't match from where
he was.

"What if we moved to South America and became fluent
in Spanish? Or hiked all of the world's tallest peaks? Oh! Or we
could create a travel couple's Instagram! We could sleep under
the stars in Jordan or see the glowworm caves in New Zealand
and ride hot air balloons over Myanmar. I've always wanted to
move to Europe but Asia would be more off the beaten path

— we obviously have to ride motorbikes across Mongolia and through Vietnam!" I'd email into the void, trying to erase the memory of how frustrated GI Joe had been with the cultural differences in Brazil and how embarrassed I had felt because of it.

As I pulled away, I fell deeper into what was unfolding in front of me — a community of kindred spirits equally drawn to the unknown and a new person who seemed capable of walking this path beside me.

January 24, 2020
PUERTO NATALES, CHILE

I've been thinking about it so much and a lot of it has to do with going through all of these really good but hard, scary and ballsy situations together. ie. cliff driving, bridge jumping, ziplining, etc. And the closer I get with these people, the further I get from those that aren't here. Which is really hard for me to comprehend.

That night, under the dim lights of a rooftop bar and the thrum of Galantis' Never Felt a Love Like This, I crossed a line I couldn't uncross: I cheated on GI Joe.

The next morning, still tangled in sheets next to someone else, with my mouth dry and my heart aching, I prepared to board a plane to Mexico — the final stop on my Remote Year journey. I couldn't even look at my journal as I threw my things into my suitcase. Writing it down would make it real, and if it was real, I would have to face what I'd done. I left the outfit I'd worn the night before in the bathtub, as if abandoning it there could somehow erase the truth — as if not seeing it meant it didn't happen. Instead, I spiraled — fast and hard. In Mexico, I drank whatever was poured. Snorted whatever was passed. Slithered under the gate of a closed tattoo shop and let someone pierce my nose. I bribed a cop to avoid getting arrested with trembling hands and broken Spanish. Picked a fight with GI Joe when he sent flowers. The closer I got to myself, the more I resented the version of me he loved — the one who didn't exist anymore.

Every night, I sat on my rooftop with my legs dangling over the edge and watched the sun dip below the Mexico City skyline, wondering what the hell I was going to do when this fantasy faded away and reality came roaring in.

So I did the only thing I knew to do — instead of going home, I ran. I booked a one way ticket to Costa Rica, hoping I could outrun the plane crash waiting to land on my life.

At the airport, a piece of reality found me. I passed through security and the emotional weight equivalent of a dump truck slammed into my chest. I crumpled to the floor like I'd been physically body slammed, right there in the middle of the airport terminal. Tears I'd been bottling for months exploded from me. Sorrow. Guilt. Despair. But more than anything — grief.

Perhaps I was grieving the girl who had tasted freedom — who had found slivers of her truth on mountaintops and inside someone else's smile, in the deep conversations under South American stars and yes, even in the wildness of Mexico City. But where would she fit in Virginia? Was this her funeral? I wasn't ready to let her die.

More sobs wracked my body. How could I go back? After all that had happened and who I had become, how was I supposed to go back to a life that felt like a shoe two sizes too small? To a man who didn't really know me? To a promise that no longer felt like mine?

And the terrifying part, that choked my sobs in my throat was: I didn't know who I was going to be next.

FIVE

WHAT HAPPENS IN LOCKDOWN, STAYS IN LOCKDOWN

A week in costa Rica didn't bring me any closer to figuring out who I was. If anything, it sharpened the edges of everything I didn't want — but I wasn't ready to listen. I clung to distraction like a life raft, ignoring each poke from my intuition deep in my stomach.

So the Universe intervened.

I landed back in the U.S. in early March 2020, just as the undercurrent of COVID began to echo into reality. A few days later, GI Joe's deployment was extended. I feigned heartbreak, playing the dutiful wife, but deep down I was relieved. His delay felt like borrowed time — a little more space to figure out what the hell I was doing and who I was doing it for.

And then, like clockwork, I tried to flee. I opened my laptop and attempted to book a flight to Guatemala the very next day. But the purchase wouldn't go through — my card kept getting declined. I took it as a glitch while the Universe took it as an opportunity. Within 24 hours, the world shut down.

I was in limbo back at my parents' house, trapped in the same childhood bedroom that had watched me grow into someone I no longer recognized. I told myself I was stuck because of the pandemic, because of the military, because of the economy. But really, I had zero intentions of taking responsibility for my own life. So the Universe gifted me exactly what I asked for — space. Too much of it.

My work, mostly tied to events and travel, came to a screeching halt. Days stretched out endlessly, time folding in on itself like a cruel joke. A day felt like a week, a week like a month. I filled the void with travel YouTube video rabbit holes and making big plans — like visiting all 195 countries before I turned 40 or buying a van and driving into the unknown. Anything but sitting still. Anything but facing myself.

Weekly Zoom calls with my Remote Year crew became my lifeline — not just a social escape, but a tether to the version of myself I'd met abroad. The one who danced barefoot at sunset, who jumped off bridges, who spoke her truth and chased freedom. The one who cheated on her husband and was too scared to unpack what that really meant. Those calls kept me emotionally connected to that wild, untamed self — the one that felt impossible to fully embody now that I was back under my parents' roof, numbed by the constant background noise of the news, pretending I hadn't broken something sacred. I wasn't happy.

And I couldn't keep pretending.

Just a week into lockdown, GI Joe informed me that he was going to be relocated. We discussed the possibility of moving across the world via email — it felt more like a transaction than a heartfelt conversation about our future. While he was suspended in time on the ship, clinging to the idea that everything between us was steady and secure, I was in motion — evolving, questioning, living. Our realities were split and what felt like stability to him felt like confinement to me.

March 23, 2020
CHICAGO, ILLINOIS, UNITED STATES

I need to have a conversation with him. About these feelings that are so frequently rising.

Questions to ponder:

- *How can we bring our lives together more even though they are so separate?*
- *Are we on the same path in life?*
- *Do we want the same things?*
- *What are our goals personally and in our marriage?*
- *How can we take responsibility for his debt and lack of organization?*
- *How can we have more life changing experiences that aren't due to the military?*

Unfortunately, I didn't have the time to execute this conversation in person — we had to make a decision about where we would relocate and his deployment kept getting extended due to COVID. So I punched up an email and sent it out into the ether, hoping that whatever GI Joe's response was, would somehow ground me — or at the very least, quiet the growing unease I didn't yet know how to name.

March 25, 2020
CHICAGO, ILLINOIS, UNITED STATES

He's telling me what I want to hear but it's not making me happy for me or us, just him. I feel so disconnected and so emotionally removed. Is it because I'm over it? Is it because I haven't seen him in over five months?

If I had a choice right now that had no negative implications, I'd buy the damn van and drive away.

Is marriage right for me? Or are these feelings natural in situations like this?

And I'm so scared to open up and talk to anyone about it because I need to always be perfect.

March 26, 2020
CHICAGO, ILLINOIS, UNITED STATES

I sadly keep thinking towards a divorce. I'm just truly unsure if he can fit into the life I want or if I even want him to.

On the flip side, do I actually know what I want or am I ruining something good?

April 2, 2020
CHICAGO, ILLINOIS, UNITED STATES

I am angry and frustrated.
I don't want to talk to him.
Everything he says, I fight.

I don't trust him.
I don't feel supported.
I am not feeling good and it is infuriating.
Unsure where to go from here.
I'm mad at him for being in the military.
I'm mad at myself for being weak.
I'm mad that if we were just dating, I'd say bye.
I'm mad I jumped into this,
I'm mad at my constantly changing feelings.
I'm mad I'm quarantined.
I just... FUCK.

The following week, we said yes to a relocation to Japan that fall. In my mind, this was his final opportunity to prove himself — to show me we were still on the right path. He kept his eyes and our conversations fixed to a future he believed was secure, while I was stuck in the present, living a life that felt increasingly misaligned.

So I started anchoring into my own future. I landed a full-time digital marketing strategist role at a remote progressive political agency. This created a further divide between me and my conservative parents as tensions had already started mounting from being in the same space for far too long.

Then, the announcement of GI Joe returning from deployment after nearly eight months came both as a relief and a shock — it symbolized a step forward and also a step toward personal responsibility I wasn't sure I was ready for.

June 15, 2020
CHICAGO, ILLINOIS, UNITED STATES

It's the day before GI Joe is supposed to come home and

all I'm feeling is anxiety. Which is really difficult because I want to be excited but so much has changed and I'm just not sure we're aligned anymore. I worry that we rushed into this without actually knowing each other and now it's coming to bite us in the ass. And while I'm over here doing the deep examination, self reflection and being realistic, his head is in the clouds that we are perfect. I'm not perfect, I've proven that, but he doesn't know that. Rightly or wrongly, I feel as though we are on two very different levels and view the world through very different perspectives and while that doesn't mean we can't work, it's also not my ideal situation because I'm always looking for more. I get bored easily and if he can't keep me spiritually, emotionally, mentally and sexually engaged, I lose interest. And put that on top of military life, it's a damn disaster. Key points to examine:

- *Rushed into marriage without checking full alignment.*
- *Giving up my dreams for him.*
- *Unsure if I can see him in the future I want.*
- *Inability to be together and dealing with more years of the military.*
- *I don't know how to live like this.*

GI Joe returned from deployment to our home in Virginia, while I stayed back at my parents' in Chicago, using my new job as an excuse. In truth, I needed a few extra days of reprieve — time to mentally prepare for having him back in my orbit. No one talks enough about the difficulty of reintegration — how jarring it is to go from your own carefully built rhythm to suddenly sharing intimate space again. The shift is abrupt, especially when you don't know if you want that person in your space anymore.

June 25, 2020

VIRGINIA BEACH, VIRGINIA, UNITED STATES

I fell in love with myself in a way that I didn't know was possible. I fell in love with friends in a way that I didn't know was possible or who could bring out the best and know the worst in me and still love me. I don't know how to let GI Joe in without taking away from the magic of that and I'm terrified because I don't want to lose myself again. I don't know how to be GI Joe's and be mine all at the same time.

I spent the summer in Virginia caught in a silent war between my head and my gut — logic battling instinct, practicality clashing with truth. I wanted to be who GI Joe saw, the person my parents could be proud of, the version of me my friends supported. A cheating divorcee didn't fit the bill. So I played the part, masked my doubts and ignored the whispers of my own desires, convincing myself that if I performed well enough, maybe I'd start to believe it too. I even found a therapist, thinking maybe she could help me untangle the growing knots inside me. But even there — the one place that was supposed to be safe — I lied. I edited my story, softened the truth, painted myself as more certain than I was. I was so afraid of what my real feelings would mean, of what they might destroy, that I kept performing even in the spaces meant for healing.

I hung on all summer to the role of dutiful military wife,

because I couldn't bear to be the one who failed. The one who gave up. The one who said, "This isn't it," after all we had sacrificed. So instead, I performed even harder, giving all my energy— to the image, the idea, the illusion — hoping it would somehow make it true.

But deep down, I knew: I wasn't just lying to him. I was lying to myself.

SIX

A JAPANESE FEVER DREAM

In october, the military came to our apartment in Virginia and boxed up our life. Every couch cushion, Crate & Barrel plate and scented candle was wrapped and loaded onto a barge set to cross the Pacific. All that remained were two suitcases each — the essentials for a life we were about to start halfway around the world. GI Joe would fly to Japan for the next three years and I would join him after the election in November; I couldn't stomach working U.S. night hours during the most demanding season of the year. That decision felt practical, but it was also something else.

Because the moment he boarded that plane, the weight of our marriage quietly lifted from my shoulders. And in its absence, something stirred — space. Breath. A spark of possibility. I had room to dream again.

Technically, my job required me to spend at least six months and a day in the U.S. for tax purposes. Emotionally, I needed that time to rediscover who I was outside of our marriage. GI Joe would be deployed for much of our time in Japan, so we agreed: I'd be with him when he was there and in the States when he wasn't.

During Remote Year, I had discovered just how healing the mountains were for me — their groundedness, their invitation to rise. I couldn't go back to feeling stuck in my childhood bedroom or boxed in by a city that no longer reflected me. If I was going to be stateside, I wished to expand. And for me, that meant Colorado.

So, it was decided. A week before I left for Japan, everyone knew the game plan — it was agreed upon, logical, approved. But my body disagreed. It revolted.

Suddenly, everything in me was screaming. I was having daily panic attacks — the kind that folded me in half, breath sharp and shallow, vision narrowing to a pinpoint. The sobs came hard and fast, uncontrollable and consuming.

And it wasn't just the panic. My body had been trying to warn me for months. I got a urinary tract infection after every time I begrudgingly gave into sex with GI Joe. At first, I brushed it off — stress, dehydration, maybe the change in routine. But eventually, I couldn't ignore what it was really saying: "No. This isn't safe." Not because he was unsafe but because the connection was. My body had been screaming the truth my heart wasn't ready to hold.

My mom would perch beside me on the edge of my bed, worry lines etched deep into her face while mine twisted with the effort of drawing in a full breath. I clutched my baby blanket like a lifeline, knuckles white, while Lu pressed close, licking the salt of my tears as they fell.

Softly, like a lullaby, my mom would guide me back to myself: "Relax your jaw," she'd whisper. "Let the weight fall from your shoulders. Unclench your hands. Breathe into your big heart. Relax your strong legs that have carried you through so much." Her voice was the only steady thing in a body that felt hijacked by panic.

When the storm passed, I'd lie on the floor, wiped clean of energy. Just a few moments to reset, to pull myself together, before remembering it was still the middle of the day and I had a job to do. So I put on my brave face, masked the cracks and pretended nothing was coming undone inside me.

When November 11, 2020 arrived, I found myself once again stepping up to an international gate — this time, flying from Chicago to Tokyo. But nothing about this felt like an adventure.

The jumbo jet was nearly empty due to the strict COVID travel restrictions — rows and rows of untouched fabric and silence. I had my pick of seats and claimed a lonely corner at the back, hoping the solitude would somehow soothe me. As I clutched my passport with trembling hands and sank into the seat, my chest caved in. The tears came fast, hot and unstoppable. All I could whisper between sobs was:

"I don't want to go.
I don't want to do this.
I don't want this life anymore."

I landed in Japan the next day, dehydrated from crying, my arms and legs numb with dread. Seeing GI Joe for the first time was disorienting — we embraced without passion, a far cry from the early days when he'd twirl me off the ground in airport terminals, eyes lit up like I was everything. This time, it was a quick kiss, a stiff hello and a quiet shuffle into the apartment. He wore baggy sweats that did nothing to stir any longing in me — not even familiarity.

Our high-rise apartment on base was eerily sterile. Our

things hadn't yet arrived from Virginia and the space echoed with emptiness. A scratchy polyester rental couch. A basic rectangle oak table. A desk. A queen bed. That was it. I laid down on the unfamiliar mattress, sleepless and hollow, unaware that this moment would become the defining tone of my time in Japan.

I woke up a few hours later, determined to take on my first workday in Japan. Midnight to 8am — that would be my new normal. I needed to keep my job and I needed some semblance of structure. At 11am, I'd crawl into bed, trying to lull myself into sleep before the cycle began again at 11pm.

On weekends, I wouldn't let myself adjust. I told myself it was discipline, really it was self-punishment.

I was set on torturing myself.

For my infidelity.

For my weakness.

For my inability to love.

For my life choices.

For everything.

The schedule didn't work — not even close. We didn't have blackout curtains, so the sun poured in unapologetically. The mattress still wore its plastic like a protective shell, crinkling with every restless toss. The base blasted the national anthem over loudspeakers at sunset each day. GI Joe would get home from his standard work hours just as I was finally drifting off, then wake me again when he crawled into bed. Groaning, I'd roll over, avoiding his touch, squeezing my eyes shut against the tears ready to spill over.

I was lucky to get three broken hours of sleep a night.

And I rarely saw GI Joe, not in any real way.

The sleep deprivation, the silence, the sterile, uncozy space and the emotional whiplash — it all chipped away at me until I hardly recognized the person I was becoming. My mental health deteriorated, slowly at first, then all at once. I stopped trying. My hair stayed tied up in a greasy, unwashed bun. I didn't bother with contacts, choosing instead to wear my smudged glasses, which sat heavy on my face. Deep bags hung under my bloodshot eyes and my skin had begun to lose its color, dulled by exhaustion and despair. I wore the same oversized fleece sweatshirt every day, like armor or apathy — I'm not sure which.

November 24, 2020
YOKOSUKA, JAPAN

A lot has happened that I've wanted to write but just couldn't get the pen to paper. This truly has been the hardest season of my life. I'm exhausted, lonely and depressed.

Thankfully, my two week arrival quarantine ends today (!!!) I'll finally be able to leave this apartment, see base, see Yokosuka, maybe see a shrine before I have to get home and in bed.

That liberty didn't last though — due to the pandemic, base locked down two weeks later and I was confined to the one and half mile radius. Each day, I'd go to the grocery store on base just to get some human interaction with the cashiers.

The walls started closing in.

I began questioning everything — not just why I was in Japan, but why I was here *at all*.

We lived on the 10th floor. Most days I'd stand on the balcony and wonder:

"What would happen if I went over the edge of the balcony?

Would GI Joe blame himself?
Would my parents miss me?
What would my friends say at my funeral?
Where would Lu live?
What would it be like to die?"

December 21, 2020
YOKOSUKA, JAPAN

Will I ever sleep again?
I need meds. And a therapist.

Christmas Eve was spent with a 1.5-liter bottle of wine, Christmas Day was spent with a hangover. GI Joe's shift — four days on, two days off — had landed over the holiday. He was gone and since my therapist couldn't work outside of the country, I was left with nothing but silence and spiraling thoughts.

December 24, 2020
YOKOSUKA, JAPAN

I've been listening to "Underneath The Tree" on repeat for the last hour. My wine is nearly gone. 2020 was hard. 2021 scares but excites me. I want to be me and live up to my dreams. I will hurt people. I won't like it. Me > everyone. Sorry in advance to anyone that gets in my way.

The new year arrived, but instead of relief from the pandemic, it brought another wave of lockdowns. The world was still shuttered, and my reality in Japan was starting to feel more like a cage for a feral animal than the love story once cited on social media and national television as "perfect." With rumors circulating that Japan's borders would close again, I booked a flight that would leave in just two days.

We didn't talk much in those final hours. Instead, we dragged the mattress out to the living room and laid it in front of the brand-new flatscreen I'd bought him as a leaving present — a gesture wrapped in guilt more than love. We curled up under a blanket and let Netflix fill the silence, the flicker of the screen doing the talking for us.

That night, we had sex for the first time since I'd arrived in Japan more than two months prior — not passionate or romantic, but something quieter. Resigned. It felt like a bittersweet goodbye disguised as intimacy, a way to say what we couldn't with words.

On January 8, 2021, with the haunting ache of You Were Good to Me by Chelsea Cutler and Jeremy Zucker echoing in the back of my mind, I zipped up my two suitcases and took one final breath in our fluorescent-lit apartment. GI Joe wasn't allowed to leave base and take me to the airport, so he hugged me in the entryway of our building — arms tight, eyes unreadable. Then the taxi pulled away, carrying me past the gates of the military base and into the unknown. I wasn't just heading home, but toward the reckoning I could no longer outrun.

SEVEN
DISHONORABLY DISCHARGED

February 4, 2021; The Pattern App

Freedom needs to be a top priority for you. Your values aren't mainstream — you're intended to be on a more spiritual path.

AFTER LANDING BACK in the U.S., I collapsed into a few weeks of nothingness at my parents' house. I slept. A lot. When I wasn't sleeping, I was numbing — filling online shopping carts, spending thousands to replace everything that had been sent to Japan but never reached me. It was as though I thought new clothes and cozy throws could wrap around my grief and turn it into something softer. My limbs felt heavy, like I was moving through molasses. I spoke in a flat, monotone voice, assuring friends that GI Joe and I would work things out — even though I couldn't remember the last time I'd truly laughed. It wasn't devastation that gripped me. It was delusion.

Avoidance. The ache of everything unspoken settling into my body like a second skin.

Eventually, I packed my GMC Acadia to the brim and pointed it west. Seventeen hours of driving later, I arrived in Denver — exhausted but craving momentum. I threw myself into apartment viewings, trying to anchor myself in this next chapter. After a whirlwind week, I signed a lease and got right back into my car. I needed space — not just a new zip code.

I drove south — Moab, Sedona, Albuquerque — chasing something I couldn't yet name.

Sedona stopped me in my tracks. The energy there buzzed under my skin, stirring things I hadn't let myself feel fully. I booked a session with a healer, hoping she'd help me cut the cord with the man I met during Remote Year — the one who had started out as my best friend and then became something more. Over the past year, we had continued a relationship, though I never knew what to call it. We talked often, confided in each other and I clung to the connection even though it felt like a betrayal to GI Joe. I didn't know if it was love, friendship or just unresolved possibility that kept me holding on.

But when I walked into the healer's room — its air thick with the scent of palo santo and sandalwood, the walls lined with tapestries and shelves of crystals — something shifted. She wore layers of rings that clinked softly when she moved and oversized, colorful glasses that made her eyes seem impossibly present. Without knowing my full story, she suggested a cord-cutting ceremony. I expected to speak about the man from Remote Year. But when she prompted me to hold one end of a string to my heart and invited me to imagine her as GI Joe — to speak to him truthfully, without filter — my body folded in on itself. I sobbed so hard I could barely sit upright.

Through tears, the words spilled out: "I'm sorry, I'm sorry, I'm so sorry I cheated on you. I'm sorry."

To GI Joe.

To myself.

For saying "yes" to a life I no longer wanted.

For forcing a future that was never aligned with my spirit.

For betraying us both with my fear.

As the wave passed and I could form sentences again, everything tumbled out in a voice both broken and clear: "We rushed into our marriage, not realizing what forever actually meant. I wanted to try — I really wanted to — but something in my gut says this isn't right. And I need to listen to that. You are an amazing human, but you are not my human."

And then I cut the cord. Physically, emotionally and spiritually.

I drove to a nearby sanctuary, sitting alongside a burbling river and threw the rope pieces in, watching the current carry them away.

February 23, 2021

SEDONA, ARIZONA, UNITED STATES

I'm not surprised by anything that happened today but it doesn't mean it wasn't tough. It felt really heavy afterwards and then the hike felt magnifying and powerful but now I'm feeling paralyzed. I need to open to my angel guides, relinquish control and be honest — this isn't the marriage I want. I'm sad. I have cut the cord on the old and given my intention of love and happiness to the Universe.

Rather than fully embracing the truth that revealed itself, I defaulted to my avoidant tendencies. I buried myself in Denver

— a new city with endless distractions. I picked unnecessary fights with GI Joe, said things without really saying anything at all, hoping he'd read between the lines and end it for me.

With the time difference, our conversations dwindled to scattered texts. When we finally managed to FaceTime, it ended in silence and a mutual agreement to take a break.

March 11, 2021
DENVER, COLORADO, UNITED STATES

I'd be lying if I didn't admit that it shook me to my core — it's been over an hour and I'm still shaking and my heart is pounding.

Universe, make it easy please.

We agreed to take the next month to sit with ourselves, to feel into what we truly wanted.

I threw myself into nature — skiing, hiking, grounding in the quiet wisdom of the mountains. I leaned into astrology and my spiritual practice, trying to make sense of everything going on beneath the surface. And somewhere in that stillness, I started building a life I never actually intended to invite GI Joe into.

I was steadying myself enough to finally tell him the truth. To have the strength to walk away from him and toward something I loved.

I took a screenshot from one of my favorite astrology apps:

March 18, 2021; The Pattern App —

While you can't ever go back and relive post glories, there are always better ones gathering.

March 24, 2021; The Pattern App —

You haven't messed anything up. You haven't taken the wrong path. You haven't sabotaged your destiny; you're living it. All that you have endured was, and still is, part of the master plan. Your impatience is a sign of your spirit drifting away; reel it back in. At times like this, when your soul feels tired, gratitude is the best antidote to turn to. At times like this, when your heart feels lost, faith is how you'll find yourself back. At times like this, when your mind is going off in different directions, stillness is the only answer to your questions. You're being prepared for something grand, that's why your soul has been put through one test after another. Raise your head to the sky and thank the Universe for the blessing that's coming, your time in the dark is ending. A new chapter with light, love and abundance is about to begin.

As our month apart came to a close, I knew there was only one course of action.

I propped my phone up on a pillow in the middle of my bed, took a deep breath and pressed the button to FaceTime GI Joe.

When his face filled my screen, I could tell by the somber look in his eyes that we were finally on the same page — perhaps for the first time ever.

In the quiet of that conversation, he acknowledged what we both already knew: I had been preparing him for this all along. Teaching him how to budget, encouraging separate purchases, keeping him at arm's length from my Remote Year friends, dreaming of futures that didn't make sense with his lifestyle.

I wasn't building a life with him. I was building a life for myself.

We stared at each other in silence, tears rolling down our cheeks, knowing this would be the last time we'd see each other.

And just like it began — through a screen, across an ocean — our relationship ended the same way: distanced by more than miles.

Exactly three years after he set off on his first deployment, our marriage came to an end. I had always carried a quiet suspicion that my first marriage would end in divorce. And now, I had fulfilled that prophecy — not out of failure, but out of finally telling the truth.

April 13, 2021
DENVER, COLORADO, UNITED STATES

Everyone keeps asking what they can do for me and honestly, all I want is to be held. I'm in so much pain and feel worthless.

Guilt hollowed me out in the months that followed. I had told so few people about my infidelity — not because I didn't want to be honest, but because the shame felt unbearable. As a result, my grieving was incomplete, suspended in a purgatory of omission. Without the full truth, I couldn't fully heal.

I went dark on social media, silencing the version of me that had once broadcasted every milestone. I stopped reaching out. I shelved conversations before they even began. I sheltered myself in a self-imposed isolation tank — like if no one could see me, they couldn't confirm what I already feared about myself.

When I finally found the words to tell my extended family, the divorce papers were already filed. The decision had been made, but that didn't stop the pushback. They didn't understand how a marriage that looked so stable from the outside could collapse without warning. They didn't understand how I could throw away something "good enough."

"You shouldn't be doing this," my aunt said, her voice calm but clipped. "He's good. He's kind. He loves you. That should be enough."

But beneath her words, I heard something else. A quiet fear. A warning. As if what she was really saying was: "Don't end up like me." Divorced. Alone. Still trying to make peace with a story that didn't turn out the way she'd hoped.

The questions, the disappointment — it all deepened the self-inflicted wounds I was already nursing. I knew, with absolute clarity, that ending my marriage was the right decision, even as my friends and family questioned my choices and cast their doubts like stones across a fragile path I was barely holding together.

But what haunted me most was how I got there. How had I lost my integrity along the way?

All my life, I had worn the public persona of the "good girl." The perfectionist. The smart student. The standout athlete. The one with big potential and even bigger dreams — the kind everyone assumed would take me far. And yet, beneath the polished surface, there was always a quiet rebellion brewing. By sixteen, once I had my own car, stealing became a habit — a thrill I chased in secret. I'd skip soccer practice and stroll into Macy's with empty hands, walking out with a designer purse slung over my shoulder, stuffed with stolen clothes and accessories. At Target, I'd hide lingerie and swimsuits under baggy sweatpants, then check out with nothing but a pack of gum. I slipped lip gloss and nail polish up my sleeves at the local pharmacy like it was second nature. I spun my car on black ice once, landing in a ditch on the way to driving school — punishment for a speeding ticket I'd already shrugged off. I drank every chance I got, hotboxed my car before school, smoked hookah every afternoon after. My ears were heavy with oversized hoops, my belly button pierced before senior year, my nose done shortly after. I got my first tattoo at eighteen — a pink and orange hibiscus flower with the word "faith" inked across the top of my right foot. Not long after, I added my second: "it was then that I carried you" scrawled along my ribs. My rebellion wasn't loud, but it was constant. A steady defiance tucked beneath the image I'd learned to project.

But those seemed minor in comparison to this — this was the ultimate rebellion. And it didn't feel thrilling. It felt like betrayal. Of him. Of myself.

Had I ever had integrity? Had I ever truly known who I was beneath the roles I played?

I sat with these questions. I battled myself. I blamed others. I broke apart. I took responsibility.

And then I took myself to Guatemala.

EIGHT

TAKING BACK MY NAME

I READ THE EMAIL twice before leaping out of my desk chair and doing a full-body happy dance. Remote Year was making its post-COVID comeback — launching a series of week-long retreats to reignite its community and recover lost revenue. After nearly escaping to Guatemala the year before, this invitation felt like divine timing. My spirituality had deepened in recent months — I carried crystals in my bag, tracked the moon phases and read signs into everything. This wasn't just a trip; it felt like a call. A wellness retreat didn't just sound good — it felt necessary.

The itinerary was vague: daily wellness activities, personal growth sessions, group bonding. It was my first retreat, so I didn't know exactly what to expect or what to look for but something in my gut said yes. I didn't know how things would unfold — only that I had to be there. That it would change everything.

On the first full day, we were asked why we were there. My voice shook as I read aloud from my journal, silent tears streaking down my cheeks:

"I'm going through a divorce. I had this life thought out for myself and ourselves with goals, dreams, timelines and then I realized that wasn't going to happen, he wasn't right for me. I could have been the dutiful military wife but that would mean giving up on myself. I could have waited his contract out but I knew a divorce would happen regardless. I always knew I wasn't traditional but being in a marriage with extra military hardships was too much. Being on Remote Year, I saw what I could have. And ultimately, I love myself more than I could love someone else and I need to honor and take care of that. So why am I here? I'm going through a divorce and I crave returning to the things I love doing and loving myself."

Later that day, I kept asking the same question in my journal, over and over, like a chant:

"I lose myself in relationships, why is that?
How can I stay present and involved and selfish all at
   the same time?
How do I not let someone else's energy consume
   mine?"

Midway through the week, something shifted. For the first time in months, I felt strong enough to reclaim something that had been lingering just out of reach: my name. Constance Nicole Kulczycki.

I scribbled it everywhere — in my journal, on the wall of a local bar covered in graffiti, across my social media profiles. I proudly introduced myself wherever we went: "Hi, I'm Connie!"

I was no longer tethered to my marriage. I was no longer performing a version of me. I was my own sovereign being. And my name — that full, true, fierce name — was my power.

On the second to last night of our retreat, a fellow participant, Lauren O'Connell — better known as @themoderna-
strologer — led us through a new moon ceremony under the
starlit Guatemalan sky. It was a moment to pause, to manifest,
to call in everything we desired for the next moon cycle.

June 24, 2021

LAKE ATITLAN, GUATEMALA

New moon, new name.

Something shifted in me. I could feel it — a rising, a reclaiming. The version of me who had arrived in Guatemala had
been transformed. I wasn't just healing anymore; I was expanding. I was ready to leave this place and step into the world as the
woman I had become.

But first, I needed to hike a volcano. And I had someone I
wished to invite along with me.

Throughout the week, I'd found myself gravitating toward
the retreat leader — not just because of his presence, but because his energy pulled me in like a magnet. There were these
small, undeniable moments: the way he spoke about spirituality, the ease of his laugh, the way he moved through the world
with curiosity and intention. His sense of adventure. His home
on wheels.

I texted my best friend Kelly after the first day, "What happens when you want to fuck your retreat leader?"

But it wasn't just lust. He didn't just check the boxes —
tall, dark, handsome with a beard and fit body; traveler; for-
ward-thinking and financially grounded; spiritually aware and
emotionally intelligent. He felt like my **mani**festation list come
to life. I had written in my journal just weeks earlier: "I yearn

for an open and honest and passionate and adventurous partnership."

And more than the resume, it was the feeling. I felt like I
knew him deeply the moment I met him. Like our souls had
already met. Something in my gut nudged me that McDreamy
would matter — that his presence in my life wasn't a coincidence but fated.

I lay in the hammock at the retreat center, eyes half-closed,
heart open and let myself drift into the daydream I couldn't
shake — the one where he was mine.

In it, being with him felt like stepping into pure possibility. He wouldn't confine or clip my wings; he'd expand my sky.
With him, I didn't have to shrink to fit. I could be more —
more curious, more creative, more me. The future stretched out
like a canvas we could paint together: stitched with adventure,
soul-stretching conversations, slow mornings in unfamiliar
places, inside jokes and shared dreams. He was the kind of man
I had always imagined walking through life with — a partner,
a mirror, a co-creator. The one I could grow old with without
ever growing bored.

And, like always, my imagination outran reality.

When I meet someone I'm interested in, I've always had
this reflex — this cinematic mind that fills in the story before
the second scene. I could paint our home, our travels, the way
we'd move through life together — before we even picked out
the color scheme. I did it with the Man in Finance. With GI
Joe. I fell fast, in love with the idea more than the actual person
in front of me. And even now, despite all my awareness and
intentions to move slowly, I could feel myself doing it again.

I blinked my eyes open, reading Kelly's response, "Don't get
into another relationship anytime soon."

In the off-moments of the retreat — at meals, walking between sessions, on the boat rides between the towns on Lake Atitlan — McDreamy and I started to open up to each other. It wasn't grand declarations or sweeping romance. Just quiet honesty shared in passing, in presence.

"Well, I've never had a relationship longer than six months, to be honest," he told me one evening on the way to dinner.

I nodded, filing that away.

His stories hinted at a familiar pattern: when things got intense or uncertain, he pulled away. Intimacy didn't seem to root him — it spooked him. And as much as I wanted to lean in, I could feel that subtle tug — the quiet warning that maybe I was dreaming of the potential, not the reality. Of the man he could be, not the one he actually was.

In that haze of longing, I opened my journal and wrote:

I want a different kind of relationship — one where two people come together because they connect on a different level. Where we're constantly exploring and adventuring, never settling down, at least not in the traditional sense. I want to live on planes and trains and vans and beaches and mountaintops. I want to talk all night, laugh all day and have sex wherever and whenever we damn well please. I want to hike and kayak and surf and run and ski and meditate together. I want to be together because we choose to be — not because we're bound by a piece of paper. I want a love that's alive, that expands me, that makes me feel like I'm living in full color. A relationship that's rooted in freedom, in choosing each other again and again, in making the most of our time here on earth.

And then, on the final night of the retreat, something shifted.

While the others sat around the table, McDreamy and I slipped away, finding each other in the quiet of the kitchen — sharing a microwavable bowl of Kraft mac and cheese like it was a secret.

"Want to summit Acatenango with me?" I asked.

He smiled. "Hell yes."

The next day, we took a crowded bus to Antigua and checked into a tiny room I'd pre-booked. But the moment the door clicked shut behind us, a wave of panic rose in my chest — I had only known this man for a week, and we were about to spend the night together then hike and camp together on a volcano. I hadn't been with anyone since GI Joe in January. We sat on the bed, the only place to sit, and when our eyes met, the world stilled. His expression shifted — curiosity, then awe, then hunger. As he undressed me slowly, it felt like the final layer of my old life as a wife was being shed too.

He was wildness where I had known routine — open where I had known restraint. His hands were sure but reverent, like he was discovering me and something sacred all at once. There was no rush, only presence. Every kiss felt like a question I wanted to say yes to. And I did — over and over, until I collapsed against him, breathless and awakened. The sex was amazing, yes, but it was the energy beneath it — the curiosity, the care, the rawness — that lingered.

We set off early the next morning with a group of hikers. I'd found a local tour company that handled all the logistics — gear, food, guides — so all we had to do was show up and climb. Our first official date was summiting Acatenango, a 3,976-meter volcano.

There was an ease between us — the kind that only comes when intimacy has already cracked something open.

We laughed every time our eyes met. We sat side by side at dinner, legs brushing. And as Fuego erupted in front of us, we talked long into the night — about past partners, how we had and hadn't shown up in love and what we both longed for next.

Later, in our tiny, elevated A-frame cabin, we unzipped our sleeping bags and made one. The air outside was crisp, but inside, we kept each other warm. Voyage Libre by Thievery Corporation pulsed softly from a nearby speaker — a French song, fluid and hypnotic. Our bodies moved like one to its beat, as if the music, the mountain and the moment had fused us into something new. The volcano rumbled in the distance and I could feel my own heart echoing its rise.

It felt fitting: the chaos, the beauty, the danger. Something inside me had been quietly rumbling for years. And now, standing on the edge of everything I had ever known — I was ready to erupt.

June 29, 2021

FLYING FROM GUATEMALA CITY, GUATEMALA
TO CHICAGO, ILLINOIS, UNITED STATES

I've had the faintest smile on my face all day, not because I'm only slightly happy but because it's an even-keeled feeling of bliss and happiness. I went on this retreat in order to find some hope and remind myself of the things I love to do, I'm walking away with more than I ever could have asked for — I know I made the right choice, I know I'm going to be just fine — better than fine, I feel mentally, spiritually and sexually alive. I want to figure out how to keep this feeling no matter where I am or what I'm doing. I want to align with friends, my home, my soul. I don't

*have it all figured out but for the immediate future, this is
what I'm seeing:*

- *Finding a career that is better aligned.*
- *Portugal in October for the Remote Year retreat and
then extend for another week.*
- *South Africa in December for the Remote Year retreat
and then extend for a month.*
- *Putting my stuff in storage and high-tailing it in
February to somewhere in Central or South America,
maybe Argentina?*

Things to take away from this week:

- *I am very energetically open — I need to protect that,
and stop morphing to fit the people around me.*
- *I crave deep human connection, and there's no shame
in that.*
- *Men are attracted to me — that's amazing, and I can
also be alone.*
- *Shared experiences are magic — they amplify joy
tenfold.*
- *Vulnerability is my superpower — sharing my truth is
a part of my purpose.*
- *I'm here to hold space for others, to listen deeply and to
stay soft.*
- *I want to practice stepping back emotionally and viewing
situations with clarity.*
- *I don't want my life to continue being a sob story — I'm
writing a new narrative.*
- *I want to live fully in my feminine and continue to
embrace my magnetism.*

As a side note, I would love to see McDreamy again. However, if I don't, I'm thankful for the time we had together and him providing a space where I could open up and be pretty vulnerable. It was amazing to see that there are men out there that are successful yet spiritually connected and working on themselves. He pushed me and challenged me which is something I haven't had in a minute. I don't want to admit this but he is my perfect guy on paper, yet his lack of commitment and withholding is troubling. So my love, stay grounded and go with whatever life decides to give you.

NINE

COLORADO CLARITY CODES

I LANDED BACK IN the U.S. and into my first official Colorado summer — a season of hikes, concerts, kayak trips, moon ceremonies with Lauren and first dates with new people who reminded me how alive I could feel again. One year into my job at the political media agency, I was promoted — a small but satisfying affirmation that I was building something steady, something that felt like progress.

Each day, I tracked my dreams from the night prior, I meditated, I journaled whatever came up. Slowly, those quiet moments began laying the foundation for what was next — not just where I wanted to go, but who I was becoming.

For the first time in a long time, I could see my future clearly — and it wasn't weighed down by GI Joe. It was mine.

But that didn't mean the present was light. The drama of disentangling our lives lingered like smoke in a room I had just escaped. Everything I owned was still in Japan, and I found myself begging him over email and text to send it back. I was still living out of the same two suitcases that had traveled from Virginia to Chicago to Japan and back again — patched together with a few new pieces I'd picked up since landing in Denver. The divorce paperwork was in limbo, and every day that passed without a signature felt like a string still tying me to a life I no longer claimed.

Even though he was no longer part of my path, the remnants of our story still clung to me like that smoke — heavy, unfinished and demanding to be reckoned with.

I emptied these thoughts and more into my journal:

July 13, 2021

DENVER, COLORADO, UNITED STATES

I feel like I'm missing the magic of Guatemala already which is what I was scared of — I know I need to find it within myself but damn I'm feeling like I'm missing something in my life. I don't like this feeling. So throwing it back at myself — find the magic within.

It was a weird paradox. I was finally stepping into my power, building a life I was genuinely proud of, but I could feel the edges of loneliness creeping in. I wanted adventure. I wanted the thrill of independence. But I also ached for someone to share it with — someone who could meet me in the bigness of this life I was crafting.

July 14, 2021

DENVER, COLORADO, UNITED STATES

Primal loneliness — feeling it deep in my soul... I thought of McDreamy but he also scares me. He'd lose interest and get bored too quickly. Or he wouldn't fully open up and then push me away. I don't want to hold out for him to happen... but I'll keep the space open while exploring other possibilities.

Then, one night — wine-drunk and tired of my own spirals — I called the guy from Remote Year. The one I had clung to for too long in my mind. I told him it would never happen between us. That I didn't want him — just the idea of him. The fantasy had been more comforting than the actual connection ever was. Hanging up, I felt both shaky and free.

In the weeks that followed, I kept journaling.

August 11, 2021
DENVER, COLORADO, UNITED STATES

I want to go to Bali for yoga teacher training.

August 17, 2021
DENVER, COLORADO, UNITED STATES

Connie, I am so damn proud of you. It was messy as hell getting here but I have so much joy now. It's not all perfect but here's to living your truth.

August 19, 2021
DENVER, COLORADO, UNITED STATES

Maybe I'm not supposed to be free as in single but free from the worry to be perfect. Maybe I should just quit everything. Maybe I should just go to Argentina.

I rode the waves of my emotions, letting them crash over me without trying to grasp too tightly. That had been my problem before — I had tried to control everything, to force things into boxes they didn't belong in. I had over-exercised, over-analyzed, over-stylized and had it worked in my favor? Not once. This time, I was committed to flowing with life.

And life had plans for me.

I had left the door open, telling McDreamy that if he was ever in Colorado, he should reach out. He did. I took a week off work at the political media agency and curated an epic van trip through the Rocky Mountains — every stop, every scenic detour, every cozy overnight carefully chosen to show him my world.

We laughed our way south through Frisco and Vail, Leadville and Salida, winding through Montrose and all the way to Telluride. The sun brought out the freckles that dusted his nose and arms, his already tan skin deepening into gold. He wore his baseball cap backwards, a look so effortless and boyish it made my heart skip. His wardrobe was exactly what you'd expect from someone who lived out of a van — soft, sun-worn tees, well-loved shorts, hiking boots.

There wasn't much silence — in the best way. We talked for hours about everything and nothing as we soaked in the alpine views: childhood memories, big dreams, the weird habits we thought no one else would understand. Every conversation felt like another door opening.

At night, we curled up in the van, limbs tangled atop the blankets, high from gummies and flushed from rounds of You & Me: A Game of Love & Intimacy. The questions turned us toward each other slowly, then all at once — teasing glances, playful touches, stories that slipped into desire. Conversation blurred into foreplay and sleep was always the last thing on our minds. I felt sexually and sensually alive in a way I hadn't before — not just wanted, but awakened. Like my body was remembering something it had been waiting years to feel. The same body that had shut down in past relationships, always knowing they were over long before my heart or mind could catch up.

I made the trip so good, he stayed an extra week.

I made the trip so good, he invited me to Montana the next month to meet his best friends and celebrate my 30th birthday.

I made the trip so good, he decided to use his last week of vacation from his full-time UX design job to lead a retreat in South Africa and I signed up as a participant for it.

I made the trip so good, the Universe responded in kind — my paperwork arrived from the courts. I was officially divorced. Officially free.

Like a soft-spoken mantra, John de Soto's lyrics threaded through the air, singing to the Universe:

"Before this song is over,
We be wild and free,
More than you imagine,
More than just lovers for the weekend."

Everything about this partnership felt expansive. It held the kind of tension I had been dreaming of — adventure and stability, passion and play, purpose and presence. And now, without legal ties to the past, I could finally imagine our futures intertwining in full color.

And yet, a part of me urged caution. "Reel it in. Stay here. Don't lose yourself in the dream." It always came just as I was drifting off, in that hazy space between waking and sleep. But dreams are seductive. And this one? It was just beginning.

September 9, 2021

Our connection is wildly special. I don't know where this thing will go but I'm thankful for it regardless. That he showed me what is possible. That he showed me who I can be and what I can have. That he accepted me for who I am. I am so excited to be back with him in Montana. Making each decision for myself and my heart and my magic. I am thankful, always.

I wasn't sure what we were, but I knew what I felt was real. Every moment with him expanded my world — made me think bigger, feel deeper, push myself further. But despite the magic, there was a lingering uncertainty. It crept in during the quiet moments, like when I checked my phone to see if he'd texted and felt my heart sink into my stomach when he hadn't. A slow drop. A subtle ache. A knowing that, as much as we pulled each other in, something was keeping us from fully landing. And maybe it wasn't something — maybe it was him. Maybe I was already sensing he wasn't it. Not all the way. But I'd gotten so good at ignoring that feeling. I'd done it before. *Almost* right had become my baseline.

September 13, 2021

DENVER, COLORADO, UNITED STATES

The Co-star app has now told me to not fight my feelings, wear my heart on my sleeves, and to share my thoughts with you so in an effort to be more secure, here we are:

Being with you expands my world. You make my wildest

dreams seem possible while simultaneously encouraging me to think even bigger. With you, nothing is crazy except not saying yes to adventures or following my heart. I feel comfortable being vulnerable with you — showing you my ugly truths or exploring different fantasies. The challenge of keeping things interesting is one I welcome with open arms since there are so many things I want to do and places I want to go. However, I would be lying if I didn't say it also terrifies me. I know we could be amazing together and mentally, emotionally, physically and spiritually explore together yet your relationship history of not fully opening up and your relationship ideas scare me:

History — not fully opening up, avoidant, getting bored, nit picky

Ideas — open, non-monogamy (open to trying and yet worried I won't like it and you will or vice versa and having a soul crushing breakup OR my personal inner battles of jealousy not letting it work)

We also communicate very differently and I worry that you don't always hear me even though you are listening. I don't see this as a deal breaker, yet it's something that needs to be made aware of. All of this is me getting ahead of myself though and I truly do like where we stand but we're toeing the line and it's already getting hard to ignore my feelings that are trying to escape the very tight box I put them in. And that's before we have two more grand adventures together. I don't want to scare you off or tie you down (classic Sagittarius avoidant) but I think it would be helpful, and quite frankly the thing for both of us to think of where we want this to go — it will help me to not be anxious and you to grow out of avoidance so we can both be more secure. In my head, we keep it chill for now as it has been when we're not together, allowed to date others but also receptive if one reaches out. Then when we're in Montana and South Africa, we're 100% in. Come the new year, you could spend February snowboarding with me and I could spend March surfing with you. From there, we see what the Universe has in store for us and if it wants us together or not. I'm here to give us a chance.

I never said the words out loud — too afraid of what might happen if I did. So instead, I retreated into my imagination, clinging to the potential instead of the reality.

September 16, 2021
DENVER, COLORADO, UNITED STATES

I could so easily love you. Holy shit fuck.

On our road trip, McDreamy and I had hours to fill with conversation — and we didn't waste it. We dove deep into the books Attached by Rachel S. F. Heller and In Sync with the Opposite Sex by Alison Armstrong, trying to understand how our different relationship patterns played off one another. He owned his avoidant tendencies. I admitted to being anxious-avoidant, floating between the two as a classic indecisive Libra does. We didn't run from our dynamics — we studied them, laid them out like a map, trying to figure out the route forward.

We explored what it meant to be in a partnership versus a

relationship. We talked about masculine and feminine energy, about showing up with integrity, about what it means to truly hold space. And, perhaps most surprisingly, we talked about open and poly relationships.

I had considered them before — during the lonely stretches of my marriage with GI Joe. But I never brought it up then, too afraid of rocking the fragile boat we'd built. After my infidelity, I started to question if monogamy was truly aligned for me. And now, here was someone asking the same questions. Someone curious, open, intentional. It felt like the Universe was listening.

And as if that weren't enough to process, a new job opportunity fell into my lap — I was sought out for a leadership role at a well-known political agency. They had built their reputation on communications and PR, but were now expanding into paid media, and I would be helping shape and lead the team. The Vice President title was impressive, the offer of $150,000 nearly double my current salary. The company was based in Washington, D.C., with offices there and in New York City — though neither had reopened post-pandemic. I negotiated to stay fully remote, with a home base in Denver should they ever return to in-person work. I wasn't in love with the company culture, but the financial freedom it promised? That was hard to walk away from.

September 23, 2021
DENVER, COLORADO, UNITED STATES

I am going to take it — for the position, title and money.
I will have work life balance and set firm boundaries.
I'm going to save like crazy in order to buy a home base,

create my dream space to host retreats and then quit so I
can spend time getting my yoga teacher training in Bali.
I'm going to travel the world and be happily in love with
McDreamy.

As I tried to process everything that had unfolded over the
past few months, life refused to slow down. I was already packing my bags for the next adventure — two weeks in Montana
with McDreamy to celebrate my birthday and the end of my
job, a brief stop in Colorado to drop my sweet pup Lu off with
my parents who had recently moved to Arkansas, then a multi-
week trip to Colombia with McDreamy, followed by a visit to
his parents in Florida before I finally looped back to Denver. It
was a whirlwind and I was doing my best to keep up, hoping I
wouldn't lose myself in the rush.

After Montana, something shifted. Not just in our relationship, but in me. I had flown out to meet three of his best
friends — and from the moment I arrived, they pulled me into
their world like I'd always belonged. We spent the two weeks
hiking through breathtaking trails, where our conversations
ran deep, guided by prompts from the Vertellis card game —
we reflected on our childhoods, shared our fears and our greatest dreams. With every mile and moment, I felt myself shifting
into the version of self I wanted to be.

On my birthday, we paused at a scenic lookout mid-hike,
and the guys surprised me with heartfelt wishes. Varun — Mc-
Dreamy's best friend and someone I'd connected with effortlessly — was the first to speak, telling me how deeply he believed in my energy and potential. The others chimed in, saying
they could feel I was meant for big things — that my beauty
wasn't just in appearance, but in presence. That night, we ate

at a cozy Italian restaurant, followed by drinks at a local bar where a stranger bought me a beer and led the entire room in singing "Happy Birthday."

McDreamy gave me a camping stove — a nod to our van trip through Colorado the month prior — and in that moment, it felt like he saw the whole of me: the dreamer, the adventurer, the one who wanted to build a life outside the lines.

We talked about our future. Decided we would be together — in an open relationship for now, knowing we each had individual travels ahead of us, but trusting what we had was real. At the end of the trip, we all exchanged small gifts and hand-written cards, keepsakes to mark a two weeks none of us would forget.

On the flight home, I found myself writing and rewriting a letter to McDreamy, trying to put into words everything that had stirred in my heart. I jotted it onto a Whitefish postcard, tucking it safely away in my bag — saving it for when he joined me in Colorado the following week:

I've rewritten this about 20 times because how do you put something so special and indescribable into words? On top of that, it's hard to believe we've only truly been together on three separate occasions, yet we have such a strong connection on so many levels. It all leaves me speechless. The thing I can say with confidence though is that you make me so happy. This trip was so beautiful, and my birthday was one I will never forget — and that's because of you. The vulnerable places we both went were inspiring, and I'm so proud of you for going there and honored that you did so with me. I'm so excited to see where the Universe takes us. Here's to being more secure, together. And all of the adventures, planned and unplanned, to come.

It felt like the beginning of something real. Something that couldn't be explained — only felt.

And I was finally ready to feel it all.

TEN

LOST IN LOVE, FOUND IN A COW PASTURE

A S QUICKLY AS the summer had gone by, the fall passed even faster — blurred by movement, but anchored by something that felt sacred. It was the last night of our trip in Colombia. We'd spent the day wandering Medellín, squeezing the final bits of adventure out of our time there. That evening, we decided to go out with a bang — ordering a small bag of cocaine, something wild and reckless that felt like a nod to the freedom we kept chasing. We ended up hooking up in the bathroom of a club, a chaotic mix of laughter, passion and adrenaline. When the drugs wore off, we slipped back to our hotel room and picked up where we left off — slower now, more tender.

Afterward, tangled together, his body draped over mine, nose to nose, I could feel something hanging in the air between us. A tension. A truth trying to push its way out. I gently nudged, "What's going on in that head of yours?"

He deflected, brushing it off, then got up and disappeared into the bathroom. When he returned, he crawled back on top of me, bracing his weight with his forearms, his face just inches from mine. There was a pause — and then his eyes searched mine, steady and unblinking.

"I think you're my person," he said quietly. "I love you."

The words hung between us, electric and disorienting. On one hand it felt right and on the other I wasn't expecting them — not from him, not yet — but as soon as they landed, I felt my heart surge in response. Not with certainty, but with the undeniable knowing that something between us was real. That whatever we were building, it wasn't casual anymore.

"I love you too," I murmured, pressing my lips to his.

The dreams of financial freedom, the sexual fantasies, the plans of traveling the world together that I had tried so hard to tame, came rushing forward. A future stitched together with inside jokes, shared sunrises, van road trips and lazy Sundays. A life where I didn't have to choose between freedom and partnership — I could have both. I could have *him*.

As This Too Shall Last by Anderson East played through the speaker, its soulful ache wrapped around us like a promise. The lyrics clung to the air — not in pain, but in the belief that love, this love, could endure. That the goodness could last. That we could build something real, wild and lasting.

It felt like fate. Like every heartbreak, every detour, every soul-stretching ache had prepared me for this moment. For *him*. For a love that felt like coming home — not the home I was raised in, but the one I'd always been searching for.

And yet, the afterglow dimmed faster than I anticipated.

November 12, 2021
DENVER, COLORADO, UNITED STATES

It's been one week since he told me he loved me. One week

since I told him I loved him. One week since it was never spoken about again. I haven't slept much this week and I think that is contributing to it. I love him but he is not everything — I am. I will not lose myself. I will be elevated. I will not be dependent on him. I will welcome him into my life as an equal. Thank you Universe for bringing us together — I look forward to all of your plans for us together and individually.

It sat there between us, unacknowledged — like a fragile object neither of us wanted to touch. After the confession in Colombia, I thought the air between us would be warmer, softer, surer. But once we were apart again — him in Naples, Florida with his parents, me back in Denver — something shifted.

Our text messages were inconsistent. The phone calls, not as often as I would have liked. And then one night, after a quick check-in, he said, "Alright, I'll talk to you later," and hung up.

Still no I love you.

November 15, 2021
DENVER, COLORADO, UNITED STATES

The word "trauma" has come up so much in my thoughts and words today and yesterday — with the Man in Finance, with GI Joe, with those from before even. I'm terrified that these thoughts and fears will work their way into my partnership with McDreamy and that's the absolute last thing I want so I'm going to focus on getting it out then manifesting the good in:

• Not hearing from the Man in Finance and him disappearing every other weekend.

- *The Man in Finance not wanting labels.*
- *The Man in Finance calling me crazy and gaslighting me.*
- *Not showing the Man in Finance that I wanted him.*
- *The Man in Finance cheating on me.*
- *The Man in Finance being on dating apps while we were living together.*
- *GI Joe deploying.*
- *Cheating on GI Joe.*
- *Not being able to settle with GI Joe.*
- *Leading the man from Remote Year on.*
- *Being told I'm not loved anymore.*
- *Suicidal thoughts.*

I have all these traumas and I want to move forward and grow and be my best self but how? Remembering these instances truly breaks my heart and I don't want to repeat these. I'm just as scared of McDreamy breaking my heart as I am of reverting back to that weak, lost version of myself. I want to be strong and independent, someone who can fully give to a relationship without losing herself. I want us to be open and honest with each other, supportive and loving and inspiring. I want routine and adventure. I want to love each other like we've never experienced before. Cracked open, vulnerable, visceral. I want to be aligned and feel the power of our love radiate to every corner of the Universe. I want to be two individuals who choose a life together every single day.

So I dove headfirst into personal development. If I wasn't working, I devoured self-help books like they were lifelines, journaled obsessively and filled my ears with podcasts about secure attachment, conscious communication and how to stop sabotaging healthy love. I didn't just want to show up for myself — I yearned to show up for us. I wanted to prove to him — and to myself — that love didn't have to be something we guarded against. That this could be different. It could be safe and expansive.

November 20, 2021; A Note from the Universe
DENVER, COLORADO, UNITED STATES

Speak positive words into your life every single morning. Think big. Think healing. Think success. Think happiness. Think growth mindset. Always start the day with positive energy.

I tried. I really did. But the splinters were forming. His avoidance hadn't disappeared — it just quieted. Waiting. And on top of that, our open relationship was beginning to stir some of my deepest insecurities.

When a new COVID strain emerged in December, just days before our scheduled flight to Cape Town, South Africa for the retreat, we made the difficult call to cancel. Instead, we rerouted to Costa Rica — his heart home. He had spent most of 2021 in Santa Teresa, a surf and yoga town on the Nicoya Peninsula, and he had recently returned to lead a retreat over Thanksgiving. I thought being there with him might ground us, bring us closer.

Instead, I felt myself start to fall apart.

I noticed how women looked at him — curious, flirtatious, lingering. And then my mind spiraled: "Had he already been with them? Were they still talking? Was this "open" agreement just an easier way to never commit?"

We had settled on four rules:

◆ If one of us isn't asking the other for details, then don't tell them.
◆ Stay safe — physically, emotionally and energetically.
◆ When we're together, we're together.
◆ Tell an interest on the first date or before hooking up about the open partnership.

The rules were clear. But boundaries don't always quiet the mind — especially when past wounds are still raw.

I *wanted* to trust him. And on many levels, I did. But the ghosts of betrayal — not just by others, but by myself — hadn't been exorcised.

And Costa Rica, with all its magic, was starting to become the mirror I didn't want to look into.

December 8, 2021

SANTA TERESA, COSTA RICA

The amount of worry spiraling in my head this morning and last night was ridiculous. And really frustrating. I know this is how I inactively push everyone away and that's exactly what I don't want to do. So let's visualize what the rest of this trip will look like:

◆ *In love.*
◆ *Happiness.*
◆ *Content.*
◆ *Purpose.*
◆ *Adventure.*
◆ *Some routine — working out, healthy eating, etc.*

‹ *Affirmation.*

I just want out of bed and to stop self-sabotaging.

It's one of those days that I have so much to say but unsure how to say it so I'm just going to start with:

I choose happiness.

The Universe responded.

That day, on our way to a waterfall, our four wheeler broke down in the middle of a cow pasture. No service. No way out. Instead of letting it ruin the moment, we hiked in and spent the afternoon floating in the natural pools, laughing at the absurdity of it all. By the time we made it back to the road, we noticed a sign for a tow truck that we had somehow missed before.

McDreamy rode up front and I climbed into the truck bed on top of the quad in my hot pink thong bikini, waving at passing cars as we were towed into town. And in that moment, I realized — this is us. This is how we make it. As long as we can remember our essence, our lightness, our laughter, we will always find our way back.

But the Universe wasn't done testing us.

Two weeks later, I caught strep throat. And after barely recovering, we both got COVID. My symptoms lingered longer than expected — a deep, relentless cough that wouldn't let up. I brushed it off, thinking it would fade with time, but as the weeks passed and we returned to Colorado, it only got worse. One morning after struggling to catch my breath, McDreamy insisted I go to the emergency room. I left with a round of prednisone, an inhaler and the unsettling realization that my body wasn't bouncing back as quickly as I wanted it to.

Still, I pushed forward. McDreamy and I threw ourselves into ski season, spending every free moment on the slopes and every evening packing up my apartment, putting all of my possessions into storage because our next adventure awaited us. Even as my lungs reminded me to slow down, I ignored the warning signs, determined to keep up with the pace of the life I had built.

February 21, 2022; A Note from the Universe
DENVER, COLORADO, UNITED STATES

Of all the wonderful places you'll go, of all the happy times you'll have, and of all the adventures that now call unto you, each will be enhanced and will more quickly come to pass with your absolute immersion into today's places, times and adventures.

And as I closed the door to my empty apartment, I believed it. Because no matter what was ahead, I was still chasing the life I had dreamed of.

ELEVEN
BUILT ON A BUBBLE

O N FEBRUARY 27, 2022, McDreamy and I stepped out of my empty Denver apartment and into the terminal at Denver International Airport, bound for Buenos Aires. It felt surreal. We weren't just heading on another trip — this was the beginning of something deeper. First, we had planned two weeks with his family and attending our first wedding together. Then, three months exploring the country on our own.

Just eight months earlier, I had written about Argentina in my journal, a vision shown to me by the Universe. And now, I was here in the "Paris of the South" — not just as a traveler, but as part of a story bigger than my own. Through his Argentine father's eyes, I saw the country not as a tourist, but as a place steeped in love, history and family legacy. In those first two weeks, we ate more empanadas than I thought humanly possible, drank deep red bottles of Malbec under wide-open skies and hiked a glacier that made me feel small in the best way. My social media posts affirmed the reality — it was the trip of a lifetime — and it was only getting started.

March 1, 2022; A Note from the Universe —
BUENOS AIRES, ARGENTINA

What if every single decision you ever made was the right one? They were. Legend.

While my mind was content, my body was telling me otherwise. During the first week of the trip, what we thought was a spider bite morphed into a quarter-sized cyst right below my eye. McDreamy's father accompanied me to the doctor for medication and later the emergency room to get it lanced. I walked around with a black eye for weeks afterward, the swelling casting a constant shadow across my face. McDreamy tried to keep things light, joking that he had committed "It's just a spider bite," in Spanish to memory since we had to explain it so many times.

When McDreamy's parents flew home, we settled into a rhythm: work in the mornings, long Argentine dinners at night, weekend escapes into wild landscapes. Before they left, his mom and I shared a quiet moment. She beamed at me and said, "You two work out because you met doing something you love, and you keep doing what you enjoy. Your hobbies are the same, and you're not asking each other to change." Her words lingered. There were moments I'd pause mid-bite, mid-laugh, mid-street-wander and think, "This is my life. I built this." I was traveling the world, working remotely, living alongside someone who dared me to expand — to believe that more was always possible.

March 22, 2022
BARILOCHE, ARGENTINA

2022 — the year of living out my dreams.

As the initial euphoria faded, my job, which had promised remote flexibility, began tightening its grip. With return-to-office mandates creeping in, I hid the fact that I was abroad. Every WiFi issue sent my anxiety skyrocketing, and worse, I started to direct that stress toward McDreamy.

One morning, when the internet cut out at the house, I snapped. I hastily threw my laptop into a bag and barked at him to get a move on. Without waiting, I stormed out, power-walking the two miles along a dusty road with no sidewalks to the only coworking space in town, leaving him trailing behind. A stray dog began following us, weaving through traffic and nearly getting hit. But I was too wound up to notice. It wasn't until I finally sat down, sweating and breathless, that the adrenaline gave way to shame. Tears welled up. I turned to the dog, to McDreamy, and apologized through sobs. "I'm so sorry," I whispered. "I lost it. That wasn't fair."

Instead of embracing the adventure, I was grasping for control. I needed everything to be perfect — the WiFi signal, the schedule, the illusion that I had it all handled. Instead of being a wonderful backbone of my dream future and juicy savings, my job was draining me, slowly siphoning the joy out of our days. I could feel resentment creeping into our relationship. The longer I sat in that tension, the harder it became to talk openly with McDreamy — about work, about us, about what we really wanted from this lifestyle we were supposedly building together. Before doing a new anti-anxiety meditation I found on YouTube I wrote:

March 23, 2022
BARILOCHE, ARGENTINA

I've been pretty anxious, frustrated and resentful the last

*few days and this meditation is to counteract that hotness.
Trusting and knowing that the Universe is working for me
in ways I can't understand just yet.*

But trust felt impossible when I was living in a constant push and pull — craving freedom and flexibility, yet terrified of losing stability.

It wasn't just work that was stirring my unrest, I was missing my sweet puppy Lu in a way that caught me completely off guard. I had imagined myself thriving in this nomadic dream, but I hadn't accounted for the ache of separation — the way leaving her behind with my parents felt like leaving behind a part of myself. I could still see her face when I closed my eyes, feel the weight of her on my lap, the familiarity of our rhythm. We were living in a mountain town and the guilt of enjoying hiking without her was weighing me down.

March 25, 2022

BARILOCHE, ARGENTINA

*Lulubear's birthday — feeling a lot of emotions and I
am thankful that dogs don't have time awareness as that
would break my heart even more.*

The guilt was heavy, but not heavy enough to make me go back. I wanted this life too much to give it up. I wanted the challenge, the beauty, the expansion. I wanted to see what I was capable of and what we were capable of — even if it hurt.

Despite the friction, despite the exhaustion, Argentina was waking something up in me, like a seed of confidence. If I had made this life — even imperfectly — what else could I create?

March 29, 2022
BARILOCHE, ARGENTINA

Last night and then again this morning, "I am alive. I feel alive," kept coming through. It's wild what can come true if you just focus on it. The power of manifestation is so real so I want to plan out some more right now:

- *I want to buy a rental in Denver and have it pay for itself plus some.*
- *I want to travel.*
- *I don't want to feel work stress.*
- *I want a healthy, loving, sexual, supportive and spicy partnership.*
- *I want connection.*
- *I see myself in Bali in one year.*
- *I see myself organizing travel retreats on the side.*
- *I am abundant.*
- *I am light.*
- *I am love.*
- *I am dream.*
- *I am a writer, a leader, a source.*
- *I am Constance Nicole Kulczycki.*

I saw my future unfurling before me, but my dream life was rubbing up against my fears like sandpaper.

McDreamy and I had obviously discussed open relationships before, but I was still trying to wrap my head around it. I had just finished reading a book on polyamory, and while I didn't think that lifestyle was for me, I found myself intrigued by the concept of sexual exploration within a committed partnership.

"I don't want a commune of relationships, just to sexually explore together or when it's long distance," I wrote. "I want to understand his drive behind wanting an open partnership. I don't think there's a wrong answer — I just want more understanding."

To me, an open relationship was a way to expand and explore *together* — to deepen our trust, navigate edges with intention and strengthen our connection through honesty. But I had an inkling there was more to it for him — that beneath the surface of progressive ideals and freedom-speak, he was using openness as a shield. It was a way to avoid the emotional intimacy he wasn't ready to face because casual encounters didn't require vulnerability. They didn't ask him to be fully seen.

What felt expansive to me was, for him, a means of staying safe and unexposed.

And I didn't always know how to articulate that. These conversations left me fumbling, unsure if I was saying what I really meant. Because despite all my growth, there were still parts of me that were wildly unconfident. Was something missing in our relationship? Or was this simply a new layer of myself I was being called to explore? I wanted to meet it with curiosity — and I tried — but each time I approached the conversation, a knot of fear tightened in my chest.

But I couldn't sit with those thoughts for too long because my job was rearing its head again. I had a full day of meetings — completely blocked from 9:30am to 5pm — a few of which I was leading and others where I was scheduled to present directly to clients. But that morning, the power at our house cut out without warning. Panicked, I threw on my backpack and we sprinted out the door, once again power-walking to the only coworking space in town. But when we got there, the power was out there too. I tried to hotspot off my phone, but it died just a couple of hours into the day. I borrowed McDreamy's phone to keep going, but then my laptop battery started flashing red. We raced to a café rumored to have electricity, but when we got there, they were dark too. Defeated, we poured alcohol into our coffee cups and sat at a corner table in the sun as I missed the rest of my meetings, including the ones I was supposed to lead. I never found out what caused the outage — just that I had lost a full day of work and every ounce of composure I had left.

Despite the struggles, I couldn't ignore how deeply grateful I was. I was in Argentina. I was free. I was experiencing love, travel, creativity and personal growth in ways I never had before.

Our house in Bariloche looked like it had been plucked from a European fairytale — all old-world alpine charm, inspired by the chalet styles of Switzerland and Bavaria. Giant, wood-lined windows framed a lush garden filled with trees and flowers that shifted with the mountain light. Inside, the space was warm and welcoming, with a fireplace we lit most evenings and a well-worn couch that seemed to hold the shape of our bodies. The kitchen was small but complete, and without even trying, we created a ritual: sautéed vegetables, pasta and pesto — our signature dish. Bariloche was quiet at night, the stars sharp and clear above the mountains, but during the day it hummed with hikers heading to the trails and cyclists streaking past along the main road. Life moved gently here, wrapped in fresh air and slowness. And for a little while, it was enough just to be — tucked away in a house that felt like ours.

But even as his hands closed around my waist as I boiled the pasta one typical Monday night, even as he kissed my neck and a smile blossomed involuntarily, I couldn't shake the feeling that something wasn't quite right. As a nomad, staying connected with my community back in America was becoming harder — the life I was living felt worlds apart from theirs. And because I was traveling with my partner, I wasn't putting myself out there in the same way I had when I was solo.

Without realizing it, I had created a bubble — just me, McDreamy and the life we were stitching together. I kept planning future travels, filling our shared calendar with flights and Airbnb bookings. A part of me believed that as long as we kept moving, kept booking, kept building the dream, the bubble wouldn't burst. McDreamy wouldn't have a chance to get scared and leave.

My mind kept looping: gratitude for everything I had, the stress of work, the beauty of Argentina, missing Lu, wanting to deepen my partnership. But instead of sharing these feelings, I held them inside, convinced I had to process them alone.

And my body confirmed it — this time, with another bump, this one buried in my armpit. It was as if my body had been chatting quietly to me all along and now, it was screaming.

I just wasn't sure if I was ready to listen yet.

TWELVE
THE COSTUME OF CALM

AFTER THREE MONTHS in Argentina, it was time to move on — to leave the sweet, slow bubble we had unintentionally created and re-enter the rhythm of American life. And I was ready for it. First stop: Florida, for the second wedding of the 2022 season. From there, we'd head to Arkansas so McDreamy could meet my family for the first time.

My relationship with my family had always been a mix of deep love and unspoken pressure — the kind that comes from being an only child. I had spent most of my life trying to be who they wanted me to be: good, responsible, successful, polished. I had tried. Back then I had wanted to try.

As we folded our clothes and packed up our bags in Florida, McDreamy glanced over and asked casually, "So, what are your parents like? What was it like growing up solo?"

I paused, my fingers smoothing the edge of a sweatshirt. "Soccer was my job," I said, half-laughing. "My mom used to say if you're not aiming for the Olympics, what's the point?"

He raised an eyebrow, waiting for more, but I just shrugged.

That was the thing about pressure — it rarely came from yelling. It came from silence. From expectation.

By this point, I was getting tired of trying. I wasn't satisfied with the subtle rebellion of tattoos and crashed cars that could be taken for an accident. I wanted to fuck shit up. I wanted to trust my intuition and follow it with reckless devotion — without the guilt, without the fear of consequences.

But my upbringing always lingered like a soft warning in my ear, mocking me "Girl you know that freedom isn't safe. Stability is the goal. And once you have it, you better have a backup plan, because eventually, it will all fall apart."

My parents had lost everything in the market crash of 2008 — their business, their sense of security. That experience wasn't just a chapter in our family's story; it was a scar that shaped every decision that followed. Even years later, that lesson echoed through our house like gospel: "Don't risk too much. Don't dream too big. And whatever you do, don't let it all slip away again."

Knowing how differently McDreamy and my family saw the world, I went into the visit with an open heart and a cautious kind of hope. I knew they still carried reservations about my divorce from GI Joe, but I wanted them to see what I saw — that walking away from something misaligned had made space for something beautifully, undeniably true. We wanted to show them the life we were building together.

Our reunion was made even more sweet by seeing Lu — when she realized it was me that walked through the front door, she launched herself at me. I dropped to the floor, giving her full access to spread kisses all over my face. She was the warmest thing in the house though.

At first, everything seemed fine. Hugs were passed all around and basic pleasantries were exchanged. My parents asked about our travels, giving us the chance to tell stories from Colombia, Costa Rica and Argentina.

"How's the new job going, honey? Are they okay with you galavanting around the world like that?" I nodded vaguely, pretending to be too busy playing with Lu on the floor to respond.

"And what do you do, McDreamy?" They inquired.

"I'm a UX designer. Kind of like an architect for websites." He responded.

But that's where the questions ended — a dead end, filled with silence and awkward glances toward Lu. And in that silence, old patterns crept in: the fear that I wasn't good enough, not interesting or deep enough to truly connect with, to fit into the mold they had in mind. I felt myself closing down under the pressure of trying to make everyone comfortable, until I no longer felt like myself.

We left Arkansas wrapped in an unspoken tension. Nothing had exploded, but nothing felt resolved either. I didn't feel seen. I didn't feel understood. And while that hurt, I also knew it was no longer my job to twist myself into someone they could understand.

Luckily, Chicago was next — wedding number three of the season and a chance for McDreamy to meet my hometown friends. My friendship circle had been tested over the years — ups, downs, growing pains — but we had made it through. Now, we loved each other without conditions or expectations. They had become the backbone of my chosen family, holding space for all the versions of me.

Chicago also gave me something else: answers, or at least the hope of them. I went to the doctor to figure out what was going on with the recurring angry bumps on my face and in my armpits — these strange, persistent reminders that something inside wasn't right. I left the doctor's office with a prescription for doxycycline, a broad-spectrum antibiotic for infections caused by bacteria and certain parasites, and a vague suggestion to "Hope for the best."

From Chicago, I flew to Washington D.C. for a work trip while McDreamy headed to New Hampshire to spend time with his friends. I arrived early in the weekend, excited to explore the nation's capital for the first time since childhood. I had a few free hours, a sense of adventure and the belief that this chapter of my life — the career growth, the love, the independence — was finally aligning.

And then I turned off airplane mode. I heard the ping ping ping of messages like machine gun fire lighting up my phone.

Waiting for me was the dreaded "Hey girl..." direct message on Instagram. My stomach dropped before I even opened it to read it in full. I knew what it was, I knew that tone. I had received enough of them in my past life with the Man in Finance to recognize the shape of betrayal before the words even appeared.

After a few exchanged messages, the truth surfaced: McDreamy had slept with her while he was in Florida and I had returned to Denver that previous November. She hadn't known we were in an open relationship. But after seeing a recent social media post, she started connecting the dots — realizing the timing overlapped and reached out because she didn't want to be the other girl.

Technically, this wasn't a breach of our agreement — we were in an open relationship and we were only together when we were physically together. That part wasn't the betrayal.

The betrayal was in the silence. He hadn't just forgotten — he had chosen not to honor my one request: "Tell the person about our open partnership before anything happens." That wasn't just a preference; it was the boundary I had set to protect my heart. He had agreed.

And in choosing to bypass it, he told me everything I needed to know. I wasn't worth the discomfort of a five-second conversation. My feelings weren't worth the awkward pause it would've taken to say to this girl, "Hey, by the way I have a partner."

A lie by omission is still a lie. And that omission, however small it may have seemed to him, felt like a violation to me.

He showed me, in the quiet he chose, just how little space I truly occupied in his world. Ouch.

Shaking physically in the baggage claim area, I called him. Straight to voicemail. Of course. He was somewhere deep in rural New Hampshire with no cell service. No contact. No explanation. No comfort.

I wanted to scream and tear his gorgeous beard to shreds. So instead, I cried in the Uber and cancelled my sightseeing plans for that afternoon. I sat with it.

I had to process it alone — the rage, the heartbreak, the sting of disappointment that throbbed like a bruise under my skin. I paced the hotel room work had paid for, circling the bed like I was trying to outrun the reality clawing at my chest. I tried to journal, but the pen trembled in my hand, and the words came out garbled, frantic. So I turned to my phone — breath shaky, voice cracking — and started recording. I talked in circles for minutes, sobbing mid-sentence, begging the Universe for clarity, for justice, for something to hold onto.

I caught my reflection in the bathroom mirror — mascara streaked down my cheeks, lips trembling, a wildness in my eyes I barely recognized. My face was flushed, blotchy, too honest.

I gripped the sink and stared hard at the woman looking back. "Okay," I whispered, voice hoarse. "Right. I have to take responsibility for my own nervous system. This is my reaction. My well-being. Even if he isn't here to hold space for the pain he's caused."

I'd always known how to take care of others in crisis — but this time, I was learning to tend to the crisis I had created by not being true to myself sooner. This was the work I had signed up for.

Radical self-responsibility.

Even when it hurt like hell.

When I finally got a hold of him, my voice was shaky but measured.

"I created that boundary for a reason," I said. "To protect myself. To feel safe. And this — this is exactly what I was trying to avoid."

He exhaled, unbothered, "I didn't think it was that serious."

Holding my ground, I replied. "You didn't tell her about me. That's not openness — that's omission."

I could hear his shrug through the phone, "I just didn't think it was a big deal."

"It is when I find out from her," I said, my voice tightening. "I didn't want to be in some tangled web where random women are reaching out to me, thinking they're doing the right thing — thinking they're helping. I don't want to be blindsided. I don't want to know."

Somewhere in the back of my mind, another voice rose — one I didn't want to hear. "I can't do this again." I couldn't relive the spiral of secrecy and second-guessing. I couldn't survive another version of the trauma I'd barely untangled from the Man in Finance.

There was silence on his end. No urgency. No real apology. Just the low hum of defensiveness.

"It's not about rules," I added. "It's about respect. And right now, I don't feel like you respected me at all."

That was the first time I saw it clearly — we viewed freedom differently. He saw it as detachment, as never having to explain himself or consider how his actions might land. I saw it as truth — as the ability to be fully seen and still loved.

That difference cut deeper than I expected. It forced me to re-examine everything about our agreement.

What had once felt expansive and intentional now felt murky and cracked. The version of "open" we were building didn't feel open-hearted — it felt exposed in a way that didn't feel comfortable in my body anymore. I curled into a tight ball on my bed, the covers pulled up to my eyes like armor. My journal was nestled into the little fort I had built, the only safe space I could find. I wrote slowly, deliberately, trying to anchor myself back in truth:

June 21, 2022
WASHINGTON D.C., UNITED STATES

I feel very alone and I know I need to tell someone but this feels too exposing and I'm scared of being judged, especially after him meeting all of my friends, how am I supposed to explain this?

This was scary because it did show our cracks and reminded me how fragile a relationship could be despite the magic it has. It shook me to talk and face my trauma and our cracks and I'm excited, which doesn't quite feel like the right word because I'm also anxious, to move forward and grow together.

Other things that are coming up for me:

- *What is the happy medium between "don't ask, don't tell" and transparency? Because I don't want to be blindsided again. Maybe this version of open isn't right for us. Maybe participating together is a better fit.*
- *For McDreamy — Does this only happen when it's organic and in the moment? Or are you actively seeking it out? Because the idea of you on apps makes my stomach drop. There's more trauma there than I realized.*
- *For McDreamy — How can I make you feel more secure in us? More adventurous in us?*
- *What I need to feel secure: more communication when we're apart, more "I love you's," more appreciation. Space to process. Permission to feel without being rushed. A photo of me posted on your Instagram every once in a while — because, yes, even if it sounds ridiculous, I sometimes feel like I'm being hidden. Deep talks more often. Less needing to constantly be "on" and sparkly or be in planning mode. I want the weird, the wild, the wandering thoughts. I want all of it.*

Despite the pain, I wasn't ready to give up. I sat in my company's boardroom, surrounded by colleagues in button-downs and blazers, my own business casual mask perfectly in place. No one around the table had any idea that beneath the surface, my heart was splintering. I nodded at the right moments, chimed in when needed — all while trying to piece together how to move forward without collapsing. I knew that my typical next step — charging ahead while secretly carrying resentment — wasn't going to work here. If we were going to keep going, I had to find a new way. A healthier way. I just didn't know what that looked like yet.

So I looked backward — flipping through the pictures on my phone. A solo shot of me, wrapped in wonder, taking in the stillness of Lake Atitlán. A video of the volcano erupting in the darkness. A selfie of me and McDreamy curled together in our tiny cabin. The multi-colored buildings of Antigua glowing beneath the sun. A group shot under a waterfall. I studied each frame like a roadmap, searching for the version of myself I had been then — the woman fresh from Guatemala, clear-eyed and confident. I wanted to find my way back to her. Back to the part of me who believed in possibility, who trusted her own truth. The one who hadn't yet been bruised by the reality of how complicated love — even conscious love — could be.

My week in Washington D.C. ended as quickly as it began. Other than a quick dinner with a friend and half a day of sightseeing, most of my time was spent with coworkers — connecting their Zoom faces with their physical selves, slipping between small talk and strategy, making sure I showed up as the calm, capable professional they expected. And while I was still undoing the knots in my stomach, I didn't have the luxury of time. I had to meet McDreamy in Rhode Island for wedding number four — this time, with his immediate family and close friends. So I did what I've done a thousand times before: tucked my feelings deep inside and put on the mask. Chose the sexy yet tasteful outfit with great shoes. Curled my sun-kissed blonde hair into effortless beach waves. Smiled, laughed, found the charming thing to say and held his hand like nothing had happened.

June 28, 2022
BLOCK ISLAND, RHODE
ISLAND, UNITED STATES

One year after the best first date of my life on the volcano and the most blissful week I can imagine and that's still what I want to call in. This past week has pushed me to revisit what I said I wanted and asked for, revisit past traumas and work through old habits and wow I'm not perfect but I'm doing it. When I focus on myself and being in my soul's purpose, that is when the good things come. I'm almost finding bliss as we sit on the beach watching ducks swim by. It's more calm energy though, rather than the fire I felt last year. I think that's okay and it feels weird and slow and who am I? New moon, please fill me with bliss and warmth and presentness and strength and growth.

I looked at McDreamy — really looked at him. Into his green eyes flecked with brown, at his slightly crooked nose, spotted with freckles, beneath the beard I loved to stroke — and I knew: This is what I want. This life. This love. This path. And I would do anything to keep it.

So I told him. I told him I forgave him. That I still believed in us. That I wanted to keep building this unconventional, magical, messy life together. That I was doing my best.

He looked at me, eyes soft, voice low. "Thank you," he said. "I don't deserve your grace, but I promise — it won't happen again. I want this. I want us. I'm all in."

Then he smiled the smile I'd memorized and whispered, "I love you, boo boo."

I leaned in close, eyes locked on his, "Good," I said, voice teasing but sharp. "Or else I'll be the one choking you out." Then I kissed him — hard, hungry, full of every emotion I didn't have words for.

And then, I boarded a plane to Portugal.

It was my first solo trip in a long time, and after the whirlwind of the last few weeks, I could feel how foreign it felt to be in my own orbit again. In my own energy. For the first time in a while, I wasn't sure how to be alone. I had spent so much time wrapped up in McDreamy, in *us*, that I wasn't sure where I ended and the relationship began. Now, in a new country, on my own, I was being asked to remember. Who was I without him? Without the drama? Could I still hear my own voice beneath the noise?

I made coffee for one, the silence of the kitchen loud in its emptiness. I debated where to work each morning — a café, a coworking space, the Airbnb kitchen table — calculating WiFi speeds and noise levels as if those small decisions might anchor me. I booked tours on the weekends just so I wouldn't be aimlessly wandering, hoping structure might soothe the ache of solitude.

July 7, 2022
LISBON, PORTUGAL

Yesterday was hard — the loneliness crept in, exhaustion weighed on me, and I felt unmoored. Everything in me ached for stability — a home base in Colorado, a sense of grounding in my relationship.

The books by Alison Armstrong that McDreamy and I had listened to together kept playing in my mind. Her insights on attachment after sex, the way women create internal deadlines for relationships — it all felt so real, so applicable to what I was experiencing. I'm eager to unpack it with McDreamy, to make sense of the emotions swirling inside me.

And, more than anything, I miss Lu. The ache of her absence is its own kind of weight, pressing into me with every passing day.

Slowly, I found my way back to myself. I leaned into the solitude I had once craved. I walked for miles through Lisbon's winding streets, took myself out to dinner with only a book for company and journaled through the tangled thoughts in my head. I gave myself the space I didn't know I needed. I ordered too much for one person — starters, mains, always dessert — as if feeding myself well could fill something deeper. And maybe, in some small way, it did. I ended nearly every meal with a pastel de nata, the warm custard and flaky crust a small comfort I could count on.

And then I was ready for my next adventure: meeting a friend in Croatia, where McDreamy would join us. But instead of settling into the joy of a new chapter, old insecurities flared. After a full day of drinking on the Croatian coast, I watched in growing discomfort as my friend's flirtations toward Mc-Dreamy crossed into something unmistakable — her hands lingered on his shoulders, then slid slowly down his arm. She leaned in close, practically perched on his lap, casually sharing her sexual stories like it was nothing.

My stomach knotted as I sat stiffly on the towel beside

them, hiding behind another glass of wine. My jaw clenched so tightly I could hear my teeth grind. One hand absentmindedly drifted to my foot, where I started picking at the flower tattoo, wishing I could scrape it off. I moved to the words on my ribs, tracing their edges with my nail, willing them to disappear.

They reminded me of a girl who still thought love could save her. Who believed that permanence meant safety. Who inked hope into her skin before learning how slippery it could be. I didn't want to be her anymore — so naive, so easily impressed, so desperate to be seen. But in that moment, watching McDreamy with my friend, I was right back in her skin. Small. Insecure. Forgotten.

The jealousy — and the deeper fear beneath it — boiled over.

That night, everything cracked. "What the fuck was that?" I screamed, my face contorting into repulsion. "What happened to when we are together?"

He rolled his eyes at my drama saying, "Come on boo boo, you know she was just drunk. We were all drunk. It's so annoying when you get possessive and I'm right there. You can see nothing happened. You're overreacting."

On and on we fought into the early hours, both of us sobbing — breaking up, then clinging to each other moments later. We fell asleep in a tangled mess of emotion, my tears drying on his chest.

The next morning, I woke up heavy with regret. Shame clung to me like humidity. I rolled out of bed, trying not to wake him up, threw on a workout set and went for a walk around the block. As I put one foot ahead of the other, breathing through the emotional and energetic hangover it became clear: "What if I hadn't fully forgiven him? Maybe my decision to move forward was actually a bandage, not a wound healed. What if I'm still learning what forgiveness actually looks like?"

Back at the apartment we ate leftover pasta from a Ziploc bag in silence, both double checking our suitcases before taking a taxi to the airport. We left Croatia with a bad taste in our mouths. We both blamed it on the greasy food — but if we were being honest, it was emotional residue. The friction. The dregs of everything unspoken sitting in the bottom of our stomachs like cold coffee grinds no one bothered to clean up.

So we let it sit because next up was wedding number five in Maine, followed by number six back in Colorado. We were riding out the final stretch of a chaotic summer, trying to keep it together for everyone else while quietly navigating our own cracks. At the Maine wedding, one of McDreamy's close family friends pulled me aside. She admitted she hadn't wanted to get close — that she'd seen too many women brought around, only to disappear by the next gathering. But then she smiled and said, "If it's not you, it's not anyone."

I took her words to heart. They felt like proof — that I wasn't imagining the depth of what we had despite the recent threads of tension. That I was good for him. Good for us.

After she left, I sat scrolling through my photos of Lisbon. Portugal had gifted me clarity — space to remember myself. And with that clarity came a grounded knowing: in order to feel safe and sane, I needed a home base. Not a place to stay forever, but one I could return to. Something to root me as I kept flying. I spent the next week in Denver touring condos — narrowing options with my gut as much as my eyes. And then I found it. The one. I zipped up my metaphorical big girl pants, got approved for a mortgage and put in an offer.

Just like that, I was one step closer to the grounded freedom I was designing my life around. A breath of relief at the potential stability of a home of my own filled my lungs before we boarded another plane — this time to Denmark.

No more packing up all my belongings to head on adventures.

No more storage units and culling my closet only to regret letting go of stuff later.

I'm going to be a homeowner, I thought as I buckled my seat belt and squeezed McDreamy's hand with a smile so radiant, he kissed me deeply in return.

September 8, 2022
COPENHAGEN, DENMARK

New country, new habits — taking care of my body, speaking my truth, setting boundaries. I've been holding too many things in my body for too long and I'm ready to release it all.

The next month and a half was meant for us — for McDreamy and me to reset, reconnect and refocus on all the parts we had neglected during the whirlwind of summer. We'd been saying yes to everything and everyone but ourselves. This was our time to come home to each other.

So we cooked nourishing meals from scratch — roasted veggies, lentil bowls, homemade smoothies. We rolled out our mats for daily yoga and took turns guiding each other through flows, lifting weights in between meetings, our bodies reclaiming strength alongside our trust. We biked across the city, weaving past canals and cafés, laughing as we navigated cobblestone alleys. And later, when we left the city for the quiet majesty of the Swiss Alps, we hiked daily — steep trails, glacier lakes, barefoot picnics in the grass. We started dreaming aloud again:

talking about hosting retreats together, revisiting our "one-day" country list, daring to imagine a future we could co-create.

But something still felt... off.

I kept getting strange, painful bumps on my face and in my armpits. I cycled through doctors, none of them offering answers that made sense. Then one morning, I woke up with blood dripping from my ear.

He hailed a taxi and took me straight to the ER.

It was the most jarring wake-up call yet — my body screaming in a language I could no longer ignore. I had spent the past few years doing the inner work, but now the physical work was demanding to be seen. My healing couldn't be just emotional or spiritual anymore. It had to be cellular. Full-body.

And the irony? The decision I thought would give me stability — the Denver condo — was the very thing spiking my anxiety. Two weeks before closing, I shot up in bed in the middle of the night, spine stiff, warning myself aloud: "Don't do this." Then I fell right back to sleep.

September 15, 2022
INTERLAKEN, SWITZERLAND

If it feels like you're running up against a wall, dig a hole.

But I didn't want to dig. I wanted to climb. I wanted to arrive. I ignored the message, brushed off the unease and marched forward with blind optimism.

When the hot water heater of my "perfect" choice condo sprang a leak days before closing the sale, I laughed it off as bad luck. But it wasn't just a leak. It was the Universe, yet again, trying to show me something I wasn't ready to see.

I didn't listen. I had a checklist. A timeline. And I wasn't about to let intuition get in the way.

September 24, 2022
INTERLAKEN, SWITZERLAND

Dreams:

- *Fully furnished and peaceful condo.*
- *Bali.*
- *Epic hike to summit, in Nepal.*
- *New Zealand van.*
- *Updated van.*
- *Passionate relationship.*

September 26, 2022
GRIMENTZ, SWITZERLAND

One day until closing!!! Eeeeeep. I'm excited to be back with my people in my place and I don't want to wish away these beautiful next couple of weeks. I am so blessed and lucky. Thank you Universe.

By the time closing day came, I was ready — or at least, I told myself I was.

"This is good, this is a dream come true and I am so ready, I am adulting on a whole new level," I pep talked myself as I checked my email for the millionth time that day.

We were seven hours ahead of Colorado and I waited all day for the official confirmation to land in my inbox. The email came just as I sat down to dinner. I read it, smiled then popped a bottle of champagne.

I had done it, I had bought my own home.

And even though I had signed the paperwork alone, I imagined filling the space *with* someone. *For* someone. I was already picturing McDreamy there — in the kitchen making breakfast, dancing with me in the living room, dropping bags by the door after another international trip.

We continued the celebration with expensive bottles and decor shopping, as we wandered through Spain and Andorra, the final legs of our travel marathon. There was one more wedding to attend — this time in Massachusetts — the grand finale to a summer that had stretched us in ways I hadn't fully processed.

And then we could go home to Colorado.

THIRTEEN

A KEY IN MY HAND, A
QUESTION IN MY HEART

November 7, 2022

DENVER, COLORADO, UNITED STATES

It's been nearly a month since my last entry — so much happened in that time yet it's hard to grasp and reflect on it. Now I am a homeowner, with a massive credit card bill and that is okay because it's home and I am happy.

Today, I behold all the abundance that surrounds me.

LANDING BACK IN Denver felt like stepping into the life I had been working toward for years. The condo was mine. My own space. My sanctuary. It felt grounding, safe, stable — all the things I hadn't allowed myself to truly crave while I was constantly in motion. Now, with meditation returning to my mornings and routine trickling back in, I was beginning to feel it: freedom through roots, not just wings.

McDreamy and I emptied my storage unit and quickly got to work making the space feel like home while draining what was left in my bank account in the process — on a pullout sectional couch, kitchen supplies, extra towels and sheets. There was a clear urgency to get everything set up — partially because I wanted it to feel settled before we left for our rescheduled Africa trip in December, but also because I had purchased it with the intent of making it a passive income source on Airbnb while we traveled.

Even though I had designated half the closet to McDreamy, there was still this odd push-pull between his presence in my home. We had lived together for the past year, but only in the form of traveling. This was different. I had purchased the condo. I was designing and furnishing it. He didn't have a place of his own, aside from the van.

I wanted him there. And yet, I felt myself tightening around the idea of him fully moving in. I was ready for it, but was he?

November 17, 2022
DENVER, COLORADO, UNITED STATES

I don't know where this anger and annoyance has come from and I'm happy we get some space. I love McDreamy beyond and don't want to ruin it by always being on top of each other. He takes my breath away every day and I want to keep that alive and well.

Things that make me smile about him:

- *The gift of my own Onewheel.*
- *His hugs.*
- *His willingness to adventure.*

- *His restlessness.*
- *The twinkle in his eyes.*
- *His obsession with green juices.*

My person. My human. My love. Universe, keep giving it all to us.

I knew I loved him — that was never the question. But something about the way we were constantly orbiting each other, never fully landing, was starting to wear on me. We had built this relationship in motion — from one adventure to the next, one country to the next, one dream to the next. And somewhere along the way, I realized I was the one curating that motion. Not just for me, but to keep him engaged. To keep it exciting.

Stillness was good. I knew that. Stillness was necessary. But stillness scared me — not because I didn't crave it, but because I was afraid he'd lose interest once the momentum stopped.

Now, for the first time, I had put down roots.

And I wasn't sure what that meant for us.

I knew I was being short with him, but I couldn't stop myself. Snappy and guarded.

He was in the kitchen again, using the last of the peanut butter I'd been saving for my morning acai bowl. I watched as he scooped it out and put it into his mouth without even asking. Something about how he licked the spoon clean made my jaw tighten.

"Could you at least ask next time?" I snapped, more sharply than I intended.

He looked up, surprised, bottle in hand. "It's just peanut butter, boo boo."

It wasn't. Not really.

It was the dishes he always said he'd do later. The shoes he left by the door I kept tripping over. The underwear briefs he stepped out of to get into bed and let sit there for a week. The way the space I'd worked so hard to create — my space — no longer felt like it belonged to me.

He gave me that look — the one where he blinked slow, unreadable — and backed off like he always did when things got too sharp. Too real. And I knew what came next: he'd retreat. Crack a joke. Change the subject. Pretend nothing was wrong.

And I'd let him.

Because if I pushed too hard, I risked revealing the truth neither of us wanted to say out loud: that when things stopped being fun, he didn't know how to stay.

And I didn't know how to ask him to.

So instead, I just sat there — jaw clenched, throat tight — wondering how much of myself I'd have to shrink to keep this alive.

With the holidays approaching, we naturally fell into separate rhythms. I'd be spending the week with my parents in Arkansas and he'd be with his in Florida. The space felt necessary, overdue.

November 29, 2022
DENVER, COLORADO, UNITED STATES

I'm dreading going to Arkansas for Thanksgiving but the guilt of not showing up would be even worse.

Thanksgiving was supposed to be comforting — potatoes three ways, soft music, my dad's terrible jokes. But instead, I found myself gripping the edge of the couch, blinking back tears.

My dad was tall and quiet, with black hair now streaked with white and a thick mustache he'd had my entire life — his signature look. He wore the same style of glasses he had since I was a kid. His eyes were a light, sharp green — a perfect contrast to his mom's pale blue. Mine sat somewhere in between.

He was a man of few words, but when he spoke, it was usually a zinger timed with surgical precision. He loved old cars — especially the ones that rumbled like thunder — and always seemed to be tinkering in the garage. But I often wondered if he was actually happy. If he missed drag racing in the streets of Chicago with his friends, stirring up trouble, making people laugh.

I knew we all had to grow up eventually, but sometimes it felt like he had lost himself in the process — and took it out on me instead.

"We know you have an opinion, just share it!" my mom called from the kitchen, her voice already sharp with accusation.

My dad had just asked me what I thought about transgender kids — not out of curiosity, but as bait. A trap disguised as conversation. Another attempt to provoke a fight over our clashing political views, to remind me just how far I'd strayed from the way I was raised.

"I don't have one," I snapped, my voice cracking. "I came home for peace, not... whatever this is."

I fled to the bathroom and collapsed to the floor, my body racked with sobs. The grief of it all — the misunderstanding, the distance, the exhaustion of trying to belong somewhere that no longer felt like home — spilled out in heaves I couldn't control.

When I finally emerged, blotchy and breathless, my dad

looked at me with narrowed eyes and muttered under his breath, "Look who's being dramatic now."

We drove home in silence, the air between us thick with everything unsaid. Once we got back to the house, I retreated to the guest room, leaving the door open — a silent invitation in case either of them wanted to talk.

Hours passed before my mom stepped in and asked if I wanted to play cards.

"I think we should talk about what happened first," I said, my voice soft but steady. "I'm sorry for my part in things. I'd like to hear the same from you."

She stared at me, arms crossed, then replied flatly: "I have nothing to apologize for."

That night, I cried myself to sleep. We spent the next day in strained silence, avoiding each other at all costs.

The following morning, I woke up before dawn. My bags were already packed. I buried myself in Lu's warm little body, promising I'd return for her soon. I slipped out the door, the chill of morning biting at my cheeks and drove the fourteen hours straight back to Colorado in silence — Arkansas shrinking in the rearview, but the ache in my ribcage refusing to loosen.

I needed to choose something new — something that could finally free me from the weight of their expectations, their ingrained beliefs, the invisible tethers of my upbringing. Not just physical distance, but space to think, to breathe, to figure out what I truly wanted without their voices in my head. "Were you allowed to break up with your parents?" I wondered, pounding the steering wheel with a feral growl.

Driving through the mountains of Colorado the following day, trying to clear my head from the wreckage of my time in Arkansas, the Universe sent me another sign — a literal hit. I was rear-ended. A jolt that forced me to confront the question I had been trying to outrun: "What do you really want?"

In the absence of my family's support, my chosen family stepped in, any qualms I had had recently were pushed aside: McDreamy wrapped his arms around me, grounding me in a way only he could. My girlfriends Jacqueline and Kelly and Pippa and Stef surrounded me with love, reminding me that I was never truly alone.

And then, we boarded a plane to Africa.

Botswana, with its golden plains and slow-moving elephants, was a balm to my soul — a place where time itself seemed to exhale. The dry air smelled of sun-warmed earth and acacia trees, and the silence between animal calls felt holy, like nature was holding me in a sacred pause. Each sunrise washed the sky in colors I didn't know existed, and something in me began to unclench.

Zimbabwe, with its thunderous falls and endless sky, reminded me of the vastness of life beyond my worries. The roar of Victoria Falls was deafening and divine — like the Universe reminding me of its power and my place within it. I stood in the mist, drenched and wide-eyed, letting the spray baptize the parts of me that still clung to fear. There was nowhere to be but here, now, in the breath of the gorge.

The wildness of it all — the unfiltered beauty, the stillness, the way everything moved at its own pace — it stretched something open in my heart. This wasn't the kind of healing I could plan for or journal through. It was primal. Elemental. It worked its way into my bones without asking permission.

And then Mauritius — turquoise water, white sand, mango trees heavy with sweetness — fulfilled a childhood fantasy. There was something about waking up to the sound of waves outside my window, sipping fresh juice under a sky smeared with pinks and golds, that reminded me how much wonder still lives in the world. It reminded me: "You're allowed to dream again." It reminded me that anything — even joy, even softness, even a new chapter — was still possible.

And then, within our first thirty minutes in South Africa, everything shattered again.

We had just checked into our Airbnb in Cape Town — a modern high-rise overlooking the city, full of potential. We wanted to grab a few essentials, ease into our surroundings. So we set off on foot, cautious but calm, dressed in sweatpants, trying not to draw attention. I knew Cape Town's reputation and had read the warnings, but it was broad daylight. We thought we'd be fine.

We weren't.

Within a block, two men began flanking us on either side. In a quiet but urgent gesture to protect me, McDreamy slid his arm around my shoulder — but I startled and jumped, mistaking his touch for the man who had been inching closer, his eyes locked on me. The men started yelling, voices rising. Pedestrians joined in, a mix of chaos and confrontation building around us.

We ducked into the first open storefront — an Arby's — hearts racing, breath short. We waited inside for fifteen minutes, trying to shake the adrenaline. Then, cautiously, we stepped back into the street with a new plan: hold hands, stay close, don't stop moving.

We didn't make it ten feet.

A boy, no older than fifteen, narrowed in on me like he had been waiting. Time slowed. He lunged. I felt his fingers claw at my neck, scratching down my chest as he tried to rip off my necklace. It snagged on the strap of my fanny pack — the only thing that saved it. Without thinking, I bolted, sprinting directly into traffic, convinced that getting hit by a car would be better than being touched again.

We didn't make it to the store.

Shaken, we turned back toward our apartment — but not before witnessing another scene unfold. A van screeched to a halt ahead of us. Its doors flew open, a man was hurled onto the sidewalk, and another lunged in. It happened so fast, so violently, that for a moment, I couldn't breathe.

Nowhere felt safe — not the sidewalk, not the store, not even daylight. Only our high-rise felt like a sanctuary. We sat frozen on the couch, watching more robberies happen below us through the glass, the city pulsing with a rhythm we couldn't find our place in.

McDreamy jumped into action. He pulled out his laptop and began researching everything he could: crime statistics, safer neighborhoods, alternate Airbnbs, even emergency flights back to the States. He walked me everywhere after that — hand in hand, always on alert. He ordered Ubers, even in the middle of the day. He never let me feel like a burden. Never made me feel like too much.

One moment, I had felt whole. The next, my sense of safety was ripped away. The Universe was screaming — throwing sign after sign in my path — but I was too rattled to decipher what it meant. Too busy surviving to understand what I was being asked to see.

December 31, 2022
CAPE TOWN, SOUTH AFRICA

Whew, I am feeling so many things right now that I don't even know where to start. It's like so much has happened and I don't know how to process because also this perfect front is put on Instagram, but am I happy? I want 2023 to be about soul living — people, places, slowness. There's no one to impress, just myself to love my life.

1. *Wipe the slate clean.*
2. *Focus upon what you really want.*
3. *Chart your course.*

‣ *Give thanks that your life is exactly as it is.*
‣ *Decide that 2023 will be the happiest year of your life yet.*
‣ *Every day, follow your heart and instincts down new paths.*

2022 had been a year of building — a first home, a partnership, a vision. But as the year came to a close, I realized that somewhere along the way, I had lost the thread of myself. I had poured so much into making things *work*, that I hadn't stopped to ask if I was actually happy.

So I sat down and wrote out my intentions for the year ahead:

2023 —

‣ *Soul living — friends, places, activities, spending.*
‣ *Sanctuary of a condo.*
‣ *Income Airbnb.*
‣ *Deep friendships.*
‣ *Passionate relationship.*
‣ *Meaningful work.*
‣ *Inspirational Travel Diary.*
‣ *Supportive with an open heart.*

- *Pure joy.*
- *Gratitude everyday.*
- *Adventures in the ordinary.*
- *Epic trips that suffice.*
- *Health in nourishment and movement.*
- *Create magic in Cape Town after a rough start.*
- *Make Colorado home.*
- *Soul deepening retreat.*
- *Impactful and adventurous remote work.*
- *Celebrations of life.*

I didn't want another year of chasing. I wanted presence, I wanted clarity, I wanted *me*.

But first, I had to let go of perfectionism and the need to always be putting on a show, something that I was not keen on. How else did you make change?

A Note from the Universe

For a moment, I want you to think of the life you always dreamed you'd have. I mean the real deal — the one with fabulous wealth, extreme health, laughter, friends and maybe a personal chef named Hans. Plus helping others, giving, sharing, leading.

Now isn't it funny how easy it is to forget about that life when we focus on just a few goals.

Don't get me wrong, goals can be awesome, but to a degree most goals are part of the "hows" that will get you to an even bigger picture, right? Yet when life hits a little turbulence and a specific goal seems so, so far away — if you've been thinking of it as "how" everything else will happen, you'll suddenly feel powerless.

The real deal, your rocking life, is not contingent upon having any single manifestation. Your rocking life is only contingent upon your ability to keep focused upon the big picture, in spite of everything.

In order to let go though, I needed to forgive myself. The guilt and grief over my past discretions hung heavy over my head. So with the stroke of midnight, I did my best to accomplish exactly that. And by doing so, I was able to make room for the next year ahead.

January 3, 2023
CAPE TOWN, SOUTH AFRICA

Dear Connie —

Life is full of so much joy, adventure, love and goodness. It also has many regrets and wrong decisions, which in my opinion, just makes everything that much more of a reason to be thankful. However, you also need to forgive and release and move on — I give you permission to do just that.

Connie, I forgive and release you of the guilt of:

- *Cheating on GI Joe.*
- *Roping your infidelity into your uncertainty.*
- *Cliquing.*
- *Not being honest with your best girls.*
- *Not showing the full you to McDreamy.*

- *Locking McDreamy in plans.*
- *Being short tempered with McDreamy.*
- *Not having the conversations you needed to with McDreamy.*
- *Fighting with friends.*
- *Venting about friends.*
- *Not holding enough space for friends.*
- *Fighting with mom and dad.*
- *Leaving Lu behind.*
- *Not budgeting well.*
- *Not getting back into therapy.*
- *Not treating my body with respect and drinking too much.*
- *Explosive reactions.*
- *Drama.*

Connie, I forgive you. I release you from the guilt of these things.

Connie, I want you to embody the following:

- *Calm.*
- *Light.*
- *Honor.*
- *Love.*
- *Strength.*
- *Adventure.*
- *Action.*
- *Soul purpose.*

Connie, I love you. And I am so proud of you.

Love always, Connie

As I wrote the last words of that letter, something that had clenched inside me like a fist, lessened its grip. The past few months had been a storm — a battle between the life I was trying to hold onto and the truth of my dissatisfaction I couldn't ignore. But in that moment, I didn't need to fight anymore. I didn't need to fix everything, or make it all make sense. I just needed to do a trial run of what it feels like just to *be*.

And for the first time in a long time, that experiment felt like enough.

FOURTEEN
CTRL+ALT+DELETE

JUST AS I began to soften into the Universe's guidance — to listen, to trust, to surrender — reality came knocking in the form of a corporate reminder: I still had a job to do. I had accepted the role with clear intentions — build my resume, boost my bank account, buy the condo and create the stability McDreamy and I needed to travel the world freely. But from day one, I knew the company didn't align with my values. The leadership was toxic, the culture transactional and the energy was always on edge — you could feel it the moment you joined a Zoom call. Bullying happened behind closed doors, passive-aggressive emails were sent in place of real conversations and you always got the sense someone was one mistake away from being fired. No one exhaled. So I did what I had to do: I protected myself. That meant pouring into my team rather than placating executives, prioritizing people over process and guarding my authenticity like it was sacred — hiding my travels, my healing, my truth.

When review season came around, I wasn't expecting fireworks but I also wasn't prepared for what I got.

January 6, 2023
CAPE TOWN, SOUTH AFRICA

That feedback really sucked to read. New work goal is to give it all I have when I'm doing it. I don't need to be at the top and I want to show a good face.

Tears welling up — maybe I don't belong here. It's not what brings out my best. *There is a way I can fulfill my true purpose in life.*

Something better is coming!!!

I sat on a stool in the kitchen and slipped off my shoes, letting them fall with a muted thud to the side. The tile floor was cool under my feet — that dense, grounding kind of cold that cuts through the noise in your head. It startled me into the present for a second. The light overhead flickered slightly, casting a soft glow on the bottle of wine already waiting on the counter, uncorked from the night before.

The feedback wasn't brutal. It wasn't a gut punch, a red-inked rejection, or some unmistakable sign that I had failed. No — it was something worse. Mediocrity. Shrug-worthy. A "not bad" that felt like a slap. It landed in that quiet, hollow place inside me reserved for dreams that never quite made it off the ground.

And fine? Fine had never been part of my vocabulary. Fine didn't explain the late nights, the skipped meals, the dull ache in my lower back from hunched-over hours chasing perfection. Fine wasn't worth the spiraling stress that had burned holes in my gut and turned my travels — the life I had built — into something I had to recover from.

I poured a generous glass of wine and didn't bother with a toast. The first sip stung — not because of the alcohol, but because I knew exactly what I was doing. The glass hit the counter a little harder than I meant it to.

I stared at the sink for a while, then took another drink. A long one.

I told myself it was just to take the edge off, but I could feel the familiar rhythm settling in — the glass that turns into two, maybe three, the dull warmth sliding into my chest like a weighted blanket over discomfort I didn't want to name. I wandered to the fridge, then back to the stool, restless in a space that suddenly felt too still. The silence pressed against my ears.

I drank because it was easier than calling someone. Easier than admitting I was disappointed. Easier than asking for reassurance or telling the truth: that I was afraid maybe I was just average. That all the years of striving, all the sacrifices, all the curated courage — might not amount to the version of success I had been chasing.

I drank because I didn't know how to sit still with the version of me who wasn't extraordinary.

January 9, 2023
CAPE TOWN, SOUTH AFRICA

Sobriety. Scary yet necessary. Let's flow to see how it works.

Something about declaring myself sober felt different and real this time. I accepted that drinking wasn't the escape it used to be. The way my body recoiled the next morning, the way my mind spiraled into self-loathing the next day— it wasn't sitting right with me anymore. I had used alcohol as a crutch for years, a way to smooth over the edges of my discomfort but now, all it did was make the discomfort worse.

Still, the idea of letting it go completely terrified me. Drinking was woven into the fabric of my social life, my relationships, my identity. It was the glue that held me together in spaces where I didn't quite fit. It was a backbone during the hard moments. Without it, what would I lean on?

And yet, I couldn't ignore the questions bubbling up beneath the surface:

> "Was I unintentionally creating distance because I couldn't fully show up when I drank?
> Was the hangover dimming my light — the sparkle in my eyes, the depth in my presence?
> Was this the barrier between me and the deeper connection and higher purpose I craved?"

The truth was, I didn't know who I was or what I was capable of without alcohol. But as our time in South Africa came to a close, I was starting to wonder if I'd ever fully know — or love — myself with it.

January 18, 2023
CAPE TOWN, SOUTH AFRICA

Reflection era to call in that good good for the month ahead —

Cape Town has been full of life lessons and reminders of what I do and do not want from my life:

- *Deep, soulful connections.*

- *Body health: workouts, good foods, less alcohol, routine.*
- *Travel: home base blend.*
- *Job alignment.*
- *Me time: journaling, reading, meditation, movement.*

I think I will always be searching and I want to use my slow periods and settle into them with gratitude rather than looking forward to the next thing. That is a toxic trait of mine.

There are so many words that don't make it onto these pages as they are rushing through my heart and my hand can only go so fast — I hope that the energy gets put into these pages though — a release, a growth, an acknowledgment.

I am proud of you, you lucky girl.

Even as my thoughts churned while I packed my bags to head back to the States, there was an undercurrent of gratitude and knowing beneath it all — a deep trust that, despite my uncertainty, I was still on the right path. I just had to let myself see it, to take the first step towards it.

After six weeks in Africa, I finally exhaled. I hadn't realized how much I'd been holding — the tension in my body, the constant forward motion.

Back in Colorado, thin winter light filtered through the blinds of my condo. I made coffee barefoot in the kitchen, watching steam rise, trying to feel settled. It should've felt like home. Like safety.

But something was off.

The condo, once a symbol of stability, now felt sterile. Mc-Dreamy and I had built a life together, but now it felt like I was holding it up with my bare hands. I lit palo santo, hoping to shift the energy, but the space felt like it was waiting — for something to begin, or maybe to end. The furniture was still arranged just how we'd left it, but suddenly I saw how much of it I'd chosen. His presence barely lingered.

We had done the thing — traveled the world together, lived the life we once only dreamed about. But now, the next chapter felt blurry and far away. Our dreams had started to drift in different directions, and what once felt expansive now felt... lackluster. Just okay. And for a while, okay had been enough. We shared values. We loved to dream. But somewhere along the way, we'd gone from dreaming to planning — from magic to strategy.

I kept adjusting the tent poles, tightening the stakes, hoping it would hold. But deep down, I could feel it shifting. And for the first time, I wasn't fighting the change.

If I wanted a life different from the one I'd been handed — full of freedom, creativity, aliveness — I couldn't keep choosing what made sense on paper. So I loosened my grip. I let the relationship become whatever it needed to become, even if I didn't know what that meant yet.

At the same time, I started returning to myself. I'd been coughing for nearly a year, breaking out in the painful bumps no one could diagnose. It was exhausting. So I tried acupuncture — and after the first session, my cough disappeared. The bumps vanished. It felt like a miracle.

I started listening to my body. I booked a Wild Women's retreat in Mexico, hoping it would help me reconnect with my purpose — to find some spark in my career again. I set my sights on yoga teacher training in Bali. I was finally bringing Lu home. I journaled, meditated and began caring for myself in deeper, more intentional ways.

I was creating a life I loved. But that didn't mean it was perfect. The tiny irritations stacked — the toaster always left on the counter, the pile of gear that never made it to the closet, the way McDreamy tuned out mid-conversation to check Redfin. Or how I'd say I was "Fine" when I wasn't, expecting him to just know.

None of it was huge. But they were the pebbles in my shoe — easy to ignore until you've walked on them long enough to bruise.

Since Thanksgiving, I'd taken space from my parents to prioritize my healing. The silence brought relief, but also an unexpected loneliness.

Meanwhile, my motivation at work had flatlined. I'd been given a lackluster review weeks earlier, but I couldn't summon the energy to care.

And Kelly, in her usual no-bullshit way, called it out for what it was:

> **ME:** I literally can't focus on anything. I stare at my screen for hours and get nothing done. Then I feel guilty for getting nothing done. Rinse and repeat. I'm exhausted all the time but sleep doesn't help. And my anxiety is like... feral. Just clawing at me from the inside out.

> **KELLY:** Sounds like you're burned out...

I had been powering through for so long — convincing myself I could just hold on a little longer. But I was finally admitting where I was at. And it wasn't pretty.

Something had to change. So I opened my journal and started writing:

March 6, 3023

I want a soul job. I want to be able to freely travel and for the most part, not abide by time zones. I want coworkers I can be honest with and inspire passion. I need a yearly salary of $150,000 minimum. I want to work on process and strategy and people development. I want to be in-house at a travel or wellness company. I want to break ground and lead by example and elicit fire. I want one in-person meet-up a year. I want fewer meetings and more flexibility. I want a home where I can equally settle and adventure. I want this in the next year. I will not work another election cycle.

Universe, today was hard. Help to heal and transform me. Introduce me to the woman I am called to be.

I am love.
I am light.
I am strong.
I am wild.

Oh baby, am I so excited to be ignited. Mexico, you are calling me loud and clear. Let's do this thing. Let's routine and health and love and strength and build that foundation for what is to be built because it's going to be damn good. Breathe in, hold, breathe out. You strong bitch. Go get the Universe's wildest dreams for you. It's going to be epic.

I was determined to build a life that felt good from the

inside out. To shed what wasn't working and to move toward what was.

But growth doesn't always feel like progress. Sometimes it shows up as tears on a random Tuesday night.

McDreamy was flipping through real estate apps on his phone while I sat curled on the couch, surrounded by the pillows we bought in Guatemala, clutching a mug of peppermint tea I couldn't bring myself to sip. Across the room, he stood up from the kitchen chair and sighed, placing his phone down on the table. Arms crossed, gaze fixed on the mountains barely visible in the dusk.

"I think I'm going to put in an offer on the mountain house tomorrow," he said gently, not meeting my eyes.

I nodded and sniffed. "Okay. Yeah. That makes sense."

But it didn't feel okay.

There was a long pause — the kind that makes the air feel heavier. My throat tightened as tears spilled down my not-so-tan-anymore cheeks. I focused on the faint hiss of the tea kettle behind me, trying to stay composed.

"So... does that mean you're moving out?" I asked, my voice barely audible.

He finally looked at me. "I think we both need some space. Just to... reset, boo boo. Find a new rhythm, you know?"

I wanted to say I understood. I wanted to say I supported him. And part of me did. But the truth was messier. It felt like something precious was slipping through my fingers while I pretended to allow it to flow in a new way, one where we only partially lived together.

That night, after he went to bed, I sat on the kitchen floor and cried silently yet so hard my chest ached. Was I grieving the version of us I thought we were building — the one where we bought groceries together and whispered goodnight every night under the same roof? Or was I finally letting go of the illusion that love had to look a certain way to be real?

Everything I'd feared — the old karmic stories of abandonment, the loss of stability, the ache of not being "normal," not being "chosen"— it was all here. Not as punishment, but as a mirror.

We had always said we wanted to build something different from traditional relationships. Something sacred and untethered. But we had no map. And now, standing at the edge of uncertainty, it showed. The tension between us lived in every quiet pause, every missed attempt at connection.

Still, as I finally crawled into bed next to his sleeping body I whispered into the stillness: "Universe, guide me. I'm scared and open. Let me stay with love, even in this unraveling. Let him feel it, too. That whatever happens next... we can still choose love."

March 21, 2023
DENVER, COLORADO, UNITED STATES

Small wins yesterday that mean the world:

- *Continuously putting my health first and getting good numbers at acupuncture.*
- *Making the hard decision and moving ahead with getting two tattoos removed.*
- *Flossing consistently and my cavity getting smaller.*
- *Pilates for my body and soul.*
- *A solid night of sleep.*
- *Chicken nuggets and good conversations with McDreamy.*

Continue down this path. I trust in you Universe — guide me.

When so much of what grounded me was starting to feel shaky — my family, my partnership, my job — I focused on the small things. I needed those tiny moments of clarity, of control, of gratitude.

And then, before I even had the chance to make my next move, the Universe made it for me.

I got fired.

March 29, 2023

DENVER, COLORADO, UNITED STATES

Head up, deep breaths, you are the shit.

You are strong, independent, a fighter, a lover, the light and I am so proud of you.

Let's get this shit done.

A Note from the Universe —

One of my favorite things about time and space, is that absolutely nothing can ever happen there that can't be seen as the blessing it is.

A Note from the Universe —

I have it on good account that you will soon be called a number of inflammatory names — lucky, blessed, gifted, destined, favored, special and perhaps, most outrageously, not like the rest of us. Let's give them something to talk about.

10:58am
I know this situation is hard but I am determined to rise above it.

5:29pm
Every challenge I face is an opportunity to grow and improve.

6:44pm
Good things are coming to me.

7:00am
I attract only the best into my life because I believe that I deserve the best.

The Universe had been listening when I said, six months earlier, that I wanted to do my yoga teacher training in Bali. It had heard me when I said I would quit my job after I got my bonus. My bonus had come and gone, and yet — I had stayed. So the Universe sped things up. It didn't wait for me to make the move. It did it for me. And it felt like a gut punch.

My ego was bruised. My fear kicked in full force. How would I afford my mortgage? How would I find a job in this economy? What would my friends think? How could I fail so miserably? Is the way they fired me even legal? Who can I ask about that?

Billing hadn't been lining up correctly on one of our biggest client accounts — a discrepancy that, after some digging, revealed a small underspend. We had been actively working through a plan to roll the dollars into the next quarter. Yet, the moment a meeting with my boss popped onto my calendar the day before — vague title, no agenda — I had a gut feeling. And when we logged on and HR suddenly joined the call, I knew what was about to happen.

They cited three reasons. Two were pulled from my last performance review — vague "areas of improvement" I had already refuted and that, if truly grounds for termination, should have warranted a formal PIP. The third was the underspend.

I looked directly at my boss through the screen, voice even. "You know we've been working through that. The client will be fine shifting it to next quarter. And that underspend? It was from when you managed the account."

No response. HR simply said, "This decision is final," and just like that, the call ended. My computer locked. My access revoked.

As I told Jacqueline these details, I found myself finishing the story with a cracked voice and a half-laugh: "Do you still love me?"

Because deep down, that was the real fear. That if I couldn't succeed, if I wasn't the person who always made things happen, I wouldn't be enough.

So I did the only thing I could do to prove to myself that I still had control. I booked my yoga teacher training in Bali a few days later. I whipped out my credit card to finish the transaction online saying, "I am not going to let those assholes win. I am not going to let fear win. I am determined to make this time count."

April 11, 2023
DENVER, COLORADO, UNITED STATES

The luckiest day of the year — let's see what you got, Universe. I'm open to it all and more. Let the magic unfold.

April 13, 2023
DENVER, COLORADO, UNITED STATES

When the mind goes wild, listen and move forward. That does not need to be your story. I am so proud of you.

FIFTEEN
UNLEASHED

B EFORE I COULD make it to Bali, there was Mexico — a retreat I had booked just a few months prior with the intention of gaining clarity around my next career move. At the time, I envisioned myself reflecting on the next step while still securely employed, using the space to brainstorm new possibilities.

What I hadn't anticipated was walking into the retreat without a job to return to. I hadn't anticipated needing to speak with an employment lawyer about wrongful termination. I hadn't anticipated the scramble to rearrange my plans to be financially mindful. I hadn't anticipated sitting in the rawness of uncertainty with no plan, no safety net, no clear next move.

April 16, 2023
TEPOZTLÁN, MEXICO

Universe I'm so fucking ready for my soul's purpose — I'm literally shaking for it. The chills, the tears, my wild woman needs out and the correct path to travel on. I'm tired of the boxes, I don't fit in them no matter how hard I try or the different variations. This is my time — this is all happening like this for a reason and I'm whole-heartedly listening, ready to make it my normal. Let's do this baby. I'm proud of you for listening. I'm proud of you for taking the leap. I love you, all of you, all parts. Live, breathe, love, light in your body. No more playing small or perfect or for someone else. This is your life. Live it for yourself. Fully. Follow your heart, your passion, your pussy, your dreams, your soul. Be your wild woman self. That will bring you to your soul's purpose.

Your inner child doesn't want to be "cool" anymore, she wants to be herself and wild.

Alignment, power — step into it.

For the first time in what felt like years, I wasn't just thinking about what I should do. I was feeling what I was meant to do. It was vibrating through me, shaking loose all the old stories I had held onto — the ones that told me I had to be polished, that I had to have a clear five-year plan, that I had to be "successful" in a way that made sense to others.

I no longer cared about fitting in. I wanted to burn the box down.

April 17, 2023
TEPOZTLÁN, MEXICO

I ignite my wildfire when I empower others, when I push out of my comfort zone, when I dance, when I travel, when I love fully and without judgement, when I listen to those tiny splenic pings of gut signals and follow the open road, when I let my wild woman guide me.

Go deep, stay deep.

Birthing a new age — birthing new creations. Dreaming a new world into being.

The sun had just begun to dip below the ridgeline, staining the sky with watercolor streaks of coral and lavender. We sat in a loose circle on the woven rug beneath the open-air palapa, our bodies still humming from the breathwork ritual that had just unraveled us.

The retreat leader knelt in the center, her scarf-wrapped hair catching the golden light like a crown. She held a piece of copal between her palms and spoke gently, her voice a melodic current that tugged at something warm and restless in me.

"I invite you," she said, "to share a moment from your childhood when you first felt the need to be good — or perfect — in order to be loved. Let your body speak. Let your truth breathe through you."

I felt the familiar hitch in my throat. My chest fluttered, and not in the poetic way — more like a trapped bird unsure if it would be safe to fly. My hands rested on my knees, fingertips buzzing. And before I could overthink it, I spoke first.

"When I was five," I said, my voice shaky, "I laced up my first pair of cleats because my best friend in preschool wanted to play soccer and I wanted to do everything she did. They were too big, but I didn't care. I ran hard — harder than anyone else — because even then, I'd started to learn that if I pushed myself, if I performed well, people would notice. I would be proving I belonged and I could be the best."

A few women nodded, soft eyes on me.

"I joined a travel team two years later, and then started practicing with the boys. I was the only girl. That meant I had to be better just to be seen as equal. Every practice, every drill, I pushed. Not for joy, but for approval."

The words surprised me with their sharpness. My voice strengthened and I met the gaze of the women sitting around me, their non-judgmental gaze giving me courage to go deeper.

"One of my coaches — the one who made us run until we nearly vomited — later went to jail for abuse. Another got swept up in a national scandal. But no one asked us girls how we were doing. My parents always had their eyes on college scholarships and the Olympics — that was their benchmark of good enough. So, I just kept showing up, because to sit out was to disappear. Definitely risk not being loved."

The tears came quietly, cooling my cheeks.

"The summer going into my senior year, I blew out my knee. It wasn't the injury that broke me — because I was already broken — but what came next, added years of rebuilding. I never started another game. I sat on the bench in silence, watching my teammates play the last match of my life. And I told myself I deserved it. That I had failed. My parents barely spoke to me for months after. What could they say?"

I paused, feeling the memory in my spine, in the tightness of my jaw. "I learned then: if I wasn't performing, I wasn't valuable. If I wasn't achieving, I wasn't lovable."

I looked up at the circle. "And I've carried that belief through every job, every relationship, every dream. Even now, as I try to become this woman I write about — the wild woman — that old voice jeers at me, 'You're not enough.'"

A breeze swept through the palapa, rustling the palm

fronds above us. I breathed in deeply, letting it fill the hollow places.

"But I'm done playing that game. I don't want to be 'fine.' I want to be real. Messy. Wild. Soft. I want to show up without the mask of perfection, even if it scares me. Especially when it scares me. I am ready, thanks to you all, to experience myself as a Wild Woman."

Silence followed. Not empty, but affirming. I felt held — not for my polish and charm, but for my truth.

And for the first time, I didn't just say Wild Woman — I meant it. I was her. Not some future, perfect version. But me, here, barefoot on this rug in Mexico, speaking into the co-pal-tinted twilight.

That night, after a hot cup of tea and cold outdoor shower, I tucked into my bed and white cotton sheets.

"Did I mean it?" I wondered.

"Was I really ready to welcome in the archetype of a Wild Woman? Could I stop trying to prove I was worthy of love — even be abused for love?"

Yes.

I had witnessed myself each day in the breathwork ceremonies and other intense workshops. I saw how I was learning to let the emotions move through me, to give them space, but not let them define me.

"An emotion is only 90 seconds. The rest is just an echo." We had been taught on the first day. It felt like weeks ago now, but it was three days prior.

Unable to fall asleep, I turned on a light, sat up and chewed on that thought. I had spent years — decades — trapped in the echoes, replaying moments long after they were over, letting them dictate my worth. Looping thoughts and pushed down emotions were as routine as my morning coffee and wine after work. But what if I simply let them pass? What if I gave them their 90 seconds and then moved forward?

I was choosing to rewrite my story. I grabbed my new favorite journal with the multi-colored geometric shapes on the cover and scribbled in a final note of the day:

I love you. I want you to find your soul career. I want you to nourish the soul relationship you already have. I want to keep following the call and your emotions. I love you. And I am so proud of you. Burn the box down.

Half way through the week I had started taking long walks in the lush tropical paths around the retreat center. The more I listened — to the silence around me, to what was in my heart — the more I realized that my purpose wasn't something I had to find. It was something I had to remember. Something I had to uncover. My voice was already there. I just needed to trust it.

April 19, 2023
TEPOZTLÁN, MEXICO

It's day four and something new is within reach. I feel deeply connected when I slow down, meditate, listen and connect, share my story, make an impression, move, dance. All the things that are happening this week. Being fired was the biggest blessing in disguise — it is giving me the space to explore, to get out of the corporate grind, to create magic. That is what I want to do — create magic. Every damn day. Inspire. Travel. Share. Universe, I'm so excited for what's to come.

The need to expand and being scared, it's necessary to trust your path. The need to expand was wanting to change paths and the resistance was the fear. I don't want to live in that frequency, so instead, I welcome it. Universe, make it big, bright and juicy.

By day five, my fear of being jobless had been replaced with excitement. Instead of clinging to the idea that I had lost something, I was walking into the final day of our retreat embracing all that I had gained — freedom and possibility.

The sun had just begun to set, casting a soft orange glow across the horizon — a final kiss from the light that had warmed the tiles beneath our feet all day. It was the last evening workshop of the retreat. Around me, women wrapped in shawls, yoga pants and sarongs gathered in a loose circle beneath the open sky. Their faces shimmered with glitter, their hearts tender from a week of breathing, shedding, remembering.

Before we began, we each took a small square of mushroom chocolate — just enough to help loosen any final dregs, to soften the grip of what still hadn't been released.

Our last ritual was a sunset shake — a movement ceremony to release anything we weren't taking home with us. A small speaker hummed awake with tribal drums and low, pulsing rhythms. The retreat leader stood in the center, barefoot, arms lifted, hips swaying slowly as the music built.

"Let it out," she called firmly but gently, "Whatever is still stuck, whatever is still clinging — give it to the earth. Shake it out of your bones, now mamas!"

And so we did.

My body started stiffly at first, arms swinging in hesitant circles, knees creaking into a bounce. But as the music grew louder, so did my movement. I shook my wrists, then my shoulders, then let my head roll back as a low, unexpected sound escaped my throat. I didn't stop it. I let it rip — a primal, guttural *"AHHH"* that tasted like salt and ash.

The others were moving too — some with tears streaming silently down their cheeks, others with quiet smiles, some twerking in ancestral booty shake that felt as old as the palm trees swaying attuned above us. We weren't dancers; we were initiates. I could feel it — the electricity of being alive, of not needing to hold it together. My legs pounded the earth like roots waking up from a long sleep. My chest loosened. The old armor slid off without a sound.

After the final drumbeat faded, we all paused, hands on knees, breath heavy in the hush.

Then, as if moved by one shared pulse, we stepped toward each other into the center — sweaty, smiling, tear-streaked — and wrapped ourselves into one long, warm, tangled hug. Arms over shoulders, faces tucked into necks, hearts pressed close. The kind of hug that says: "I saw you. I see you. I'll carry this home with me."

I blinked back the sting of goodbye tears as someone whispered, *"Thank you,"* and another voice answered, "This changed me."

We slowly untangled, laughing gently through the ache of parting and padded down the worn stone path toward dinner. I curled my hands around a warm mug and sat cross-legged on the deck for a moment longer.

That's when the words came to me — not spoken aloud, but silently clear in my bones:

For years, I thought strength meant control. That if I could keep everything tidy — my emotions, my career, my relationship, my future — I'd be safe. Held. Powerful.

But the Wild Woman in me knew better now. She knew that power lives in the release, not the restraint. In the scream, in the sob, in the belly laugh. In the dancing body, not the perfect plan.

I thought I had to hold my relationship with McDreamy together — that if I could just fix myself enough, analyze enough, anticipate every shift, we'd stay aligned. But that's not how love works. Love breathes. It co-creates. It asks both people to show up, raw and willing.

It wasn't just about McDreamy. It never had been. It was about me finally understanding that my worth doesn't live in how well I manage everything — it lives in how well I let go. How honestly I feel. How fiercely I trust.

I stood up, watching the sky darken above the palms and exhaled.

I didn't need a plan.

I just needed presence.

As I packed my carry-on and felt tempted to rush to be extra early to the airport, I offered myself a pause to journal another flood of words that were pulsing through me. As my words flowed, any shame I had ever had evaporated. I realized how much I had been conditioned to suppress this part of myself — to shrink it, dull it, make it palatable for others. But I wasn't here to be palatable. I was here to be alive.

April 21, 2023
TEPOZTLÁN, MEXICO

I feel most sensual when I am in my body. And confident. When I am expecting nothing and know I deserve everything. It's the part of my wild woman that I lose the most and let life take away to smother and it is the part that I want to keep the most consistent. I want to find the magic of it being my baseline and making sure that

fire is always burning. Dancing in a dark room, red wine,
chocolate.

I feel connected to my primal nature when I let go and
dance, during sex, letting out any noises that bubble up, feel
my emotions hard and strong then let them pass, shake the
emotions away, get into nature.

So much of this is emotion based and I give myself
permission to feel them in their full intensity then let them
go, as this is the only healthy way. Express them, talk
them out, feel them but don't let them consume you and
extinguish your fire.

It's not just on McDreamy — we are in a partnership.

In the midst of contemplating my future career, my purpose and unravelling some deep childhood wounds about wor-
thiness, the weight of our dynamic had also been sitting heavily
on my chest all week. For the past months, I had spent so much
time analyzing, picking apart what was and wasn't working,
trying to make sense of the changes. But in this moment before
catching the flight home to him, I saw it clearly — it wasn't just
up to me to fix or to hold or to shift. Relationships are *co-creat-*
ed. It wasn't about what I needed to do differently; it was about
what *we* needed to create together.

I had been so focused on maintaining control — over my
emotions, over my path, over our relationship, over our travel
plans — that I had forgotten the beauty of surrender. Of releasing the tight grip I had around *how* things were supposed
to unfold and letting it bloom as nature intended-wildly. When
I had finally clipped the seat belt onto my lap aboard the jet

back to Denver, I grabbed my journal and let the processing continue:

April 22, 2023

TEPOZTLÁN, MEXICO

Whew, has this week been a journey — much more so than I ever anticipated too. I came into this week wanting to find my soul's purpose, inviting the Universe to show me the way. I asked for alignment and power, I wanted a reset, a new, better path and it has been presented to me, now I just need to follow the call — intend and create as the high priest card instructed me today. With the reminder that he is only second to the high priestess, thus I must not let this endeavor get in the way of my divine feminine, my full wild woman. This will be a challenge for you my love and I know it. It wouldn't be in front of you without it being attainable. I am so proud of you my love — for how you have handled this shift so gracefully, for pushing yourself to learn and explore and grow this week and how you will fucking prosper in this new endeavor. Let's make this happen.

The answer had been in front of me all along. It wasn't about finding something new — it was about stepping fully into what was already mine.

I wasn't lost. I had never been lost. I was exactly where I was meant to be.

SIXTEEN
WHAT THE SILENCE REVEALS

L EAVING MEXICO WASN'T easy. I had just experienced one of the most transformative weeks of my life, where I remembered how powerful and worthy I was simply by being — not doing. That retreat opened an access point to new parts of me. I felt alive, wild, magnetic. Sensuality poured through my limbs like honey — not performative, but embodied. I was open and receptive in the best way, ready to be met with that same energy.

But when I returned to Colorado, the contrast was jarring. The mountains were still there, my condo still warm and welcoming, McDreamy still loving — but distant. He was consumed by the mountain home he'd recently purchased, head down in construction plans and contractor texts, barely able to look up. I had cracked open in Mexico. I had wanted to dance that wildness into our connection, to seduce him with my softness and bring him into the magic. But he didn't have the capacity. My sensuality had no place to land — no container, no mirror. So it dimmed.

Integration post-retreat into your real life again is the part no one warns you about. They tell you to buy the plane ticket, to go to the retreat, to follow your dreams — and I did. I cracked my emotional body wide open like I'd undergone open-heart surgery. And then I came home. Not to a nurse or midwife to tend to my stitches and post-surgery routines. I returned to emails and laundry and bills and the quiet hum of my old patterns waiting for me at the door, asking to come on board again.

Bringing the wild woman home — the one who breathes through discomfort, who feels to completion, who trusts the whispers of her body — felt nearly impossible. I wanted to hold onto the magic I'd felt during breathwork and shaking rituals and quiet walks in nature where I could hear life itself speaking.

I kept asking myself: "How do I take what I just felt — who I just became — and bring her into my daily routine?" I didn't have the answer yet, but I was determined to find it.

April 24, 2023
DENVER, COLORADO, UNITED STATES

"Protect your energy."

The song I woke up with in my head this morning so I think I should take caution and listen.

Today feels different — it's a Monday, I don't work and yet I'm programmed as if I have somewhere to be. I am working on rewriting that narrative, especially hearing how women from the retreat live their days — free for themselves with their chosen structure. That is what I'm looking for and will create for myself. The magic is coming, is all around me, is in me. Let it shine. And this journal, it feels so powerful, it holds all of all my dreams and new beginnings, and intentions I feel good and embodied. I am a goddess.

Even with that magic still humming beneath the surface, I could feel the undertow of old conditioning trying to pull me back. Rest felt indulgent when my primal self yawned and asked for a nap. I resisted her, because in the city, stillness felt like failure. It was a daily choice to rewrite my narrative — one I was finally brave enough to make, even if it would be a lifelong practice.

April 26, 2023

DENVER, COLORADO, UNITED STATES

"Of all your lifetimes, do you know which ones you'll look back on with the fondest memories, the most pride, and the widest grin? The ones where in spite of challenges, no matter how daunting, difficult, or painful, you pressed on."

This is now my love, and I am already beyond proud.

I was on my favorite hike, seated on a sun-warmed patch of grass and wildflowers, Lu curled up beside me. The mountains stretched out in front of us like an invitation. A nearby creek burbled softly, offering the kind of peace only nature can. I knew I was preparing for something big. My body, my soul — they were all recalibrating for the next season, even if I couldn't yet explain it. Even if I couldn't give the kind of assurance the people in my life were quietly craving. Something was shifting. I could feel it — even here, in the stillness.

And I knew it wouldn't happen quickly. This next chapter would be long, grueling, disorienting. But I was sure of one thing: with the support of McDreamy and my chosen family, I could get through anything. I'd already survived so much in my thirty-one years. Even if this was the most transformational season yet, I wouldn't let anything stop me from making it to the other side.

So I did my best to settle into it — the stillness, the quiet, the pause I had so long resisted. I reminded myself this was the slowdown I deserved. After years spent contorting to fit in, striving to be the best, chasing some elusive version of success, maybe this was the moment to rewrite it all. Who knew if I'd ever make it to retirement — so why not savor the space I had now? This was my chance to reset. To rebuild. To start living the life I actually dreamed of.

So I boarded a plane headed from Denver to Bali.

May 26, 2023
BALI, INDONESIA; A NOTE
FROM THE UNIVERSE —

Inquiring minds want to know — have you ever felt so down you wondered whether or not you'd bounce back? Were you later surprised by how quickly you did bounce back? And then were you surprised by how far you went? Did you promise you'd never forget how amazing you are? We did.

The air in Bali was thick with humidity and the smell of frangipani and gasoline. As I stepped out of the airport, a wall of warmth wrapped around me like a damp towel — dense, alive, almost ceremonial in its welcome. Taxi drivers called out, holding weathered signs with handwritten names, roosters crowed somewhere in the distance and a motorbike zipped past so fast the breeze caught the hem of my linen pants.

I slid into the back seat of a yellow taxi and tried not to stare too long at the driver's dashboard altar — a cluster of tiny flower offerings and photos of gods I didn't yet know the names of. He smiled at me in the rearview mirror and pointed toward a coconut vendor on the side of the road. *"First Bali coconut?"* he asked, amused. I nodded, already sweating. A minute later we pulled over and I was handed a chilled coconut, opened with one clean machete slice. I took a sip — sweet, earthy, almost creamy — and let the coolness trickle through the travel fatigue.

The ride to Ubud was slow, winding past temples with red parasols, stone statues wrapped in black-and-white checkered cloth, women balancing towering fruit offerings on their heads, rice paddies shimmering like mirrors beneath the morning sun. My breath softened. My jaw unclenched. The chatter in my mind finally began to quiet.

By the time we pulled up to the jungle-shrouded gates of the yoga retreat center, my heart had begun to recalibrate.

There it was: the handmade wooden sign I'd seen on my vision board a hundred times — only now it wasn't a photograph. It was real. I was here. I had made it.

I checked into my room — a small bungalow with white linens and a mosquito net cascading like silk from the ceiling. The air smelled faintly of lemongrass and more incense. It seemed incense was a constant here in Bali. I dropped my bags, kicked off my sandals and stepped barefoot onto the cool stone floor.

Everything in my body whispered: "You are exactly where you are meant to be."

And yet — the familiar tug in my chest followed me.

Even here, in paradise, the ache of something unresolved hovered beneath the surface. Despite how strong and proud I always felt when setting off on a solo adventure, a quiet question looped inside me:

"Why can't I just be happy where I'm at? Why do I always need to leave in order to feel like myself?"

And then a deep knowing would answer, "Because you're meant for more. Settling goes against your very nature. Don't let the fear and uncomfortability hold you back from something far greater than you ever could have imagined."

I curled up on the edge of the bed, coconut still in hand and let the question be there. Not as shame, but as invitation. Maybe this time, I wouldn't try to fix it. Maybe this time, I'd just stay with it — through every posture, every breath, every unraveling.

May 28, 2023
BALI, INDONESIA

The slowness is good for you, my love. This is what you and your body have been craving so don't rush through it or waste it.

Once I found my grounding — waking early with the sun, curling up in the soft quiet of my room to journal, pulling a card for the day and walking the long way to breakfast to avoid the mischievous monkeys swinging through the trees — I felt steady enough to begin yoga teacher training.

Our cohort was large and diverse — 30 souls from every corner of the world gathered together with the same intention: transformation. We were 96% women, and I had a feeling this many ladies together, spiritual or not, was bound to bring up some drama.

June 1, 2023
BALI, INDONESIA

The first day of my yoga adventure. My love, this is going to be tough in so many ways and yet it is going to push a tremendous amount of growth and beauty into your life. This is such a special gift you are being given so please be fully present and flow with it. I am so proud of you my love, you are truly stepping into your higher self and it is so beautiful to be a part of. Remember our power, our wild, our love, our purpose.

I found myself observing each person with curiosity and compassion, noticing how they reflected parts of me I had yet to embrace or express. Some girls came off as cold or mean, stirring up memories of how I used to guard my heart with an icy edge. Others couldn't look up from their phones and I saw the part of me that still escapes into distraction when the present feels too vulnerable. A few carried an air of conceit, always needing to be seen — a mirror of the performer in me, the version that once believed being admired was the same as being loved. Then there were the people pleasers, bending over backwards to be liked, echoing the younger version of me who thought worth was measured by approval. Some mirrors showed me who I was becoming — bold, soft, open. Others showed me where I still needed to grow. It was deeply humbling — and exactly what I needed.

The schedule was intense — we rose before the sun, practiced until sweat soaked our mats, sat in lectures and studied posture, philosophy and anatomy well into the evening. We ate delicious vegan meals that nourished us from the inside out, our clothes and notebooks often drenched in the sweet, earthy scent of incense that lingered in every corner of the space. My body ached. My brain pulsed. But my spirit was alive. Fully, radiantly alive.

June 5, 2023
BALI, INDONESIA

Today ended up being the most powerful day and I just had a wave of thankfulness wash over me during our evening practice. It justified every single thing that led me to this point in my life and reinforces what I envision the future to hold. I needed this day. Thank you mama, thank you Universe.

Each day came with its own lesson — some physical, some emotional, some spiritual. The breakdown of old beliefs, the stitching together of a new identity.

June 7, 2023
BALI, INDONESIA

Wow, so we've already gone through one week of Yoga Teacher Training. Two more weeks to go. It's been quite a journey with practice, learning, some challenging group dynamics as cliques form, trigger points, growth and everything in between. There are ways I would act differently if I could but since that isn't humanly possible, I can learn and move forward with more grace:

· Talking potentially triggering subjects with a sense of caution and not to brag.
· Experiencing topics I know with humility and remembering each instance is its own journey.
· Providing others with more space to talk and asking engaged and guided questions.
· "Thank you for sharing" and "I support you in however best helps you."
· Consciously making all decisions including sitting, movement, talking, killing mosquitos, etc.

My love, I invite you to come back to yourself and breathe. I want you to remember what you want to embody — light, love, wisdom, strength and protection. Let these energies surge through your every move, even when you are having a hard day. Let yourself emanate these energies through your actions, words, movements and very essence. Call them in daily, meditate on them. And then remember you are doing your best and I am so proud of you. I am so proud of you.

The program didn't just stretch me physically — it asked me to step into emotional maturity and embodied leadership. My old tendencies to perform or prove were slowly melting away. Even as I navigated group dynamics and being around so many different personalities, I was learning to listen more deeply, speak with greater care and honor both my own experience and the stories unfolding around me.

To take that work even deeper, we were given a challenge: choose one day to practice complete silence. No writing, no asking questions, no nodding or reacting, no facial expressions to indicate agreement or discomfort. Just presence. The purpose of silent day was to encourage introspection and self-awareness by removing external distractions. It offered space to observe our thoughts and emotions, deepen our meditation practice and connect with our inner selves — ultimately strengthening our ability to guide others through their own journeys.

About halfway through the program, I felt the nudge and decided it was time for my silent day. I didn't overthink it; I simply woke up one morning, nodded to my roommate and slipped into stillness. It was meant to be a day of clarity — a personal reset. But what followed was far from serene.

Within hours, a bird shit on my mat, I spilled my coffee and a noisy conference took over the yoga shala next door. Still, I stayed committed. The chaos only sharpened the lesson. With no outlet for venting or distraction, I found myself flowing with it instead of resisting. The silence forced me to choose my responses carefully — to communicate only what was necessary, and in that, something beautiful emerged. My mouth was still, but my mind was loud, racing with thoughts. The real work, I realized, was syncing the two — expressing only what was true and letting the rest dissolve. I softened. I listened. I practiced the art of relaxing into what is.

June 17, 2023
BALI, INDONESIA

Wow, look how far we've come and yet still so much I want to do which is motivation to keep this up and embrace the lifestyle because fuck, I'm so much happier here. As always, we just have to learn how to integrate and keep expanding.

Card pull — The Amaryllis Lute

"You are growing fast and leaving fear behind." I feel that in my soul and wow that feels grand, especially to receive that validation from the Universe. Thanks mama.

I'm super passionate about helping others release and find their freedom through movement, dance specifically. I wonder how I would get there and what that would look like?

The vision was beginning to take shape — not just for who I was becoming, but for what I felt called to offer the world. I wasn't just here to practice yoga. I was here to ignite movement, healing and freedom for others.

One evening, I sat cross-legged on the couch beside the pool, the warm night air clinging to my skin, when my phone pinged.

PIPPA: How's Bali?! Are you loving the training?

ME: It's amazing. But honestly... it's not even about getting certified anymore.

ME: It's about becoming more of me. Softer. Stronger. More present. More wild. More divine. It's like I'm remembering who I really am.

And I knew — I would never go back to who I'd been. The

girl who drank to disappear, who dimmed her voice to keep the peace, who shrank herself to fit.

As the training came to a close, I didn't feel like a new person. I felt like myself, finally. Not because I had changed, but because I had come home — to my body, to my truth, to the wild woman I'd once buried beneath ambition, shame and self-doubt.

This wasn't just about yoga. It was a remembering. Of my softness and my fire. Of my power to lead, to feel, to free myself.

I didn't know what came next. But I trusted that if I kept listening — to my body, to my soul, to my knowing — the path would rise up to meet me.

This wasn't an ending. It was the beginning of everything.

SEVENTEEN
BETWEEN WILD AND ROUTINE

COMING BACK FROM two months in Bali felt like being
dropped from a cloud onto concrete.

I had spent the time fully immersed in presence — soaking up the heat, the green, the incense-filled air, the power of my body and breath and movement. I had unfolded in ways I didn't know I could. But returning to America was a harsh slap of reality. The noise was louder, the energy harder, the pace faster. And the softness I had cultivated — that sacred, subtle feminine magic — felt threatened by the harshness of Denver.

I didn't want to admit it yet, but I had changed more than the city could hold. Less than a year earlier, I had bought my condo with pride, excited to nest and build. Now, it felt like a cage with great lighting. But how could I leave something I had just worked so hard to build?

The weight of reintegration came quickly. I was sober — not because I had to be, but because I was finally comfortable enough with myself to not rely on alcohol to survive social settings. But even with that clarity, I felt bogged down — financially, emotionally, existentially. I was applying to hundreds of jobs and hearing nothing back. The market was brutal. My housing costs were designed for someone with a full-time salary — not an unemployed nomad figuring it out in real time. While Airbnb covered most of my mortgage, I was still responsible for daily expenses and unemployment barely touched the cost of living. It wasn't enough. My anxiety was in overdrive. The grind of it all was soul-deadening. And every day I walked a tightrope between trust and desperation — trying to believe there was a greater plan, while quietly begging for some relief.

July 14, 2023
DENVER, COLORADO, UNITED STATES

Time alone heals. We know that and yet we choose to ignore it. Time can also mold you and that is exactly what we don't want. Stay in this peace and love and higher vibration. Don't lose this magic and know you'll always carry it with you.

I clung to the magic of Bali like a lifeline. I tried to slow down, to hold onto the softness and the smell of incense. But my bank account didn't care about the rituals I brought home. I journaled fiercely, with a determined wild woman flare that I thought my retreat leader from Mexico would have been proud to witness.

July 15, 2023
DENVER, COLORADO, UNITED STATES

What is your dream life looking like now? Part time agency work, part time yoga teacher and retreat leader.

What would make you feel more comfortable? More retreat training, meditation training, working at coffee shops, part time living in Bali, time in Santa Teresa, India.

This is the beauty right? You get to design these hours how you want to, you can leave what isn't working and explore how to make your dreams come true. So let's think on that and make a map to make it happen.

But dreaming doesn't pay the bills. So I tried to trust, even when those around me continued to question.

One night, as we curled up on the couch after dinner, McDreamy looked over at me, concern softening his features. "So… what's next for you?" he asked gently. "I mean, I believe in you, you know that. I just… don't really get the plan."

I nodded, staring into my water bottle. "I don't totally know yet," I admitted. "But I can feel it coming. I just need a little more time."

He smiled, but the uncertainty lingered in his eyes. "Okay," he said. "I'm here. I just want to make sure you're okay."

July 16, 2023
DENVER, COLORADO, UNITED STATES

Trust. The Universe is working for me, money will flow, community will support, alignment is alive. I trust it all, even in these moments of questioning and intimidation. I am thankful I can trust so deeply. This is a gift. These feelings are all gifts and wow is it beautiful because not many can melt this deeply. So thank you Universe, nothing is possible without you.

I did my best to create structure amidst the uncertainty. My mornings were slow and intentional — filled with self-care rituals, journaling and movement that grounded me. In the afternoons, I shifted into job-hunting mode: updating my resume, scouring job boards, submitting applications into the void. It was equal parts exhausting and discouraging, but I kept going.

Yoga became my anchor — a lifeline when everything else felt uncertain. I made a point to get outside every day, letting the sun kiss my skin and the crunch of gravel beneath my feet remind me that I was still here, still grounded. I buried myself in self-help books, clinging to anything that offered clarity. The Origins of You: How Breaking Family Patterns Can Liberate the Way We Live and Love struck a particular chord — illuminating the generational wounds I was trying to untangle. Wounds that felt especially tender in the ongoing absence of contact with my parents.

I was doing everything I could to not let the magic fade. So I created something small, but powerful: teaching yoga in the park, once a week. It started as a way to keep Bali alive inside of me — the softness, the slowness, the sovereignty. But it quickly became more than that. It was a step into my leadership. A way to blend the many versions of myself — teacher, traveler, healer, seeker — into one embodied offering.

Holding space for others reminded me of the power I had within myself. Even in the in-between — when clarity was murky, when nothing external had landed yet — I was still becoming. I didn't need a title or a paycheck to validate my transformation. I could feel it in my breath, in my body, in the way I was beginning to show up — for myself and for others.

But growth didn't mean the path was easy.

I was sitting at the kitchen table, laptop open, when Mc-Dreamy walked in, holding his mug of coffee.

"You okay?" he asked, reading the tension in my shoulders.

I sighed, rubbing my temples. "I got a job offer."

His eyebrows lifted. "Wait, that's good, right?"

"It's full-time. Political agency. Good title, solid pay." I paused. "But... it's not what I want."

He sat down across from me. "So what do you want?"

I looked out the window, unsure how to answer. "I want to build something of my own. A business. A platform. A life that's mine — not just another line on a resume. But the money, the security... it's tempting."

McDreamy nodded. "That's a big call. But if it's not aligned..."

"It's not," I said quietly. "And I can't go backward. I've come too far."

There was a long silence between us, filled with all the invisible fears I hadn't spoken aloud — about money, identity, being seen as irresponsible.

"I just feel like I'm floating between two worlds," I admitted. "One where I do the safe thing. And one where I go all in on myself... and risk everything."

"And?" he asked.

"I turned it down," I said, finally meeting his eyes. "I have to bet on me."

August 18, 2023

DENVER, COLORADO, UNITED STATES

What do I have in me right now?

‹ *Meet up group.*

- *Retreats.*
- *Community.*
- *Active meditations.*
- *Integrating yoga — it's not just a flow.*
- *Masterclasses and webinars — to take and to film.*
- *Travel.*

How do we rope this all up? I need help harnessing.

The vision had always been there — quiet, persistent, tucked somewhere beneath the noise of what I thought I *should* want. But now, for the first time, it was beginning to take shape — not just in my mind, but in my reality. I didn't have a five-year plan or a perfectly polished pitch deck. I just had a feeling — a deep, undeniable knowing that this wasn't it. That saying yes to the wrong thing would be saying no to myself.

The ideas weren't just dreams anymore; they were invitations. Nudges. Clues. A quiet pull toward something I couldn't fully explain yet but could no longer ignore.

And for the first time, I was ready to follow that pull — not because I had it all figured out, but because I finally trusted myself to find the way.

It was time to answer the call.

EIGHTEEN
WHERE THE SHADOW LURKS

O UR WEDDING SEASON was about to kick off — a whirl-wind three months of van life, road-tripping across states to attend four celebrations of love, while trying not to lose our own in the process. In the lead up, I could feel my rhythm with McDreamy, which had felt routine and right for the past weeks, begin to wobble.

It was going to be a high-stress cocktail: long days of driv-ing, minimal alone time, balancing McDreamy's demanding UX workload with my own financial uncertainty and trying to stay grounded when our physical world was anything but. The van — which he had purchased before we ever met, intending it for solo adventures as a single man — wasn't exactly designed for a couple and their eight-pound dog. It lacked a sink, an in-door shower, but we had a five-gallon bucket to use as a toilet. There wasn't even enough room for both of us to stand at the same time without performing a choreographed shuffle. Living out of a van, traveling wherever we pleased, sounded romantic but the reality was a constant dance of logistics, discomfort and the unhideable exposure of who we were when things got hard.

The preparatory moments always brought out the worst in me. I wanted everything to be perfect — our route mapped out, the gear packed just right, a real bed at least once a week so our bodies wouldn't break down before our spirits did. I was trying to create structure inside a life that demanded surrender. And while there was no one else I'd rather share my days with, we had to be intentional about creating space.

August 28, 2023

OMAHA, NEBRASKA, UNITED STATES

First full day on the road — let's manifest greatness, love, existence, peace, understanding, oneness. It's hard and it's work but it's worth it. No more calling in the worst — just communication, love, patience, understanding, love always.

Do what he cannot.

As we stopped for gas and McDreamy headed inside to pay, I reminded myself that my thoughts held power. That my words shaped reality. I anchored in the belief that our partnership could be both adventure and refuge. That we could meet each other with compassion instead of defensiveness. That the freedom we had chosen would not come at the cost of peace.

I also trusted that support — in all forms — was on its way.

And then it started to arrive. Slowly, quietly — an inbox ping here, a calendar block there. Interviews were scheduled. Part-time opportunities presented themselves — not *the* thing, not the soul-aligned career I dreamed of, but a start. They gave me the financial backing I needed while still leaving space to create. A foundation to build something bigger from.

Because dreaming is brave, but resourcing yourself to make the dream real? That's power.

September 6, 2023
BREWSTER, MASSACHUSETTS,
UNITED STATES

A lot is being called in right now which is scary for the fact that I need to decipher between what is good for my soul and vision — trust my love.

Even as things started to take shape — interviews coming through, job offers on the table, the tiniest bits of momentum stirring — I could feel something inside me misaligned. An internal friction I couldn't name yet.

We had driven east to spend a week on the plot of land McDreamy co-owned with friends in rural New Hampshire. It was one of those places that looked like a postcard: lush, remote, quiet. On paper, it was perfect. But the version of me that showed up that week was anything but. I was short-tempered, negative, argumentative — all sharp edges and no softness. The contrast between who I was being and the beauty around me was jarring. And I hated how I was showing up.

One morning, as he stirred creamer into his coffee beside the campfire, he looked over at me and said, gently, "You haven't smiled in days. Are you okay?"

I snapped, faster than I meant to. "I'm fine. Maybe I'm just not as enchanted by bathing in a cold brook and bug bites as you are."

He blinked, taken aback, but didn't respond right away. Just set his mug down on the log beside him and stood in the rising light. "It's not about the brook," he said quietly. "I just miss you."

That landed like a rock in my chest. Because the truth was — I missed me too.

The truth was, something deep inside of me was screaming to be acknowledged. But I didn't want to listen. I was afraid of what that voice might say — what it might mean for my partnership, for my path forward, for the life I thought I was building. So I resisted. And the more I resisted, the more that shadow version of me took over.

Eventually, I gave myself the space I so desperately needed — from the group, from McDreamy, from the noise. I booked a spa day in a nearby town and finally sat with myself. And instead of trying to silence that dark, reactive part of me, I listened. I looked her in the eyes. I asked what she needed.

What I heard was simple but profound: I needed space. I needed to reclaim myself. I needed to release expectations and pressure and control. And in naming that truth, I began to soften. The shame started to dissolve. I made peace with that shadow, and in doing so, I cleared a path for the light to return.

September 23, 2023
RUMNEY, NEW HAMPSHIRE, UNITED STATES

Lessons of the land:

- *I need my space and time.*
- *I need to put myself first.*
- *I like showers.*
- *Cold plunges take getting used to and then they are reinvigorating.*

- *I need to release my parents.*
- *I need to release control.*
- *The magic of Bali is always within me.*
- *Friends on the same path are crucial.*
- *Happiness is within and takes work, work on it every day.*
- *Lead with love.*
- *A shakeup of the routine is a learning experience.*
- *Turn inwards, change and grow outwards.*
- *Let healing in.*

It's wild how quickly clarity follows when you finally stop running from your own truth. As soon as I acknowledged the shadow, my dreams began taking clearer form. I could see the outlines of the life I was calling in — the real one. The aligned one. The one that felt expansive, rooted and *mine*. It started with a new idea, a ritual for me and McDreamy I only felt safe enough to talk about in my new journal:

September 24, 2023
BREWSTER, MASSACHUSETTS,
UNITED STATES

The spiritual marriage has been on my mind a lot — we're not there but I know that's where I want to go. Where does it start? Year three being better together. Communicating. Leading with love. Support. Intimacy. Freedom.

- *Part one: mountain top with Varun and a photographer.*
- *Part two: A retreat abroad with our people.*

Work harmony is necessary. I prefer part-time making

$100,000 minimum. The condo will generate $7,000 per month minimum being rented six months out of the year, thus the expenses are covered while work is for play and savings.

Travel is necessary — I want three months each year in Santa Teresa and at least five new countries a year — vacation or nomad style. This comes with Lu who will adapt and love our adventures as they are outdoor and friend focused.

Relationships are thriving — I have a great and deep bond with four people I see regularly. It's very important to maintain the long distance friendships but more necessary to foster face-to-face time.

Libra season is here — another trip around the sun is near the end. This year was hard, let that enable strength and growth for the next year to come.

The vision was anchoring. The dreams were sharpening. The healing was happening — and not in the dramatic, earth-shaking way I used to crave, but in small, intentional, grounded moments. I was learning that coming home to yourself is the most powerful kind of transformation there is.

But even as my heart expanded, I kept some of these dreams tucked away — particularly the spiritual marriage. There was still something holding me back from fully expressing my wants to McDreamy. A quiet fear that if I voiced it, even with no pressure for it to happen now, he would hear it as an ultimatum and bolt.

I didn't want to scare him away. I didn't want to shatter the delicate, beautiful thing we were building by reaching too far, too fast. So I kept my deeper desires close to my chest, frantically scratching them into journal pages instead of into his arms — creating a small, invisible distance between us even as we built a life side by side.

When McDreamy and I weren't staying in hotels for weddings or living out of the van, we were crashing at his parents' house in Massachusetts. Since meeting them two years earlier, they had become an integral part of my life. We had a family group chat. We'd extend wedding weekends just to spend more time together. We went on family trips. They were the ones I turned to when I needed "an adult's" opinion on work, the condo or life in general.

They filled a gap I hadn't realized was still so tender. At the age of thirty-one, I didn't think I still needed parental warmth. But their presence offered something steady, safe and soft — a quiet reassurance I hadn't let myself want until it was there.

I was genuinely grateful — for the king bed, the private workspace, the stability their home gave us, especially with my finances on shaky ground. But no matter how cozy or cared for we were, it wasn't our space. It was another container we had stepped into, another set of expectations we hadn't created ourselves. And over time, it started to feel like we were just guests in someone else's life.

The walls, once comforting, began to close in. And slowly, they started to suffocate the wildness we had both fought so hard to protect.

So, in a fit of spontaneity and desperation, we booked a last-minute trip to Mexico for my birthday. We wanted sunshine. We wanted freedom. We wanted to feel like ourselves again.

October 8, 2023

SAYULITA, MEXICO

The final day of my 31st year, what a wild one it has been.
So much growth, step backs, pauses, learning, traveling,
slowness. It's overwhelming where this year took me and
tested me. I am learning to listen more, slow down, stay true
to myself, put others first — which is a direct contradiction
I realize but that's where I step into my power.

But instead of sun-drenched bliss, a category four hurricane barreled toward the tiny beach town we were staying in. Power lines were ripped down, water stopped running and for several days, we lived off granola bars and the water bottles we had stockpiled. To top it off, I lost one of my part-time contracts — I hadn't been able to complete an assignment on time and the company didn't care that I was literally in a natural disaster. I should have taken it as an omen. Instead, I posted to Instagram, making jokes about the chaos, still wearing my birthday crown.

But the truth was: I was tired. Tired of trying to find levity in every downfall. Tired of pretending I was fine. Tired of pushing when all I wanted to do was pause.

In a moment of desperation, I booked a session with a reiki healer. I laid on her table, barely able to speak and as her hands hovered above my skin, she asked me to envision myself as a tree — grounded, expansive, ever-changing, ever-growing, colorful.

I was reminded that I didn't have to conform to someone else's version of success. That I didn't need to hustle myself into the ground to be worthy. That my essence — wild, sensitive, intuitive — was not a liability. It was my power.

And slowly, I started to believe it.

When we finally returned to Massachusetts, I started packing for a trip I had booked the previous month — a solo birthday gift to myself. Two weeks in Albania and Romania, planned before the storm, before losing the contract, before I knew just how badly I'd need space. It wasn't just a trip. It was a reset on my relationship with myself so I could show up as my real self again. I knew if I wanted a future with McDreamy at all, let alone a spiritual marriage, I needed to find her again.

October 20, 2023
SARANDË, ALBANIA

We break and we give grace and we get back after it. The movement, the disruption, the reintegration gets in the way. How can one carry the practice throughout? How can one find the peace even when it feels hard? Let that be the focus and then the space to journal, to meditate, to move will come in stride. These moments alone allow you to regain your footing. The love is so real and raw and confusing and also so enveloping. The space is healthy and necessary and only passion and strength will come from it. Let the healing of oneself lead to the healing of the relationship.

Connie, I love you. I am so proud of you. You are strong, devoted, passionate, innovative, adventurous, kind, thoughtful. You are a light. Let that light shine always. Let it be brighter when you are sad, tired, scared or overwhelmed. Lead with your light, thus your love. Flow in love.

Remember my tree, that it's okay to change and that you just want to be yourself with no rules or objections or

judgement or shame — you're that now love, I'm proud
of you.

That trip — two weeks of wandering through cobblestone streets, crystal clear beaches and mountain-ringed villages — gave me exactly what I needed: solitude, reflection, fresh air and the reminder that I can trust myself to choose the next right step, even when the destination is unclear.

In Albania, I walked the sun-drenched boardwalks of Sarandë, the Adriatic breeze in my hair and the scent of grilled sardines and lemon wafting from beach cafés. I climbed the crumbling castle ruins of Gjirokastër at golden hour, heart pounding from the hike and the view — layers of rooftops and rolling green hills stretching for miles.

In Romania, Bucharest surprised me — all faded Belle Époque charm and buzzing cafe culture tucked between communist-era blocks. I sipped sour cherry liqueur in a courtyard bar and watched locals dance under string lights late into the night. In Brașov, I wrapped myself in a sweater against the chill of the Carpathians, wandering past Gothic spires and pastel-colored homes, feeling the weight of history beneath my feet.

Those quiet mornings and long train rides were my reset. I remembered the steadiness of my own company. I let the silence stretch. I softened the grip on needing to "know." It also gave me the space to love McDreamy better — not out of need or dependency, but from a deep well of gratitude and clarity.

October 22, 2023
FLYING FROM BUCHAREST, ROMANIA
TO DENVER, COLORADO, UNITED STATES

I'm sitting on the plane home right now, bathed in gratitude and it's such a beautiful place to be. I want to send this same feeling, wrapped in love and light, to McDreamy to give him permission to find his way to joy in however that looks for him. Not my definition.

And in that quiet flight with my headphones on and WiFI turned off, I began to understand something important: loving someone isn't about holding them tightly. It's about giving them the freedom to grow, to choose joy, to become — just as I was becoming.

The storm, the van life, the hurricane, the family dinners, the chaos and calm — it had all been a mirror. Reflecting the places within me that still needed softening, still needed truth, still needed love.

I used to think transformation came through force — through decisions that ripped me apart and demanded my evolution but now I knew better. Real transformation happens in the everyday. In the deep breaths when I want to yell. In the choice to rest instead of rush. In the quiet gratitude for a partner I'm still figuring things out with. In the courage to dream again — not in fantasy, but with strategy and surrender.

My 30s were not a story with a clean arc and a perfectly tied bow. It was messy and layered and unfinished. But maybe that's the point.

I wasn't waiting to become someone anymore.

I already was her.

Becoming, still — but rooted in the knowing that the woman I was searching for had been here all along.

NINETEEN
WORTH IN THE WILDERNESS

A FTER I GOT home from Europe, our time on the East Coast and the whirlwind of wedding season came to a close. We packed up the van and made our way back across the country. The plan was to settle into winter in Colorado — to ground into something resembling stability.

But stability, as I was learning, can be slippery.

My mortgage was still eating away at my bank account. And my income, though slowly growing, wasn't quite enough to catch up. So McDreamy and I made the practical, if uninspiring, choice to list my condo on Airbnb and live together in his mountain home — the one he'd bought with the intention of short-term renting.

One night, while we were making dinner, I finally asked, "Do you regret buying the house?"

He shrugged, chopping onions. "I mean... I thought it would be a solid investment. Rent it out, cover the mortgage, easy. But then the neighbor went full watchdog mode — threatened to report us to the county if we did any short-term rentals."

"So now we're just... here?" I said, trying to keep my tone neutral.

"Yeah," he sighed. "Guess the Universe had other plans."

It wasn't how either of us had imagined spending the winter, but we were doing our best to make it work.

Every morning, I'd curl up on the couch with my fuzzy white blanket, nestled in front of the floor-to-vaulted-ceiling windows that framed the Rocky Mountains like a painting. A cup of coffee to my right, Lu curled up to my left and my journal in my lap — ready to catch whatever thoughts needed to spill out.

November 19, 2023
EVERGREEN, COLORADO, UNITED STATES

A surge of gratitude for this beautiful life I choose daily to live how I please.

A rush of annoyance when I lose control of how I want to be.

A breath of calm when I settle in and let things flow.

A cycle. A beautiful, hard, push to be better.

But the push was starting to feel like a shove. Very quickly after our arrival, things began to fall apart. The small client base I had slowly nurtured over the past few months shared that they wouldn't be continuing their work in the new year. It marked a full year without a stable relationship with my parents. The energy in the house was heavy, like we were both quietly mourning the versions of ourselves we thought we'd be by now. We weren't fighting, but we weren't flowing either.

The days dragged — long and quiet, filled with more doubt than direction. The nights were even harder. Anxiety gripped me after dark, making sleep nearly impossible. I would lie awake, staring at the ceiling, wondering how it had come to this — feeling stuck in a life I had once fought so hard to create.

I was writing the words, affirming them on paper, trying to trick my nervous system into believing them — because inside, my patience was thinning. My energy was low. My mental strength was waning. I knew what I wanted: peace, purpose, freedom. I even knew how to get there, at least on paper. But life felt like quicksand. The more I tried to climb out of the hole I was in, the deeper I seemed to sink.

So I went back to basics. I looked at all the practices that had anchored me through other hard seasons — breathwork, journaling, movement, time outside. I made a list: the things I would do every day, every week, every month to keep myself tethered to something real, something steady. "Even if my external world is crumbling, I can find structure in the small things," I thought as I beseeched my mind to quiet at night.

December 14, 2023
EVERGREEN, COLORADO, UNITED STATES

Baby mindset shifts leading to big results. Slowly but surely my gal, we're getting there and the there will be so much better than you ever expected.

But even with those baby steps, my sense of self-worth was plummeting. I felt like I had done everything "right" — I had invested in myself, followed my intuition, done the inner work, gone on retreats, unleashed my wild woman, gotten certified as a yoga teacher, trusted the divine timing of my life — and yet I was still stuck. Still scraping by. Still waking up with a pit in my stomach.

I didn't understand how I could pour so much intention into my life and still feel so far from what I was reaching for. It was hard not to take it personally.

I had to remind myself that growth doesn't always look graceful. Sometimes it looks like lying on the floor in tears. Sometimes it looks like swallowing your pride and asking for help. Sometimes it looks like falling apart — again — and choosing to believe that maybe this is the breaking that comes before the breakthrough.

And so I stayed. I kept journaling. I kept waking up. I kept showing up — even when I didn't know what for. Because deep down, I believed: there was still something worth staying for.

Even in the silence. Even in the uncertainty. I was still becoming.

And it was noticed by the people around me.

A LETTER FROM KELSEY —

Connie,

I am sorry to hear you are going through it. Thank you for being vulnerable. It is amazing how easy it is to resort to internal criticism. When you talk about the self love piece, I cried. Until you said that, I had not realized how unkind I had been to myself. It is sad that I resort to breaking myself down instead of building myself up. I appreciate you for allowing your vulnerability to help me on my journey. Not only that, I appreciate

every time you are on my schedule. I always think of
those sunflowers you brought me when I think of you.
You are bright, worthy, beautiful and grounded and that
is the energy you leave me with every time I see you.
I know the perfect opportunity that aligns with you is
right around the corner.

Reading those words stopped me in my tracks. Her vulnerability, mirroring mine, felt like a balm. It reminded me that my openness wasn't just for me — it was healing for others too. Her message sparked an idea.

Living in McDreamy's mountain house — tucked into a sleepy neighborhood, an hour outside of Denver, 22 minutes from the nearest grocery store — had me feeling isolated and unmoored in one of my deepest seasons of need. I realized I needed support, routine and connection — so I decided to create it.

Come the new year, I would launch a meditation accountability group. Something small and consistent. A space for a handful of women to come together daily, just for a few minutes, to ground, reflect and remind ourselves that we're not alone. It would be the soft structure I so desperately craved — and a reminder that even in the middle of uncertainty, we still get to choose community.

I could feel a new energy pulsing underneath the surface. 2023 had shaken me, stripped me, humbled me. But it had also revealed so much — about my resilience, my vision and the kind of life I truly desired to build.

I no longer needed the grand declarations or resolutions. What I needed was alignment — a commitment to my truest self and a willingness to step into the unknown with equal parts courage and softness.

December 28, 2023
EVERGREEN, COLORADO, UNITED STATES

I believe that 2024 is going to be a massive turning point for me that involves a lot of growth and expansion. A lot of stepping out as my true self in places I haven't been before, which will be scary and yet so magical and since it will be aligned, the force won't be there. I'm ready for it. I'm excited for it. I've come into acceptance.

Things I want to rid myself of — distractions, checking my phone first thing and intensely scrolling, reading to avoid.

I'm not doing it all perfectly — but I'm doing it all honestly.

A Note from the Universe —

What if every no meant "not yet," every loss meant "even more is on the way," and every disappointment meant "pucker up buttercup."

The more I wrote, the more I started to believe it. Maybe everything hadn't gone to plan this year — but maybe it had gone exactly the way it was meant to. Every breakdown had taught me something about boundaries. Every stretch of loneliness reminded me how much connection mattered. Every financial stress unlocked a new kind of resourcefulness in me.

And so, on the final day of the year, I sat with everything I had survived and grown through — not just to tie it up in a bow, but to honor it. Because even in the mess, I kept showing up.

December 31, 2023
EVERGREEN, COLORADO, UNITED STATES

The last day of 2023 —

Thank you for the lessons, the hardships, the support, the growth, the good and the bad. Thank you for being alive.

This year I got lazy and let fear take over — this is no more. I lost control of my emotions — I will reground. I fell into a victim mindset — I control all outcomes.

2024, let's make some magic.

I looked back at 2023 and prayed, "I see you. I know you don't vanish once midnight hits. I'll take your lessons and grow as I need to, but please, let me. I am strong but I'm also tired. 2024, let's make some magic."

In the days that followed, I doubled down on my morning practices — not as a way to avoid the pain, but to stay tethered to myself through it. I had to find my own grounding when everything around me felt unstable.

I poured that devotion into the meditation accountability group I had started — nine women, including me, showing up each day to sit in stillness, to root, to realign. I found purpose in holding space for them. They reminded me of my light when all I could feel was shadow.

January 8, 2024
EVERGREEN, COLORADO, UNITED STATES

Unlimited and eternal abundance.

Luck is a result of awareness and intention — live in alignment with soul, spirit and source to create "luck."

I sat at the kitchen island in McDreamy's mountain house, fuzzy slippers on, staring at the wintry wonderland vista out the window. Almost a month into January and my personal winter was beginning to thaw. I grabbed my journal with cold hands and wrote:

January 20, 2024

EVERGREEN, COLORADO, UNITED STATES

Live the love you were born to live.

I want to lead in love more often — I feel as though I have lost some of that and want to reinstill it.

Today, I remember to love everything and everyone I come in contact with.

A spiritual marriage has been so top of mind for me over the last two days — not even the immediacy of it but the possibility and dream of it. I think it will happen and realistically, some things need to change in order to fully want to be there, not just the dream of there:

- *Intimacy.*
- *Play.*
- *Communication.*
- *Goal alignment.*

*This comes from us both, not just one side and I think
that's super important to note:*

- *Make moves, show up.*
- *Light up, respect schedules.*
- *Quit sassing, share more.*
- *Don't bash, respect differences and how we can get there
together on an aligned timeline.*

At some point this would be good to share.

The more I dug into what I wanted — in love, in partnership, in communication, in intimacy — the more I realized I
was no longer willing to settle for the surface. I craved depth.
And not just from McDreamy, but from myself.

Because beneath every spiral, every argument, every future
vision, there was one question I kept dodging:

"Do I believe I'm worthy of the life I dream of?"

The truth? Not fully. Not yet. And admitting that hurt.

All the unraveling around me — the roller coaster of my
relationship, the financial struggle, the career confusion —
they were mirrors. Each one was reflecting back an invitation
to look deeper. To go inward. To sit with the parts of me that
still believed love had to be earned, that stability meant control,
that asking for what I wanted made me needy, or worse, selfish.

It was my inner child — the only child who learned to
make her own fun, to play alone while others had siblings to
lean on. The girl who hid her big emotions because strength
was expected, not softness. Who laced up her soccer cleats day
after day, even when the coach was cruel and the pressure relentless. The one who was always competing — for praise, for

space, for worth. Who was taught to be agreeable, polite, easy.
She was the one who needed the most love. The one still trying
to stay small, make peace and make sure everyone else was okay
— because only then could she feel safe.

And it was her fear that was keeping me stuck.

Because when I really let myself feel into the vision — the
partnership, the creativity, the freedom — it was so vivid it
gave me goosebumps. I could see the multiple heart homes, the
laughter, the retreats, the quiet mornings, the full-body *yes* to
my own life.

But I didn't know how to get there.

One night, I curled up on the couch next to McDreamy
as snow drifted outside the window, the fire flickering low, the
smell of pine in the air. He reached for my hand. I held it, but
my mind was elsewhere.

"How do I get from here to there?" I asked the Universe
silently, not for the first time.

I already knew the answer. There's no perfect map. Just the
next right step. Breath by breath. Belief by belief.

So I started there — with what I could control. A journal
entry. A hard conversation. A softer tone with myself. I led the
meditation group, not because I had it all figured out, but because I needed to remember: showing up with love was enough.

That's how I'd build this new life. Not all at once. Not with
certainty. But with courage.

January 21, 2024
EVERGREEN, COLORADO, UNITED STATES

*My deepest, truest self finds itself through compassion —
through being inspirational, relatable, playful and light —
I can create a space for others to honor themselves through*

compassion — each of my actions, travel, guidance, adventures, can be done through this lens — my own life is my inspiration, the main character energy, how can that be transmuted from conceited to love — compassion for myself and others, for our different paths and priorities and understand that we are all trying to attain joy and bliss and happiness — to hold and be held — to honor and guide,

I am proud of you my love, don't let the struggles get you down because you are above it all and meant to shine your light to guide others.

I am the medicine — we all have it within ourselves, how can I help that to be found?

This short year has already shifted so much for you, this is the right direction and fear will not stop you — it's time to release that fear, the thought that you are not worthy or loved, that there is not enough time, it is all a mindset, a shift to abundance — tiny luxuries that add up, think of the compound effect, continue to do the small things — meditation, movement, friend dates, nature and know that is what will turn into the light that emanates to all.

I love you my girl, chin up, next foot forward, you are strong and worthy and doing great big impactful things.

I didn't have all the answers yet. I still didn't know exactly how I'd get from this messy middle to the bright, expansive future I could see so clearly. But what I did know was this: I wasn't waiting anymore.

I wasn't waiting for someone to rescue me.

I wasn't waiting for the perfect job offer or a sign from the Universe written in neon lights.

I wasn't waiting to feel 100% ready or worthy or healed.

Instead, I was choosing to walk forward anyway — with tenderness, with trust, with one foot in front of the other.

Because if this chapter taught me anything, it's that the magic isn't in the certainty, it's in the courage to keep becoming.

And that's exactly what I was doing.

TWENTY
BAND-AIDS DON'T FIX DELUSIONS

I t didn't come with a grand announcement or an angel chorus or a final test. It came on a Thursday.

After months of aching, resisting, unraveling and wondering if the ground would ever feel solid again, I woke up and felt — different. Lighter, maybe. Not healed, not whole, not "better" but like I could finally breathe. Like the walls weren't closing in for once. Like maybe the Universe wasn't out to get me after all.

A new client contract was finally on the horizon — one that had the potential to not just change my career, but redefine how I saw myself in my work. It wasn't everything I had dreamed of — not yet — but it was something. A flicker of forward momentum. And after the winter storm I had just weathered, that flicker felt like fire.

One afternoon, McDreamy stood in the doorway, rubbing the back of his neck. "I talked to the county again," he said, his voice flat.

I looked up from my laptop. "Any chance they're updating the process to get a short-term license?"

He shook his head. "No license. No short-term rentals."

My stomach sank. I knew how much hope he'd pinned to that house. "So… what now?"

He sat beside me, eyes tired. "I didn't buy this place for us to just tread water. I wanted it to work — as a business and a step towards financial freedom. But keeping it now? It's bleeding us dry and we'll never make money on a mid- or long-term rental."

I nodded slowly. "So you're going to sell?"

He exhaled, the decision already made. "Yeah. It's time."

It was gut-wrenching, but necessary — and in its wake, something unexpected opened up: more mental space. More clarity. More light.

I enrolled in a 90-day mentorship program designed to help ambitious, purpose-driven women launch their dream service-based businesses. It was built for those of us who craved something more than a 9–5 — who wanted freedom, fulfillment and to create impact on our own terms. Together, we refined our business ideas, crafted irresistible offers and learned how to confidently launch into the world. For the first time, I wasn't just dreaming — I was taking action.

Leaning deeper into self-trust, I booked a return trip to Bali for a spiritual festival that had been calling to me like a familiar drumbeat. And for the first time in what felt like ages, I was enjoying time with friends — without the underlying hum of dread or scarcity.

January 29, 2024
EVERGREEN, COLORADO, UNITED STATES

Courage —

Stand in my power today, they need me, it is not the other way around.

But with that flicker of fire came some rain. The new client contract — promising as it was — had some questionable gaps and vague expectations. And even though red flags were waving, I was tired of not having enough. Tired of the financial instability. Tired of waiting. So I said yes. I negotiated terms through difficult, sometimes agonizing conversations, landing on a six-month agreement, with the promise of a full-time role and equity — a real seat at the table. If all went to plan, I could become a partner and potentially make millions when the company sold. But the trick now wasn't in the logistics — it was in believing I was worthy of it.

January 30, 2024
EVERGREEN, COLORADO, UNITED
STATES; A NOTE FROM THE UNIVERSE —

Don't be afraid to go where you've never gone and do what you've never done because both are necessary to have what you've never had and be who you've never been.

That note came at the perfect time. Because just days later, McDreamy and I packed our bags for three months in Costa Rica. Ever since our first trip there in 2021, we'd compared every destination to that little surf and yoga town on the Nicoya Peninsula. And even though the experience back then hadn't been seamless — overpriced housing, back-to-back illnesses and not quite finding "our people" — something unexplainable kept calling us back. This time, it felt aligned. Maybe it was intuition. Maybe it was desperation. But we listened.

And as soon as we landed, we knew: we were exactly where we were meant to be.

The air was different. The pace, the energy — it met us where we were. A sense of relief washed over both of us. My nervous system began to regulate in ways it hadn't for months. I threw myself into the coaching program and joined a new manifestation group. I signed new clients. I created a schedule that not only covered my expenses but allowed for creative freedom. Space to breathe. To think. To build.

That flicker of fire? It was now a steady flame.

February 27, 2024
SANTA TERESA, COSTA RICA

Routine has been weird and yet also, working for me. I feel in and out of flow in a healthy way — giving grace and space, having tiny anxieties — it will all be good though and sharing my journey is so powerful and healing — I think it will also help bring clients and build up the community and just feel good. We are in our alignment era. We are in our truth and strength era. We are coming out on top. We are building to lead and inspire and change. Amen, bless, let's get this shit done!!!

Our first month in Costa Rica felt like one long exhale — not because everything was perfect, but because I had stopped holding my breath.

We found our rhythm in the little beach town: co-working at Selina, yogilates, beach walks for sunset. I was building my business, Lu napping at my feet, the jungle humming around

me. My nervous system — that had been in a state of hypervig-
ilance for months — finally had space to reset. I wasn't chasing,
I was being.

And even though the routine didn't always look like the
Pinterest version of a "remote life," it was real and honest and
working for me. Some days I was wildly productive, other days
I just sat with my thoughts and swam in the ocean. And that
was enough.

The balance between structure and softness — between
ambition and ease — was the dance I'd been trying to choreo-
graph for years. Now, I was finally starting to hear the music.

I would wear my bathing suit to the coworking space,
shrug off my dress after a few focused hours and walk across
the street barefoot. I would wade through the low tide, the sun
warm on my back and salt water curling around my ankles.
This was what I'd imagined: building something meaningful,
while staying rooted in joy. Doing work I believed in while prioritizing presence. Healing myself while holding space for others to do the same.

But as I began to rise again, there was something else starting to stir beneath the surface — questions I hadn't wanted to
ask, feelings I hadn't yet faced, truths I hadn't spoken out loud.
And they all revolved around one thing: McDreamy.

Many of our friends in Costa Rica were either cradling
newborns or glowing with pregnancy. We watched sun-kissed
toddlers run barefoot and naked along the beach, their laughter echoing across the sand. Parents talked casually about the
green and international schools nestled in the jungle. There was
magic in how these children were being raised — barefoot, curious, untamed. And for the first time in my life, I let myself
imagine it. Us. Children.

What had once been a hard no inside my body — a conviction I had held onto with fierce certainty — had slowly, quietly begun to melt. The more I softened into this partnership with McDreamy, the more I wondered if my resistance to motherhood had less to do with children and more to do with the container in which I thought I'd have to raise them. But this life? This version, with its wild freedom and deep presence, with our black-sheep love leading the way? It started to look like a yes.

And it wasn't just the kids I could see — it was the whole picture. A life sculpted outside the box. One where we honored our individuality and still showed up for each other every day. Where we created rituals and carved out sacred space. Where the weight of tradition didn't drown us but the truth of alignment carried us forward.

I knew without a doubt that I wanted McDreamy to be the father of my children, if I chose that path. I could feel it in my bones, in the way my body relaxed around him when he was fully present. But how was I supposed to bring that truth to light when I knew it would ignite the avoidance in him? It was as if I was living in a parallel dimension — a different version of our lives where we were both secure enough to speak freely, where the future didn't feel like a threat. If everything in life was a choice, why couldn't we both choose that secure path for ourselves? Why were we both so resistant to it?

Dreaming is easy. Speaking it out loud is harder.

We danced around the topic, tiptoeing near the edges, skimming the surface without ever saying the things that really mattered. Fear kept us quiet. Vulnerability didn't feel safe. And instead of deepening our intimacy, the silence curdled into distance.

We started overscheduling ourselves — dinners with friends, too many errands — anything to avoid being alone together for too long. When we *were* alone, the silence felt louder than ever. We barely touched each other anymore, sex dwindling from something passionate to something perfunctory... or nonexistent. Our bodies, once magnetized, now hovered like strangers sharing space.

We began bickering over logistics and routines — whose turn it was to buy groceries, how long the dishes had been sitting in the sink, what time we were leaving for the cowork. Petty things that barely mattered on the surface, but underneath, were all symptoms of what we weren't saying:

That we were slipping.

That we were afraid to look too closely at the cracks.

That neither of us knew how to bridge the growing space between us.

And when things started to break, I turned to my journal.

March 12, 2024

A LETTER TO MCDREAMY —

I am simultaneously numb and heart-shattered. My heart hurts. All I want to do is build with you. Love with you. Explore with you. And these tiny things keep getting in the way. These stupid little fights that blow up. I take my accountability — I learned as a child that the only way to fight is loud and angry and with vengeance. I also learned that's the only way to love. To get in explosive arguments that create hate and fall back into love. It's been something I've seen a lot of in these inner child modules these past few days. It's a pattern I want to break. It's a belief I want to rewrite. I need help though, I can't do it alone. I'm so sick of this cycle. Please, can we break it? I just want to love you and build what I know we can together. I want you to let me in and allow for this creation. Give yourself over so we can be fully open and transparent and on the same page. Sometimes I feel like you are a stranger even though I know you because you hide — behind the house, the phone, the plans. Just let the wall come down and not be scared of what's on the other side. Give us the fucking space to be able to build how we want and in line with our values. I don't want what other people have, I want what we have but we can't have it if we don't break this cycle so please, can we do it? Together?

We were lying on the bed of our tiny studio apartment, the midday sun spilling through the windows in golden streaks. Lu was curled between us, her soft breaths rising and falling in sync with the quiet around us. I held my journal in my hands, the edges slightly crumpled from my grip and read it aloud — voice steady, even when my heart wasn't.

When I finished, the silence stretched.

He reached for my hand. "You're right," he said quietly. "I haven't been listening the way I should."

I nodded, not quite ready to soften. "I don't need you to have all the answers. I just need you to meet me in it."

"I know," he said, his voice barely above a whisper. "I'm sorry."

We sat there, words drifting between us like smoke. "I miss us," he added after a beat.

I gave him a half-smile, tired. "Me too."

He pulled me into a hug — longer than usual, gentler. And for a moment, the weight lifted just enough for me to exhale.

But that was it. We didn't dive in. We didn't peel back the layers or touch the core. We just stayed on the surface — skimming across the ache.

A band-aid. Soft, careful and not quite enough.

And I let it be. Not because I didn't care, but because I didn't have the capacity to peel it all back right then. I had daily practices to maintain, clients to onboard, a coaching program and manifestation group to show up for and the pressure of making my business work in real time. The part of me that had once spiraled into self-abandonment in relationships was now fiercely determined to stay anchored in my own growth. So I put my energy there — not to ignore the partnership, but to stabilize myself.

I kept telling myself, "We'll revisit this when things are less chaotic." But when is that, really? The truth is, part of me feared what we might find if we pulled it all apart. I had started to see this future with him so clearly — a life built on intention, freedom, play and purpose. A life I hadn't believed was possible until him. And I was scared that digging too deep might cause it to fall apart before we had the chance to create it.

But life rarely waits for us to feel ready. And the more I focused outward, the more I realized I would eventually have to come back inward — to him, to us, to the vision that still lived inside of me but was starting to blur around the edges.

The last few weeks in Costa Rica moved both quickly and slowly — a paradox I'd grown used to. Mornings were spent grounding: morning surf sessions, card pulls on the porch, fresh fruit McDreamy would cut for us that tasted like sunshine. Afternoons often slipped into creativity and connection: client calls, content creation, yogilates, a sunset beach walk and dinners with new friends. On the outside, things were flowing. On the inside, I was learning to let the flow hold me even when parts of my life still felt uncertain.

McDreamy and I shared some beautiful moments in those

final days. Bonding over my newfound love of surfing, belly laughs over shared meals of rice, beans and tacos, the quiet kind of companionship that feels like home. But there was also distance — the unspoken kind. The kind that lingers even when you're sitting right next to someone. We never did fully come back to that letter. Never peeled off the band-aid. Not because we didn't care, but because the pace of life — and perhaps our own fear — didn't allow us to.

Before we left Costa Rica, something settled between us — not a fix, but a quiet alignment. One afternoon after a house showing, I hopped onto the back of the quad, the salty breeze tangling my hair as he climbed on in front of me. I wrapped my arms around his waist and leaned in close.

"I could see us living here," I murmured, pressing a kiss to his cheek. "I could see me hosting yoga sessions on the patio, us having get-togethers with our friends. It feels like it could be ours."

He smiled, one hand reaching back to squeeze my knee. "Yeah. I see it too."

When we landed back in Colorado, the cold hit immediately. We returned to the mountain house and sat down to map out what needed to be done so McDreamy could list it in the coming month.

I tried to lean into the comforts — dinner with friends, Lu snuggled at my feet, the familiar luxury of a fireplace and a full kitchen. But my spirit was already pulling me elsewhere. Toward something slower. Wilder. Deeper.

Bali was calling again — not just the place, but the version of me that had come alive there.

So I packed my bags, hugged Lu tightly and kissed McDreamy goodbye at the airport, promising I'd be back soon.

Then I boarded a plane for another solo journey — one that wasn't about escape this time, but return.

Not a return to a destination, but to myself. Bali, round two.

TWENTY-ONE
WHEN THE BUBBLE BURSTS

M<small>Y SOLO MONTH</small> in Bali was equal parts growth and grit — it stretched me in ways I didn't expect. During that time, I wrapped up my final coaching call and prepared to officially launch my business, *mind body world*. The first offering? The Butterfly Effect — a four-month program rooted in the belief that small, consistent shifts can lead to massive transformation. It was designed to guide women through nervous system regulation, emotional release and embodied practices, helping them reconnect to their truth and build lives that felt expansive, grounded and free.

I had an empowering photoshoot with my friend Lisa who I had met during my retreat in Mexico just a year earlier — a full-circle moment that reminded me how far I had come. As I stood barefoot in the warm Balinese earth, sun on my face and fabric billowing around me, I felt entirely at home in my body. Strong. Soft. Alive. It wasn't just about capturing a photo — it was about claiming this version of myself.

And in that moment, I thought of all the places this body

had carried me. I thought of how it had once braced itself for the cold silences of the Man in Finance. How it had held steady while GI Joe told me love meant sacrifice, not freedom. I remembered the shaking ceremony in Mexico where I first let go of control. The silence and sweat of Bali, round one. The heartbreak in Albania and the rebuild in Romania. The cold mornings in Colorado, coffee in hand and questions still unanswered. The deep love I had found and the deep grief that followed. The return to Costa Rica, and now, here again in Bali — a new chapter, the same vessel.

This body had held it all. Moved me forward, even when I didn't know where I was going. Every breakdown, every breakthrough — it had been there. And now, it was helping me build something new. Not just a business, but a life. A life rooted in truth, freedom and a homecoming to myself.

Still, even in all that growth, the beauty of Bali couldn't shield me from the loneliness. I struggled being away from McDreamy, our time zones completely opposite. While he was fast asleep, I sat on the edge of my bed, the fan humming softly overhead, and typed out a text:

> **ME:** Hi boo boo. Bali's been beautiful — the festival was so freeing, and I'm really proud of the way I've been showing up here. But I miss the little moments with you. I miss sharing my day, hearing about yours, just... being in each other's lives in the small ways. It feels weird doing this much life without you in it. Just wanted you to know.

I stared at it for a while, debating whether it came off as too clingy — too much. But then I remembered what I'd promised myself: truth over performance. So I took a breath and pressed send.

To make matters even more tender, a friend from my first job out of college had just gotten engaged. I wanted to be happy for her — and I was — but the news unearthed a wave of jealousy I wasn't prepared for. It confused me, especially because I didn't even want another traditional marriage. Still, it forced me to confront the questions I had been trying to outrun: "Was I on the right path? What did commitment look like for me? For us? Was I still trying to shape McDreamy into something he wasn't ready to be?"

Mama Bali gave me the space to sit with it all — to let the questions rise without immediately needing answers. Amid the temples and terraced rice fields, I could feel myself softening. I was learning to hold the ache and the awe at the same time.

During a particularly moving yoga class, our teacher guided us to meet our future selves. I saw her — 60 years old, with long graying hair, a radiance that softened every line on her face. She looked me straight in the eyes and commanded, "Don't waste it." Not this trip, not this love, not this life. Every moment matters and every breath is sacred.

I carried her words with me as I landed back in America, heart still half in Bali, half in limbo. I had one week to decompress, to ground, to integrate. Then McDreamy and I packed up the van once more — this time, heading west.

As we made our way toward Oregon, we were once again tasked with creating routine and stability inside a moving vehicle. This time, it felt easier — like we had worked out the kinks from our last van journey. We were more in sync, more forgiving, more fluid with the inevitable messiness of life on the road. It didn't feel perfect, but it felt possible.

And that possibility gave me confidence — not just in us, but in myself and the course I was launching. I was living the very work I was teaching, putting my own tools to the ultimate test. Could I maintain rhythm, regulation and ritual in some of the most unstructured and unpredictable circumstances? If I could do it here, in a van, with spotty service and shifting terrain — I could guide others to do the same.

I wasn't just launching The Butterfly Effect, I was embodying it.

As the anticipated start date of The Butterfly Effect drew nearer and enrollment stubbornly remained at zero, my anxiety began to quietly spiral. Living in the van — once an adventure — was starting to wear on me. The lack of space, privacy and consistency was beginning to feel suffocating. I was fighting with my insurance company over coverage for a new IUD — a basic women's right and yet still something I had to beg and battle for. That helplessness was compounded by a traumatic fall off my Onewheel, a self-balancing electric skateboard McDreamy had gifted me — a fall which not only rattled me emotionally but left my body split open and bloodied, layers of skin scraped from my elbow, hip and knee as if I had been peeled open.

At the same time, the client contract I had once seen as my ticket to financial freedom had completely disintegrated. What was promised as stability had become a source of legal stress — I was chasing money I had already worked hard to earn. Spoiler alert, I never did get fully paid.

Then, an unexpected call from my cousin reignited a long-simmering war with my family — one I hadn't realized I was still fighting. One that I had accepted many months ago that may never heal.

McDreamy and I were on the backroads, driving in and

out of service, when a text from my cousin pinged through: "Hey, call me back when you can."

My stomach dropped. My intuition flared — something was wrong with my grandma.

I answered immediately, knowing we'd lose signal again soon. "Hi, sorry — we're driving through the middle of nowhere in Oregon and my service is shit. I can call you back when we get to our destination in about two and a half hours?"

When we stopped to get gas an hour later and I saw full bars on my phone, I knew there was no point in waiting.

She answered on the first ring. "Hey, how's it going?" I said lightly, trying to brace myself.

"Grandma isn't doing well. They admitted her."

I inhaled slowly. One Mississippi. Two Mississippi. Let the breath drop into my belly, into my feet. "What does that mean?"

"I don't know," she snapped.

Questions swirled: Had my mom asked her to call me? Was this her way of extending an olive branch — or was she cutting me off for good because she didn't tell me herself? Was this the moment I'd feared all along — being shut out entirely? Unworthy. Unlovable.

"Why are you the one telling me this?" I asked. The words slipped out before I could filter them, before I could explain that I was trying to understand my mom's silence, not blame my cousin.

The frustration in my cousin's voice came out sharp and fast — not just hers, but my mother's too. I heard it all: the judgment, the resentment, the same biting edge I'd grown up flinching at. "I just don't get it," she said, exasperated. "They're your family. You don't just cut people out because things get hard."

She wasn't yelling, but it felt like a slap anyway. There was disbelief in her voice, like she couldn't fathom how I could step away — like choosing myself was some kind of betrayal.

"You and I aren't that close anymore," she added, a little quieter, but no less cutting. "And honestly, I don't know how we're supposed to be if you're not even talking to your parents. It's just... weird."

Her words mirrored all the things I hadn't said out loud — the guilt, the ache, the lingering doubt that maybe I *was* the problem. But under that was a quieter truth: I hadn't cut people out because it was easy. I'd created space because it was necessary. Because I had spent too many years trying to be the daughter they wanted — the version of me who kept the peace, no matter the cost.

I felt my own anger rise, hot and familiar, but buried it under silence. She didn't want to understand. She wanted me to conform. To come back into the fold and keep pretending everything was fine.

But I also heard something else in her voice — something small, unsure. A truth I hadn't wanted to admit: she would never truly understand me or the life I was trying to create.

And I realized, I had to stop needing her to. I had to stop needing *any* of them to.

When I gave way to that small truth, a bigger one came through: I never wanted to live life the way my family was intent on. Sheltered in a small town, saving for a future that might never come, always bracing for the worst.

I closed my eyes. My heart thudded. This was the fork in the road — the moment I'd usually defend, explain, try to fix everything. But I remembered what I learned in Mexico: emotions only last 90 seconds if you let them move. Witness. Breathe. Don't abandon yourself.

"I hear how hurt you are," I said, voice catching just slightly.

"And I'm not going to argue with your feelings. Just know I'm doing the best I can. I love you. And I support whatever you need to do for your health and your happiness."

There was silence.

When we hung up, I stared at the screen, my hands trembling — not with anger, but tenderness. It's easy to run. Harder to stay soft when others think you're cold. But that's the work. Showing up with love, even when love is misunderstood.

I slid back into the passenger seat, as deflated as a week-old helium balloon. The news about Grandma finally landing.

That night I left my journal untouched in the drawer. The next morning my oracle cards went unpulled. More undoing seeped into my days. My once sacred routines — morning practices, grounding rituals, creative bursts — began to slip through the cracks, leaving me feeling unmoored.

July 8, 2024

VANCOUVER, BRITISH COLUMBIA, CANADA

How the time passes without caring for myself. This needs to be a continued and dedicated practice, with grace and love in between.

I choose to be:

- *Light.*
- *Love.*
- *Abundant.*
- *Aligned.*
- *Inspirational.*

With enrollment for The Butterfly Effect still at zero, I fi-

nally did the thing I had been avoiding — I shut down applications. I made a public announcement that I was hitting pause
to reevaluate my business priorities and revisit the program's
structure. My emotions swirled in contradiction — one part of
me felt like a complete failure, the other part knew I was gaining something invaluable: clarity, humility, a lesson I couldn't
have learned any other way.

July 18, 2024
BEND, OREGON, UNITED STATES;
A NOTE FROM THE UNIVERSE —

*I know you already know this but the only way one can find
their way is to be lost first. To make it big, start out small.
To fall in love, first feel none. Yet when these adventures
begin and the dreamers suddenly find themselves lost, small
and alone, any feelings of lack are simply a sign that you've
made a really big and daring wish, and its manifestation
has already begun.*

And maybe that was exactly it — this wasn't the end. It
was the murky middle. The lost part of the story before the
light breaks through.

August 5, 2024
WHITEFISH, MONTANA, UNITED STATES

*I know you can do the hard things, now I just need you
to put in the work. The work is the mundane and the
specific — two things you struggle at, especially with no
framework. That's the beauty though, right? You get to
create whatever you want, whatever you love. Be willing*

to challenge the matrix, because that is what people love.
That's what they connect with. That's what will expand.

I also want you to give yourself grace.

Except it didn't feel murky anymore. It was pitch black.

After nearly three months in the van together, McDreamy and I were bickering more than ever. Everything felt tender, like we were constantly touching invisible bruises. Deep down, I knew something was breaking, but rather than admit it, I picked petty fights — about directions, logistics, the internet.

One night, we had pulled off into the woods just off a quiet road in the Canadian Rockies. It was dark and thick fog was rolling in. As we nestled the van in between tall pines, the tires skidded slightly on the earthen floor and I couldn't help myself.

"Can you please slow down?" I snapped, white-knuckling the handle on the passenger door.

"I am slowing down," he said, jaw tight.

"Then take the turn slower. Jesus."

He exhaled sharply through his nose, saying nothing.

I huffed loudly and reached over to steady the book on the dash like it might fly away. "You never listen to me when I say something. I don't feel safe when you drive like that."

"I've driven this thing through mountain passes and across the country multiple times, Connie," he bit back. "You think I'm trying to crash us?"

I stared out the window, my breath fogging up the glass. I didn't want to keep doing this, but I didn't know how to say what I was *really* feeling — scared. Not just of the road, but of us. That we were drifting. That it wasn't working.

But instead, I sulked. Grabbed my phone. Dramatically opened the van door to get some air, letting the cold rush in.

When we finally climbed into our cramped bed — the one so small we were usually tangled up without trying — we stayed rigid, backs turned, each clinging to our edge like it might give us more space than reality allowed. It was impossible not to notice how hard we were both working to avoid even the slightest touch.

And that heaviness didn't stay contained. I carried it with me into the world — into cafés, hikes, conversations with strangers. We met up with friends in Banff National Park, and even surrounded by laughter and beautiful views, I couldn't quite shake the tension. It clung to me like smoke. My smiles felt forced, my answers short. I wasn't as warm or open as usual — like I was watching myself from the outside, going through the motions but not really there. I wasn't grounded and I was desperate to pin it on something — anything — outside of me.

After a week of deflecting with friends, McDreamy and I were alone together again. As we settled into bed in the mountains of Alberta, the air cool and still around us, it all bubbled up again.

"Is it so hard to find a place to work and make sure we're there by 10am? Look on Google Maps one more time." I asked in a huff.

But what I really wanted — what I was really begging for — was for him to see through the ask and address what had been bubbling beneath the surface for months. I wanted him to pull me close and say he still chose me. That we could weather anything — unstable incomes, mounting uncertainty, the messiness of growth — as long as we did it together.

Instead, under the weight of the night and the cover of darkness, he said it like a question he wasn't ready to answer: "Maybe we should take a break."

And just like that, the foundation I had been clinging to shattered beneath me.

August 15, 2024
CALGARY, ALBERTA, CANADA

Seeing the pattern in myself, is heartbreaking.

Knowing I need to address it and change is scary. And doable.

The question is why? Why is this what I do? The explosive love is what I've seen through life, that's what I know. I don't want that. Do I have the opportunity to change that? Always.

But will it be enough to save this?

TWENTY-TWO
THE SLOWEST GOODBYE

T OO STUNNED TO speak after hearing McDreamy's confession, my tear ducts answered for me — a silent downpour that said everything I couldn't. "That's not what I want." I thought we were in this together, building a life that could weather anything. But maybe I had mistaken consistency for commitment.

It echoed a pattern I'd seen before — loving someone for their potential and hoping proximity would become intimacy. Hoping that if we just spent enough time together, if I stayed patient and steady, eventually he'd meet me fully. But love doesn't work that way.

We tiptoed around each other for the next few days, everything unsaid buzzing like static between us. It wasn't until we finally got out into nature for a hike that I felt enough space in the air to bring it up again. I paused on the trail, took a breath, and turned to him.

"I'm not saying things have been easy," I began, voice steady, "but I know what's real. I see you as the person I want to build a life with — not some version we're supposed to chase, but our own version. A life full of freedom, adventure, growth. Our values are aligned. We have plans, dreams, a rhythm that works. I still believe in us. I want the spiritual marriage, the multiple homes, the retreat business, the baby. I want it with you."

I looked him in the eye, holding my ground.

But McDreamy couldn't be swayed. He wanted a break. We would take the next weeks to explore life without each other, to reassess if we wanted to move forward together or separate.

So we drove — in silence, in sadness, in strange new territory. We spent that next week still sharing the van, still sleeping under the same roof of stars, making our way from the quiet roads of Canada down into Montana. I was set to fly back to Colorado, as planned. But what hadn't been part of the plan was the aching knowing that I might not be flying back *to him*.

Originally, I was meant to meet him on the East Coast a month later — a string of birthday celebrations for his mom, his brother, his sister-in-law and mine — before heading off on a solo birthday trip across Thailand, Vietnam and South Korea. Then I'd meet him in Mexico and we'd go to Costa Rica from there. It had all been planned. A full circle from our van life summer to a future that, until now, had felt so vivid.

But nothing felt certain anymore.

August 20, 2024
CANMORE, ALBERTA, CANADA

What do you do when the future makes sense — the homes, the lifestyle, the celebration, the baby — but today isn't working?

How do you pull yourselves from the outside stressors —

the job, the house, the failures, the confusion — to recognize what is already in front of you?

When and why did the love become conditional?

Is it you? Is it him? The us? Or are we simply lost on expectations that we're out on what is already there?

The judgement.
The drama.
The sadness.
And confusion.

What is it that people have to surpass this but we can't? Is it how we're built — the need for new and more and magic?

Why is it that the future makes sense but today doesn't?

I asked the same question over and over, hunched in the passenger seat like a ball of yarn unraveling. The heartbreak wasn't about love — we had that. It was timing. Pressure. Two people still trying to grow roots, hoping to braid them together before they were ready.

And yet, somehow, the week that followed was both the hardest and the most beautiful.

We stayed in the van — there were no distractions. No "later" to push feelings into. No real space to hide, so we didn't.

We cried. A lot. Sometimes silently, sometimes sobbing into each other's arms. We held hands and let the silence speak for us. We tried to cook our favorite meals, to sleep, to make jokes when the weight became too much and to play our favorite card games. We laid in bed with our foreheads touching and confessed our fears in the dark. It wasn't just a breakup — it was an unweaving. A soul-level separation from something we had built together, thread by thread.

There were moments where we forgot we were breaking. When we danced to music in a gas station parking lot. When we watched the sunset over Canmore Reservoir, barely breathing. When he reached for me in the middle of the night without thinking and I let him.

But the anxiety in my chest never fully left. It pulsed like a second heartbeat — tight, suffocating, ever-present. I didn't know how to live in a world where we weren't "we" anymore.

And maybe the scariest part was that neither of us wanted to let go… but we didn't know how to keep holding on. It felt like trying to grip water.

We talked about everything — our patterns, our families, our fears. The parts of us we had hidden from each other and even from ourselves — marriage, having children together, what our ideal partnership looked like. We were more vulnerable in that final week than we had been in months. Maybe ever.

It was too late to fix it, but not too late to honor it.

And so we did. In every stolen glance over our laptops in cafés. In every pot of our signature pasta, stirred together on the tiny propane stove in whatever gravel lot we landed. In every brush of his hand against mine that said, "I still love you. I just don't know how to do this anymore."

We drove south in silence, through Glacier, through rolling farmland, through long winding highways that looked like freedom and felt like grief. Each mile brought me closer to the airport in Montana and closer to the moment I'd walk away from the life we had built. The one I thought we were *still* building.

August 24, 2024
GLACIER NATIONAL PARK,
MONTANA, UNITED STATES

The thing I've always loved most is control,
Probably due to the lack I felt as a kid.
This chapter is a challenge to release my hold,
And let life play out as it should.

And that control? It was slipping — or maybe being pried from my clenched fists — one unmet expectation at a time.

August 25, 2024
WHITEFISH, MONTANA, UNITED STATES

Things I grew up hearing:

· *You're not like us, maybe you were adopted.*
· *What's the point of having a kid if you don't fuck with them.*
· *I had it worse than you.*
· *Birth control baby.*
· *Your only job is soccer.*
· *I don't like you right now but I still love you.*

The echoes of childhood phrases I thought I had long since silenced came roaring back, uninvited and unrelenting. No wonder I was searching for something — anything — to hold onto. No wonder I thought love had to be earned through performance. That I had to choose magic over groundedness. That stability was dangerous because it could vanish just as quickly as it came.

I had worked so hard to rewire these narratives. And yet, here they were again — resurfacing not to destroy me, but to be fully seen. And maybe that was the next lesson: that healing doesn't mean forgetting. It means facing. Again and again, until the sting softens and the roots finally deepen.

And then, it was time to leave.

The airport felt like a slow-motion goodbye. McDreamy hoisted my two bags — packed with only what I could carry, the rest left in the van's drawers — while I reached for Lu, curled in her crate. And suddenly, I was transported. It was eerily reminiscent of those final moments leaving GI Joe in Japan — the same weight in my chest, the same uncertainty about whether I'd ever see him, or my things, again. My mind flickered, caught between timelines, unsure if this was really happening or some glitch in the matrix — a flashback bleeding into the present. We stood outside the van on the curb of the departure terminal, arms wrapped around each other, bodies shaking as the tears came — quiet at first, then uncontrollable. The world blurred around us. Time folded into a bubble where it was just us, suspended between what had been and what might never be again.

We held on for as long as we could.

Final words came through his trembling lips: "I love you."

"I love you too." I breathed back.

And then I had to let go.

I had to force one foot in front of the other, walking toward the sliding door that would separate me from my person.

Left foot, my hero.

Right foot, my soulmate.

Left foot, my adventure buddy.

Right foot, my safe space.

Left foot, the love of my life.

Right foot, my best friend.

Left foot, my emergency contact.

Right foot, Lu's dad.

Left foot, the man I wanted to be the father of my children.

Right foot, my life partner.

Left foot, my home.

Each step felt like betrayal. Like walking away from everything I had spent the last three years building. But there was no other choice. This was the kind of heartbreak that didn't explode. It ached. It throbbed. It unraveled slowly, with reverence.

"There ain't a drop of bad blood, it's all my love,
You got all my love."

Noah Kahan's words echoed in my mind, not through a speaker but from somewhere deep within me — a song that had become a part of my bones. I had given McDreamy all of it. Every piece. Every breath. Every chance.

I didn't look back. I couldn't.

Because if I had — I wouldn't have gone.

TWENTY-THREE
NOTES I'LL NEVER SEND

I NUMBLY SHUFFLED ONTO the plane. Into my friend's waiting car at the Denver airport. Into my condo. Onto the couch. Through the first week.

Everything felt hollow — like I was living in a museum of my own life. Familiar objects, familiar routines, but none of it held warmth. It was all just *there*, echoing with what used to be. I moved through the days like I was underwater — slow, disoriented, barely able to breathe.

My mind looped on repeat — memories, regrets, what-ifs, unfinished conversations. I couldn't keep them all inside. So I created a thought log in the notes app on my phone — a digital dumping ground for the things I burned to say to McDreamy but couldn't. I wrote like it might save me, like it was the only thing tethering me to the ground. Because the only way out was through. And this was me, crawling through the fire on my knees.

August 26, 2024
DENVER, COLORADO, UNITED STATES

Not much in me to write.

*My head feels heavy. As does my heart. There's a weight
on my chest, trying to break my ribs and crush my lungs.
Being without you is like being unable to breathe.*

You've not chosen me.
You can still.
But I may be gone by then.
I hate that this is where we're at.
I hate that the future is clear but today is foggy.

*I want the commitment and I want to be strong enough to
walk away if I need to.*

McDreamy wanted time — time to explore life without
each other, to see if what we had could withstand space. I wanted clarity. I knew I wouldn't find it with his voice in my ear,
softening every edge, igniting every flicker of hope. So I asked
for no contact against his wishes. It was the hardest boundary
I've ever set.

We hadn't decided when we would speak again and I had
cancelled my trip to Asia. We agreed he would return to Denver with the rest of the things that couldn't fit in my two bags
before I left for Mexico in two months. Beyond that, everything was up in the air.

But I *did* know this: My love wasn't going to disappear
overnight. I couldn't imagine fully detaching in weeks or even

months. This break wasn't a goodbye. It was a surrender. A final attempt to find myself inside the wreckage.

August 31, 2024
DENVER, COLORADO, UNITED STATES

I got my rook pierced today, which is apparently one of the most painful ear piercings, and if that's not a reminder to myself that I'm strong, I don't know what is. Today was hard and that was a needed reminder. I miss you. Though, I'm not ready for you yet.

Kelly arrived as the first week of our break concluded. With her blonde hair and eyes that sparkled like mischief itself, she carried the kind of laugh that made everyone in the room join in without knowing why. Her sunshine pierced through the numbness. She joined me on the couch, cooked, hugged, distracted, listened. And with her arrival, the grief finally found a way out. It flooded me — every cell, every muscle, every inch. I cried, not just tears, but sobs — the kind that shake your whole body, that leave you gasping.

The kind that make you wonder if the pain will ever stop.

September 2, 2024
DENVER, COLORADO, UNITED STATES

I have melted and I hate it here. I don't know how to exist without you. I hate that that's where I am. I hate how much this hurts. I hate how much I want you. I hate that I say I only want you and yet my body feels such need. I hate this. I hate this so much. This is the hardest day I've had.

As the sadness settled into my bones, another emotion began to rise — sharper, hotter. Anger.

Not at him. Not even at me. But at the place where this unraveling began — the job that pulled the rug out from under me, that shattered my stability and my self-trust. The job that made everything after it harder.

It wasn't just grief anymore. It was rage. And for the first time ever, I was ready to feel it.

September 4, 2024
DENVER, COLORADO, UNITED STATES

I've been angry for the last year and a half, and disguising it as flow and trust and growth. But here's the thing, fuck that situation — that job took my power, that job upended and destroyed my life, that job took my security and trust, that job turned me into someone I didn't want to be, and with a position I never really wanted. Fuck you. This hasn't been fair, and, in that same breath, thank you, this is where I come to prove myself. I refuse to let that job waste another second of my life, to try to take down anything more. I will be stronger for this, and aligned. Thank you. I release you.

I had to let the anger have a voice so it wouldn't calcify inside me. And once I gave it space, I began to remember what actually mattered to me — movement, community, growth. The core pillars that had always brought me back to myself.

I walked Lu through the park daily, soaking in the changing light and the rhythm of our steps. I went to yoga, even on the days I didn't want to and stayed even when the tears inevitably flowed in the middle of class. I made friend dates, surrounded myself with safe people and spoke to Jacqueline for hours each night to help fill the quietest, scariest part of the day. I leaned on my network of healers, one session at a time, letting them slowly stitch me back together.

As I recommitted to myself, marketing contracts for election season started pouring in — a healthy distraction from my grief and a wave of financial stability I didn't realize I'd been craving. It felt like the Universe was offering me a small reprieve: a chance to focus, to earn, to steady myself.

After a particularly poignant conversation with my astrologer, a new call began to rise inside me — firm and clear. The call to sit with Ayahuasca. It had been on my radar for years, but I'd always said, "When it's time, I'll know." And I knew, it was time.

September 8, 2024
DENVER, COLORADO, UNITED STATES

I want to love you how I want to be loved — so fully and respectfully and unconditionally. I want to love you for who you are, who you want to be and who you were. Fuck the love languages, I'll give it all. I want to love you without restraints and roadblocks.

I grounded in the water today. I want to go back so I can do a full plunge. I had woken up in the middle of the night and had the deepest urge to be in the ocean, to be surrounded by water, to be held. It brought up Santa, how healing it is. And it reminded me of you and your love of cold plunges.

On Ayahuasca — if I want any chance of us, I need to do this self-work.

The decision wasn't about saving our relationship — not entirely. It was about saving myself. About facing what I hadn't yet faced. About finding out what lived beneath all the layers of heartbreak, anger, longing and loss. If I wanted to become the woman I dreamed of being — for me, for McDreamy, for whatever future waited — I had to go deeper.

Each week, our group gathered on Zoom calls to prepare for the journey ahead — a journey that would demand full surrender. We weren't just learning about the medicine; we were learning how to open ourselves to it. To her.

We were told Ayahuasca was not simply a psychedelic — she was a spirit, a divine feminine force, lovingly called *Mama Aya*. She would show us what we needed to see. Strip us down. Reflect us back to ourselves.

And she began her work on me before I even arrived.

Mama Aya amplified my emotions:

Anger is taking hold — not loud and wild, but in this twisted, quiet martyrdom. I challenge that. Anger is allowed. Every feeling is valid. Nothing is owed. Everything is of your own volition.

She amplified my questions:

What would I do if it were for myself only?

Where would I live?

What would I own?

Who would I be?

Mama Aya amplified my mental loops:

Everything I see reminds me of McDreamy. The grocery store where we got your green juice. The stretch of road where you kissed my forehead. A Vuori shirt. A van on the highway. A song in a café. Couples holding hands like nothing could ever go wrong.

McDreamy was everywhere. And yet, he was gone. And my brain couldn't reconcile the difference.

Mama didn't let me look away. She made me sit in it. Swim in it. Almost drown in it.

Because to get to the other side, I had to feel it all. And I was just getting started.

As the days dragged and the weeks flew, my grief stretched beyond McDreamy. Curled up with my weighted blanket and a cup of decaf coffee, wearing McDreamy's flannel and a pair of leggings, I let myself feel it all. The weight of old heartbreaks rose to the surface — grief I had buried from GI Joe, the Man in Finance, even my high school boyfriends. I wrote to each of them — apologizing, asking for forgiveness, sending love. I didn't need to rekindle anything. I just needed to release what was still clinging to me. The versions of me that hadn't yet healed.

Revisiting those relationships made me reflect on mine with McDreamy. Yes, our love was deep. It was different. It was real. But had it truly been enough? Had I mistaken comfort for compatibility? Had I outgrown the way he was capable of loving me? Or was I still trying to get someone else to fill a well that only I could fill?

Some days, the truth felt clear. Others, it slipped through my hands like sand. But this much I knew — I had already proven to myself that I could walk away.

The moment I boarded the plane in Montana, I chose myself.

And that strength? That's what led me to reach out. After six weeks of silence, I finally sent McDreamy a voice note:

I've been thinking about this all week — if I wanted to send something or not. I (1) didn't want to be performative, I (2) wasn't quite frankly sure if you deserved to know about anything going on in my life, and (3) my ego didn't want to be the one to reach out. Ultimately I came back to this — if I want to receive love, I have to give love, so here I am. I'm going into an Ayahuasca retreat tomorrow afternoon. While you were the most recent catalyst behind this decision, this is fully for myself. For my healing. For my evolution. I know if I have any chance of continuing to create the life and partnership I dream of, I have to greet my shadow head on. This obviously won't cure all, and I believe it's a massive mile jump ahead after all of the challenges and realizations I've had recently. There have already been a ton of lessons and learnings throughout my prep, but the one that matters the most is that my feelings on us have not changed. However, what I want has been clarified and my ability to walk away if you are not willing to match my energy is fortified. I will be ready to talk after this weekend — I get back Sunday night. I'm ready to get out of this liminal space we have been in and I'm ready to move on with or without you, though preferably with.

I didn't feel strong. I didn't feel healed. I didn't feel like I had found any resolution.

What I felt was like an egg carelessly cracked on the sidewalk — raw, spilled open, grieving. Still aching for him. Still missing the life we almost had. Still waking up in the middle of the night reaching for someone who was no longer there.

But as the grief swelled, so did the recognition: I wasn't just grieving him. I was grieving the part of me that kept choosing someone almost right. The girl who clung to men who made big promises and offered just enough love to keep me hoping but never enough to make me feel safe.

But I also knew I couldn't stay in this place forever. I had done what I could on my own — I had felt what I was capable of, survived the firsts, screamed into pillows, cried on hikes, written unsent notes in my phone. I had shown up for my grief. I had given it room.

Now it was time to let something greater meet me there.

Ayahuasca wasn't a cure. It wasn't an escape. It was a reckoning — and I was finally ready to see what Mama had to show me.

I wasn't walking into that ceremony whole. I was walking in shattered. And maybe that's exactly how I needed to arrive.

Still in love. Still grieving. But ready to see what's on the other side of surrender.

TWENTY-FOUR
ON THE OTHER SIDE OF THE VEIL

As the final week of September and my Ayahuasca retreat approached, life handed me yet another upheaval — I was kicked out of my condo. Since I was supposed to be on the East Coast, headed to Asia, it had been rented out. I suddenly had no home base. But my Denver chosen family didn't hesitate — they offered up spare rooms, empty apartments, quiet houses. I bounced between them like a pinball, gently caught and redirected at every corner. They made me feel loved in a time I wasn't sure I could be. They protected me. They cheered me on. They held me.

I pictured their faces as I made the hour-long drive north to the retreat center — sobbing so hard I had to pull over, my body shaking, my chest tight. I even wished someone would hit me with their car — not enough to permanently hurt me, just enough to give an excuse not to show up. That's how scared I was. Of what I'd see. Of what I'd feel. It wasn't just the purging and puking that Mama Aya is notorious for causing, I trembled in the face of what I'd have to let go of. Of who I might be on the other side.

After a blood pressure check, a drug test and a general overview of the weekend, we were led into the ceremony space. Nine mattress pads were laid out across the floor, each stacked with blankets and pillows, with a purging bucket to the side. I unpacked my own space with intention — my baby blanket, my weighted blanket, my favorite pillow, an eye mask, my power crystals, journal and pen, water bottle, an extra set of clothes. I layered up, wearing Depends adult diapers just in case and settled into my cocoon.

We began with a smoke bath — an opening ceremony to cleanse our auric fields and ground everyone into the space. Then came rapé, a shamanic snuff used for clarity and connection, and sananga, eye drops meant to enhance spiritual vision.

And then we were handed our cups. "Love. Light. Clarity." Those were the words I offered up into mine before tipping it back and swallowing.

We had to wait twenty minutes to ensure the medicine stayed down. As I sat there, I asked Mama to be gentle with me. I repeated my intention to her and asked her to guide me through it, "Please be gentle, gentle." Then I laid flat, pulling my weighted blanket over me and my eye mask down, curling onto my left side. At first, it felt like drifting — a liminal space between dream and seeing, like the edge of sleep but more vivid with deep, heavily contrasted colors.

Earlier in the week, I'd had a session with the retreat medic. He had reviewed my history and explained what might arise: deep exhaustion from years of anxiety might cause me to sleep. My anxious mind might loop. And because I leaned depressive, I might see some very dark things. It wasn't a warning — it was an invitation to prepare.

I tried to breathe. I tried to trust. I saw my best friends: Jacqueline and Kelly and Stef and Pippa. I felt them around me, protecting me. Holding the edges of the portal I was slipping into. And then I heard her — Mama Aya. Soft and steady.

"This is no different than breathwork, than yoga, than reiki. If you let it be."

I unclenched my jaw. Loosened my fists. Letting go, just a little.

What I saw was healing — not metaphorically, but literally. I watched myself heal myself. I was the medicine. The message was clear and unwavering: "Everything you need is already inside you." I didn't need alcohol to loosen up. I didn't need drugs to escape. I didn't need outside validation or even energy workers to "fix" me. The knowing, the wisdom, the power — it was already there. All I had to do was listen.

As the energy facilitators offered a second cup, I felt them pause beside me. I was still holding on, gripping the final threads of control and so I shook my head — not yet. I wasn't ready to go deeper. Not like that.

Instead, I rolled gently onto my right side.

And just like that, I was launched.

What had been soft and dreamy on my left side became a rocket ship on my right. Mama Aya wasted no time — flipping through visions, stories, memories and messages like a film reel on fast-forward. Faces I'd forgotten. Lessons I hadn't learned. Moments I thought I had buried. Visions that were my future or other lives or generational memories.

There was no time to catch my breath, no pause to make sense of what I saw. Just a kaleidoscope of truths.

And through it all, one feeling anchored me:

"You are your own guide. You are your own home. Take what you need and leave the rest."

The visions came fast and visceral: my love depicted as fire — bright, wild, alive. When I chose to direct it, it became contained and powerful. But when I let it spill unchecked, it was massive, all-consuming.

Then snakes — dozens of them — coiled themselves around my entire body. At first, it felt oddly comforting, like they were holding me together. But the comfort quickly turned into constriction. My limbs went numb. I couldn't tell if I was being protected or paralyzed. Maybe it was both.

And then the pain started.

A sharp, deep ache bloomed across my stomach and I panicked — was this the purge everyone had warned about? I begged silently, "Please, not that. Anything but that." But the pain didn't rise toward my throat. Instead, it traced a familiar line — the stretch mark across my belly that's been with me since childhood, curving from hip to hip. I looked down and suddenly, I wasn't me anymore. I was my paternal grandmother — and I was birthing my father via C-section.

Time and space collapsed. My body felt ancient. My womb, eternal.

I pressed my side into the mat beneath me, grounding back into the present, reminding myself where — and who — I was. And that's when I realized: I wasn't just *in* my body. I was *outside* of it too.

With each breath, I could exhale a layer of myself outward — first into the room, then over the others, sending love and healing. I could feel my physical body grounded on my mat and at the same time, feel myself hovering just above, watching patiently. And with another breath, another exhale, another layer of my being expanded even further — into the cosmos. I was here, there and everywhere all at once. I was multidimensional.

That's when I realized — I was on the other side of the veil. I had crossed into the space I had been seeking. And the

most surprising part? It was easy. There was no purge, no resistance, no earth-shattering pain. It felt as simple as opening a
door and walking through.

And Mama Aya was there, waiting for me, smiling with a
kind of ancient knowing: "You've already been here, my child,"
she said softly. "You exist here often. That's why human connection has been so difficult for you. Why you've never quite felt
like you belong."

The words dropped into my chest like a stone dropping
into water, ripples of understanding washing over my being.
Of course. That ache, that misfit frequency I'd carried for so
long — it wasn't brokenness. It was remembrance.

But then, just as quickly as I arrived, the light dimmed.

I was running, barefoot and desperate. Through a thick
and shadowed forest, vines hanging low like fingers reaching
to pull me under. I couldn't tether myself to the room. The veil
had shifted again, this time without warning.

I was lost in the dark — and the dark was inside of me.

I began to fidget on my mat, trying to claw my way back to
the now. Tears leaked down my cheeks in silent surrender. And
then the yawns began — violent, uncontrollable, primal. Each
one yanked my jaw open so wide it felt as though the top half
of my skull arched back over my head and the bottom dropped
through the floor. My body convulsed with them, each yawn
a full-body earthquake, rattling loose what I was too afraid to
release.

I couldn't ground. I couldn't come back. All I could do was
surrender and let it pass through.

I desperately tried to flip back to my left side — my safe
side. The side where things moved slower, where I could
breathe. I shifted my shoulder, hovered in a supine twist, trying
to coax myself out of the chaos.

But Mama wasn't done with me. She shoved me back to the right with a force that said, "Not yet."

Panicked and pleading, I asked her, "This is great, but how do I apply it all? How do I bring this back to my life? How do I apply this to McDreamy?"

She didn't answer. Not with words. Instead, she shot me through the cosmos — rapid-fire flashes of color, sensation, memory, emotion. It was too fast, too much. I couldn't make sense of it. I couldn't hold on.

With everything I had left, I flipped myself back to the left side — forcing calm back into my system, clutching at the slowness like a lifeline.

And then it happened. The visions softened and the whirl-wind eased. I curled into myself, arms wrapped tight around my body, grounding back into my mat. The sounds around me faded until I couldn't hear anything but my breath. And then — faint, like elevator music in the background of a dream — I heard it.

The song I Love You by The Hanumen.

The melody floated toward me and with it came Mc-Dreamy. The lyrics getting louder as McDreamy became more clear — "I love you, I do. I love you, I do. I love you, I do." He stepped into my field of vision, glowing in a light only love could cast. Behind him, scenes began to shift: a beach, a moun-tain trail, a ski resort, a countryside lane.

He was holding the hand of a little boy — just three years old. The boy had McDreamy's perfect curls and those unmis-takable green eyes flecked with brown. But he also had my golden hair, my tanned skin, my spirit.

He turned to look at McDreamy, laughing at something he'd said. Then his gaze met mine over his shoulder — clear, pure, unflinching. "C'mon, Mommy," he beamed. "Walk with me and Daddy."

His words struck me square in the chest, cracking something open. Silent, heavy tears spilled down my cheeks like a broken dam.

Somewhere in the distance, I could hear the ceremony space being closed — soft footsteps, quiet voices, the rustling of blankets — but it all felt far away.

I peeled off my eye mask, the tears still falling in steady streams. Slowly, I sat up, facing the pale yellow wall adorned with a black and white bird banner. My jaw slack, breath caught and "Whoa" slipped out before I could catch it.

And then it came rushing out, over and over again.

"Whoa. Whoa, whoa, whoa."

The realization — the weight, the wonder, the truth — moved through me like a wave. And I let it.

I was so wired from Friday night's ceremony that I barely slept. By the time morning arrived, I was utterly depleted — physically, emotionally, spiritually. The next ceremony began at 8:30am, but I chose not to participate. I had woken up with an overwhelming sense of completion, as if what I had come for had already arrived.

I stayed curled on my mat the entire time, too drained to move, just letting everything settle.

Then, during the gratitude circle after the morning ceremony, something terrifying happened. The man whose hand I was holding suddenly collapsed — face-first, like a board — right onto the hardwood floor. It was jarring and surreal. He came to shortly after, but it shook everyone, and to me, it felt like a loud, final message: You are done here, for now.

I pulled our shaman aside and shared what I was feeling —

the completion, the strange sign, the exhaustion. She encouraged me to hold space for my brothers and sisters during Saturday night's ceremony instead of participating. So I went in with that intention, inviting Mama Aya's energy without consuming her. I begged for truth, acceptance, partnership.

But the first half of the night, I spiraled. My mind was racing. I could feel a purge rising — my body kept yawning, eyes welling with tears, my stomach unsettled. Finally, I sat up and wrote pages of word-vomit into my journal, releasing all the thoughts clawing to get out.

September 28, 2024
BOULDER, COLORADO, UNITED STATES

My vulnerability is where I come back into my power — where I am me, the best version of me. I saw it at the first retreat where I met McDreamy and now I see it here. The question now is how does that come with me — how do I integrate that moving forward? How do I go from this beautiful journey seeing this beautiful vision to real life? How does it translate? How does that become what is? Surrender. Surrender to what can be so that the magic can happen. Isn't that how the magic started. It became this beautiful thing that then got warped and turned into expectations. The expectations — that is the killer of magic. That is what takes it down. So how can I release what I saw? What I hoped? At a very deep level of surrender. Surrender to what can be so that the magic is. Let the light be your guide. Let the light bring you back to your magic. The love can still be. The love still is. Don't let the love ruin the magic. If it will be, it will be, and that is where the hope

shall lie — not on the could be, should have been, wanted
to happen, because that focus is misguided. Hope for if it
will be, it shall be. Release the control and surrender baby.

Let him go.

After that, I collapsed onto my mat and slept hard — deep,
dreamless and uninterrupted until the ceremony space closed
hours later. That night, I slept again — just as heavily — and
woke up knowing something had shifted.

When I got home the following day, the anxiety crept in.
I felt both complete and deeply unsettled — an odd combi-
nation. A friend had reminded me that this was normal. "Tap
into what you need," she said. "It's already inside of you."

Of course, that echoed Friday night's message almost word
for word. Serendipity at its finest.

So I did what I could: I ate broth and strawberries. I curled
up on the couch with Lu. I binged terrible TV, cried when I
needed to and journaled until my hand cramped.

I didn't walk out of that retreat as a brand-new person. I
wasn't suddenly healed or free of grief. But something inside
me had shifted. A quiet knowing had returned — one that reminded me I am my own medicine. That the love I long for, the
clarity I seek, the strength I think I lack — it all already lives
within me. I didn't get everything out of Ayahuasca that I had
ever wanted but I got exactly what I needed that weekend.

The heartbreak still ached. The future with McDreamy
was still uncertain. The questions hadn't disappeared. But for
the first time in a long time, I felt steady enough to hold them.

I didn't need to force answers. I just needed to keep walking — one foot in front of the other, guided by my own light.

The path ahead was still unwritten.

And despite not wanting to do so, I was no longer afraid to write it alone.

TWENTY-FIVE
IT'S MY PARTY

A S I LANDED back in the "real world" post-Ayahuasca, everything felt a little softer — but also more fragile. The air was heavier, the light brighter, the noise of the world louder than I remembered. I was in the liminal space between revelation and reality, where the visions still echoed in my mind but my feet were firmly back on the ground.

Integration was its own ceremony. And we had been forewarned it was 98% of the work.

I was doing my best to honor what I had seen, felt and learned — that I am my own guide, my own home, that everything I need is already inside me — while also preparing for the conversation I had been both craving and dreading: the call with McDreamy. He had checked in just after the retreat and we'd scheduled a time to talk later that week.

I thought I knew what I wanted from that call. I had visualized the outcome a hundred different ways. The best-case scenario replayed in my head like a movie: he'd say he missed me, that he wanted to fight for us, that he finally saw our life as clearly as I did. But expectations without grounding can be dangerous — even illusions, if they're not backed by truth. And I wasn't going to mistake magic for reality. Not again.

September 30, 2024

DENVER, COLORADO, UNITED STATES

Discerning between the truths of McDreamy and my weekend lessons is extremely challenging. I have the ingredients but not the instructions — because that is for me to apply. For me to create. Take what you need and leave the rest.

So I practiced letting go. Letting go of the outcome. Letting go of the version of us I'd been gripping so tightly. Letting go of the fear that if it didn't turn out the way I wanted, I'd fall apart again.

October 3, 2024

DENVER, COLORADO, UNITED STATES

What may be, let it.

Because this time, I knew I could hold myself. No matter what.

The day we were supposed to talk finally came — a Thursday, after work. My nerves had been humming all day, but I was ready. Or, at least, I thought I was.

Just as my phone started ringing with McDreamy's name lighting up the screen, another call came in — the shaman from my Ayahuasca retreat. I stared at the two names side by side, a strange cosmic joke. My past and my future ringing in unison. I chose the past. I answered McDreamy.

It had been nearly seven weeks since we last spoke. We caught up — briefly — but the air was thick.

Then he said it: "I don't think I want a committed partnership right now."

The words hung in the air like smoke. I couldn't speak. Not because I didn't have anything to say — but because I knew none of it would matter.

He kept going. "I just… I need more time. I've been enjoying my solitude. It's been good for me."

I swallowed hard, my chest tightening.

"I'm not saying I want to close the door on us," he added. "But I'm not choosing this right now."

Three years. Over the phone. Just like that.

I said nothing. There's no point in fighting for someone who isn't willing to fight for you. So I let the silence speak for me. And then I hung up.

Immediately, a guttural sound tore from my throat as my body folded in on itself. The sobs came loud and aching, pulled from someplace deep. I called Pippa — my most selfless friend, the kind of woman who always showed up, no matter the hour, no matter the mess. I couldn't get the words out — just breathless sobs into the phone.

"I'm coming over," she said without hesitation. "I'm packing my bag right now."

When we hung up, I texted Stef, my direct, grounded and no-bullshit but always compassionate friend: "I am a fucking wreck."

But the way I ended the call with McDreamy didn't sit right with me. I didn't want to ghost the end of something so sacred. I didn't want to leave things unsaid, not like that. So I called him back. He didn't answer.

I sent a text instead: "I don't feel like I ended the call in my full integrity and I'd like a redo of that."

He called back. And this time, I spoke from my heart: "I'm sorry — I needed a beat. But now I want a redo. Thank you for being honest with me. That's all I've ever wanted from you, and I know it wasn't easy. I still love you."

He was quiet, then said: "Wow... thank you so much. That truly means so much."

I told him I held no anger, only sadness. That I saw him. That I honored his truth. He said he had been scared to answer, worried I was going to yell — something my younger self absolutely would've done. I acknowledged that. Took accountability for who I had once been. It felt like growth, even if I hated how it came about.

After we hung up, I felt better — still wrecked, still heartbroken, but at least I had shown up in my integrity. And that mattered.

I texted Stef again: "A lot of growth, even though I didn't like how it came about. Back to taking it hour by hour and doing the best I can."

The next morning, I tried to find footing in the acceptance. "I totally respect where he's at, so now I'm just trying to accept it and I'm having a really hard time. I just think this is all so dumb. He's been in his favorite place with all his people constantly around, so of course he's feeling good alone. He hasn't actually sat with what's happening. And I'm happy he got the space he needed, but I hate how it's hurting me. I've been doing so much work, and it's still so much grief."

Later that day, I sent another message: "I know it will get

better, but accepting that he may not be my end goal is daunting. So it's just back to getting through this, hour by hour."

McDreamy and I agreed he would bring my things back to
Denver in two weeks. Nothing else was decided. There would
be no clear closure. Just logistical coordination.

In my head, I still imagined a future — a softened return.
That he'd come over for a dinner date when he dropped off
my things. That we'd have a real in-person conversation. That
maybe he'd come to Costa Rica for a week at the end of my trip.
That I'd come back to Denver mid-December, live in the condo
while he stayed at his mountain house that still had yet to sell.
That we'd date again — have fun, rebuild. And by February,
we'd go to Costa Rica. Together. Like we'd planned.

But I knew where he was at — mentally, emotionally, spiritually — that version of the future didn't exist for him. Not
now. Maybe not ever.

I told Stef: "I think this is going to take me a long time to
heal from. And I'll always love him. I won't tell him that, but
if he were to say he's ready — I'm right back there too. I know
that can change with time, but that's where I am right now."

October 4, 2024
FRISCO, COLORADO, UNITED STATES

I don't think I've ever hurt this much.

I escaped to a house in the mountains for my birthday
week, a safe haven from Stef who knew I needed space to fall
apart. It was the first birthday I could remember in over a decade that I spent alone. No parties. No dinners. No partner
beside me to celebrate the year ahead. Just me, in the stillness,
trying to find my footing.

I hiked every day. Called Kelly and Jacqueline and Pippa and Lisa. Cried on the trails. Cried in the car. Cried in child's pose. I moved slowly, intentionally — if only because there was nothing else I could do. I took myself to yoga. Made myself nourishing meals. Journaled by candlelight. Let the tears fall into my tea.

It wasn't closure. Not even close. But it was the next step in the grief. One I had to take — hour by hour, step by step — without the person I thought would be walking beside me.

October 7, 2024
FRISCO, COLORADO, UNITED STATES

Birth week — it's hard to celebrate while feeling like this. So I will focus on my community showing up for me — the gratitude and love I have for each of them.

Even without the usual birthday fanfare, I felt love pouring in from those who knew me best. Texts. Voice notes. Gifts left at my door. It was bittersweet — to be held so fully by my community and yet still ache for the one person who used to feel like home.

October 8, 2024
FRISCO, COLORADO, UNITED STATES

I feel really sad and hopeless. I don't really know how to get out of this. This hole feels endlessly deep. And endlessly dark. I guess I need to be with it.

That was the lesson the mountains taught me: don't rush it. There was no shortcut out of this grief. No magical thought, no affirmation, no ritual that would pull me back to wholeness overnight. The only way out was through. So I stayed. I let the sadness wash over me, wave after wave.

October 9, 2024
FRISCO, COLORADO, UNITED STATES

Thirty-three — it can only go up from here. My favorite angel number — that's got to mean something, right…?

I wrote that with a shaky hand and tired eyes. Not entirely believing it, but wanting to. Needing to. If nothing else, I had made it through another year. One that had beaten my heart to a pulp, challenging me to stand up and prove who I really was. And now, thirty-three was asking me to rise. Slowly. Softly. But surely.

I just had to get through the day first.

The first three texts I received that morning were Happy Birthday messages filled with loving emojis from McDreamy's dad, brother and best friend Varun — a trio of reminders that even though he had stepped away, his orbit still tugged at mine. I stared at each message with a bittersweet ache, wondering if he'd reach out. Part of me begged him not to — to give me the space I needed. But the other part, the one that still silently repeated his name in every moment, was furious at the thought of him saying nothing at all.

Late in the afternoon, my answer came — not in a warm memory or a gesture of care, but in three sterile pings, his dedicated ringtone echoing through the stillness of the house:

MCDREAMY: Hey hey. I won't be making it to Colorado until the end of the month. I want to ensure you get your stuff before your trip to Mexico and Costa Rica so I'm going to ship it to you.

MCDREAMY: I'll pay for express shipping to make sure it gets to you at least the day before you fly out.

MCDREAMY: Or if there's certain things you don't need for your trip I can keep them and drop them off once I'm back in Colorado.

No "Happy Birthday." No "How are you doing?" No acknowledgment of the day or the ache. Just logistics. Like we were nothing more than a transaction. Like the last three years hadn't existed.

And what hurt more was that this wasn't new. Months earlier, we had argued about this very day — my birthday — when I asked that we spend either the day itself together or at least the weekend before or after. I knew hunting season mattered to him, that it had become a new passion and I wasn't asking him to give it up, I was asking for a middle ground. A small gesture to show that I mattered too.

But instead of meeting me in the middle, he pushed back — saying it wasn't that important, that birthdays weren't a big deal to him. As if that somehow justified dismissing what was important to me.

So this lack of acknowledgement — this sterile string of messages with no sentiment — wasn't a surprise. It was the pattern playing out, again. A pattern of me hoping he'd show up in a new way and him proving, once again, that he couldn't.

My hands started to tremble. The grief morphed into rage, hot and fast. I replied "Are you available for a conversation?"

He called immediately. I didn't bother with a greeting. The sarcasm slid out before I could stop it. "Happy birthday, Connie... oh thank you, McDreamy. Yeah, that's today." I let it sit there. Thick in the silence, heavy with everything left unsaid.

In that moment, I realized the only gift I truly needed this year was the one I had been avoiding since my days on the military base in Japan — therapy. Not a spa day or a dinner out or some distraction wrapped in glitter and good intentions. What I needed was space to unravel it all. The childhood wounds that still echoed lies about my worth. The relationship patterns etched deep into my nervous system. The quiet, simmering anger I didn't know how to release. The grief that clung to me like a second skin — heavy, relentless, always there.

So while the conversation didn't end well, it served up a revelation. And that was my birthday gift to myself: permission to heal in a new, thorough way. To finally face the things I had been carrying for too long. Ultimately, to stop pretending I could keep holding it all together on my own.

And with that, I gave myself permission to release the pressure — especially around children. Up until earlier that year, I'd been indifferent to the idea of motherhood. But something about loving McDreamy and witnessing those joyful young families in Costa Rica had created a door where there hadn't been one previously. One that was now sitting slightly ajar. Not wide, but enough to let light in. Enough to stir something soft and curious inside of me.

I wasn't naïve to the ticking clock. But I also knew that no life-altering decision could be made from inside this grief. Not yet. First, I had to steady myself. Tend to the fractures. Rebuild what had been broken.

So I gave myself a new kind of timeline — not one based on fear or age or expectations, but on healing. I'd take the next year to come home to myself. To process the loss, the lessons, the love. And then, with a clearer heart and a grounded mind, I would revisit the question of freezing my eggs.

This wasn't the ending with McDreamy I imagined. It wasn't closure. But it was a new beginning of sorts — quiet, necessary and all mine.

TWENTY-SIX

PLANES, PIERCINGS,
TATTOOS AND THERAPY

AFTER NEARLY TWO months of swimming in the thickest waters of grief, I needed a shift. I had given Denver all I could — my tears, my routines, my inner unraveling. But something about the city felt like it was anchoring me to the past, keeping me trapped in a cycle I couldn't quite break.

Before leaving, I got a conch piercing — a small, defiant act in the cartilage of my middle ear. Why? To remind myself I am strong. That I can do hard things. That I can endure pain and still choose beauty. It throbbed a little as I packed my suitcase and zipped Lu into her carrier, a physical pulse of the promise I'd made to myself: to keep going.

My astrologer had told me it wasn't just me — even the sky was working against me. Both my Neptune and DS lines ran straight through Denver on my Astrocartography chart — placements that bring fog, energetic overwhelm and emotional entanglements, often catalyzed through relationships. I was living inside a cosmic trap and I needed to get out.

So I got on a one-way flight with Lu and left the weight behind for Mexico City.

October 21, 2024
MEXICO CITY, MEXICO

In the immensity rather than the immediacy of it. It feels bigger and scarier because of that. More daunting and darker. It's the perfect time to be right here.

From the moment we landed, something shifted. My eyes didn't sting with tears at every quiet pause as they had for the past two months. My chest didn't ache quite so intensely. But in stepping out of the familiar cocoon of grief I'd been wrapped in Denver, I felt the vulnerability of re-entering the world.

It was both freeing and terrifying — to be somewhere new, to be someone new. I reminded myself to keep it simple: tacos from my favorite stand, hugs from old friends, watching Lu sniff her way through new streets. It didn't have to be a full transformation. Just a turning of the page.

October 24, 2024
MEXICO CITY, MEXICO

Letting go, moving forward, living for my now. Where will it take me? What will I acquire? Surrender to find out. Just be.

As I settled into the rhythmic pulse of Mexico City — the street vendors shouting over each other, the smell of grilled corn and exhaust in the air, the constant buzz that somehow both energized and exhausted me — my friends and I carved out intentional pauses. One in particular, a temazcal ceremony, became a turning point.

Inside the pitch-black, mud-walled sweat lodge, surrounded by nothing but the sound of my breath, the shaman's chants and the intense crackle of hot stones, I met my grief in a new way. The heat stripped me of distractions. The darkness forced me inward. And in that silence, other wounds began to rise — old pain I hadn't yet faced, buried truths that had been too tender to touch until now.

October 25, 2024
MEXICO CITY, MEXICO

Things that came up last night:

- *Letting go.*
- *Surrendering.*
- *Flowing.*
- *More play, laughs, drinks.*
- *A baby… with McDreamy.*
- *Love.*
- *Gratitude.*
- *Forgiveness — for my parents, for myself.*

The temazcal had peeled yet another layer back. Beneath the sweat and silence, beneath the grief that had been screaming in my chest for weeks, I found something gentler: forgiveness.

It started with my parents.

The stories I'd carried — of being misunderstood, of feeling unseen, of being told I was too much or not enough — had calcified into resentment over the years. But in that pitch-dark womb of earth and steam, I saw them differently. I saw their humanness. Their confusion. Their tenderness. Their wounds. They were just people trying to figure out how to do life, how to raise a child, how to survive their own storms.

And somehow, for the first time in a long time, I could see them with love. Not the conditional kind. Not the "if only they had done it differently" kind. But the deep, rooted kind. I loved them for exactly who they are — imperfect and still trying, like the rest of us.

And just as importantly, I turned that same grace inward. I forgave myself.

For staying too long. For not speaking up. For being reactive. For breaking down. For my infidelity. For not having it all figured out. For forgetting my worth.

I realized I had been punishing myself for not being farther along, stronger, more healed. But I'm just a human too — doing this life for the first time. Trying to love, to grow, to build something meaningful.

And if I could hold space for my parents in that way, surely I could hold it for myself.

And then, there was McDreamy.

The hardest forgiveness of all. Not because he did something unforgivable — but because I had loved him so fully. And when someone you love that much can't meet you in that love, the wound cuts differently.

But in that sacred heat, I let some of it go.

I forgave him for needing time. For walking away when I wanted him to stay. For not seeing, or not being ready to hold, the future I saw so clearly. I forgave him for making promises he couldn't keep. I forgave him for the silence. For the timing. For the undoing. I forgave him because I still loved him. And I forgave him because I loved myself more.

That night, I didn't walk out of the temazcal healed or whole — but I walked out softer. Lighter. More open to what might come next.

October 27, 2024
MEXICO CITY, MEXICO

The temazcal still lingers in my bones — the sweat, the surrender, the softness that came afterward. That space cracked me open. It reminded me I can love without attachment, forgive without forgetting, and release without losing the depth of what was.

I keep coming back to the question that haunts me most: How do I make him see it?

The truth is — I don't. He needs to see it for himself. He needs to feel it in his own time, in his own body, in his own heart. And maybe he will. Maybe he won't. Do I have the patience to wait for that? Or the strength to let go if he never does?

Only time will tell.

What I do know — what the fire and steam and silence taught me — is that I can't live in the waiting. Until then: Focus on yourself. Be yourself. Love yourself.

Keep moving forward — apart, but still somehow connected. Send love. Send grace. Send light.

And trust that the Universe has a plan — even if it looks

nothing like the one I imagined. Even if I can't see it clearly right now. Even if it hurts.

I forgive him. And I keep going.

Each day I gave myself to the simplicity of being — no deadlines, no performance, just presence — something ancient began to stir inside me. It wasn't loud or urgent. It was a quiet thrum, low and steady, like the drumbeat of the wild woman I had buried beneath years of striving. A primal knowing. A flicker of truth rising from the stillness, reminding me of who I was before the world told me who to be.

It came in the stillness between pages of a book, in the way a stranger's song on the street made me pause, in the quiet conversations I had with myself over morning coffee. It was as if all the pain, all the unspoken prayers, were composting into something new.

Creation.

Not for anyone else. Not to prove anything. But because I had something to say. Because I had lived something worth turning into art.

That morning, I woke up with a feeling I couldn't ignore — not one of sadness or longing, but of purpose. I reached for my journal, heart open, pen steady.

October 28, 2024
MEXICO CITY, MEXICO

I woke up with the inclination that I needed to write a book — poetry or short stories to form chapters of lessons. With my memoir woven through. I want to dedicate time

each day to jot those things down and then when I gather
all of my past journals, to weave.

"There will be one heartbreak to end all heartbreaks."

"One day, the light will start to return to her eyes."

And slowly, almost imperceptibly at first, the light began
to return.

It flickered through the cracks in the grief — in the laughter
of friends who showed up without question, in the texts from
Kelly and Pippa and Stef that reached out with "I'm thinking
of you," in the continued nightly calls with Jacqueline that held
the weight of my silence, in the hugs from Lisa that felt more
like lifelines than greetings, in the weekly sessions with my
therapist. The light returned, not yet in the world around me,
but in the quiet trust rebuilding within myself — in my ability to rise again, to keep going, even with the ache still pulsing
beneath it all.

I marked this return with something permanent — new
tattoos, black ink curling over skin like roots and reminders.
Symbols of choice. Of self-devotion. Of what stays. Of what
I must finally let go of. My body becoming a living narrative,
proof of pain turned to purpose.

The tattoos weren't about decoration. They were declarations: "I am still here. I am still choosing myself."

And as I began to choose myself — again and again — I
loosened my grip on the old version of McDreamy and me. I
was going to therapy once a week, gently unraveling patterns of
abandonment and perfectionism that had shaped so much of
my past. Each session was a mirror, showing me where I still

clung and where I was finally ready to let go. It was the first true offering to the Universe — a quiet signal that I was preparing for what was next. That I wanted it. That I was ready to move forward.

Tucked into the corner of my Airbnb's couch, journal open on my lap and Lu curled at my side, my oracle cards were spread across the coffee table, glinting in the warm afternoon light, and beside them, a new tarot deck — deep blue with silver edges — waited to be learned. I was teaching myself to listen more closely: to the cards, to the quiet nudges within, to the wisdom that lived in my own body.

October 30, 2024
MEXICO CITY, MEXICO

I watched Coco, the animated movie, today and made an ofrenda to prepare for Día de los Muertos. I placed the old version of McDreamy and I on it — a symbolic reminder that I have to let it go in order to make space for what's to come, whatever that may be. And then today, I saw the first man I've actually found attractive. I'm not sure it means anything… but it's something. A flicker. A shift. This journey is strange and winding, but I'm still on it — step by step, breath by breath.

With this new perspective, I started observing my life from the outside — like a fly on the wall of my own story. I watched how I entered a room, how I carried myself, how people responded to my presence. I noticed the difference in how I interacted with women versus men — how much more grounded and easy I felt around women and how much more performative I became around men, often subconsciously shifting my body and voice to attract their attention.

It made me reflect deeply on my past relationships — the patterns, the cycles. One would end and another would seem to begin almost immediately, like I couldn't bear the void. Like I needed someone else to tell me I was lovable, desirable, worthy. It was external validation I'd been chasing, not love.

November 2, 2024
MEXICO CITY, MEXICO

- *The need for male attention.*
- *The shift in "I must be done" to getting attention.*
- *My Leo rising coming out.*
- *The Leo connection to masculinity and attention.*
- *The deep missing of McDreamy.*

Maybe this ache isn't about missing him. Maybe it's about learning to fully see myself. To manifest myself — my radiance, my love, my truth — and let everything else follow. It's me. I'm the focus now. The rest will come.

With this new lens of self-awareness and reflection, it was time to move on from Mexico City and return to my heart home — Costa Rica. But this time, I was arriving alone. It would be my first time in Santa Teresa without McDreamy. A place that once held the magic of "us" now needed to be rewritten by just me. I wasn't sure what that would look like but I was ready to find out.

But first, Lu had other plans.

What was supposed to be a smooth travel transition turned into an international saga. We flew from Mexico City to Miami on Sunday, then Miami to San Jose on Monday. Everything seemed fine — until we hit customs. After a two-hour stand-off with border officials, I was told we were being turned around. Lu's paperwork didn't have the correct export stamp from Mexico.

I pleaded with them: my vet could send the correct document digitally, I was willing to quarantine Lu, to quarantine us both, to take her straight to the import office in the San Jose airport, to get her cleared by a vet in Santa Teresa — nothing worked. In a final act of desperation, I even tried bribing the officer. Still, no. We were placed back on the very plane we had just arrived on and sent back to Miami.

From there, we flew to Mexico City — again. I got the correct stamp. And then, finally, on Wednesday night, we boarded one last flight back to San José. Four flights. Four days. Endless hours of navigating red tape. But we made it.

By the end, my eyes were glazed from exhaustion, my body slumped in the narrow plane seat like it had finally surrendered. I was still wearing the same black leggings, tank top and leather jacket I'd put on days earlier — now rumpled and stale. My hair was twisted into a greasy bun atop my head, and in one hand, I clutched a small bag of candy the flight attendant from San José to Miami had given me when I stepped on board in tears. I hadn't even opened it. It was just something to hold.

And somehow, I didn't care. Because the second I stepped outside into the humid night air, my body exhaled.

This place is light. It's love. It's joy. It's healing. It's growth. It's home. And now I would find out if it could still be all those things... even without him.

November 8, 2024
SANTA TERESA, COSTA RICA

Intentions for Santa:

- *Healing.*
- *Creativity.*
- *Sharing my voice.*
- *Joy.*
- *Establishment.*

What I hadn't planned for, though, were the days of endless downpour. The usually dusty roads turned into rivers of thick mud. The air reeked of mold and nothing — not towels, not clothes, not even my skin — ever seemed to fully dry.

The rain was relentless. And it began to mirror something deeper. It asked me to sit still, to feel. To confront what I'd been so carefully avoiding. In our weekly sessions, my therapist gently kept guiding me back to this stillness — to notice what I reached for when the discomfort rose, to trace the patterns rather than outrun them.

The rain is challenging me — to confront what I'm stifling. That being here without McDreamy feels empty. That I'm not sure how to find my way. That I'm lonely. That I don't know how to be alone. That I don't understand how to move forward. That I feel weak. Weak that I don't know how to do this, to survive, to be alone. That I'm so bored. That I run. That I keep running. That I don't know how to settle. That underneath it all, I'm avoidant and scared and looking for someone to fix me. Because I lost my strength so long ago. Life became so hard and draining that it seemed easier to make someone else do it. To lean on in the hardest of ways that I drain them too. Leech the life out of them. Until I'm left alone again. And unable to hold my own energy. It's ugly. I'm ugly. And yet I still wonder if being able to see it, really fucking see it, is what makes me beautiful. The ability to confront, to be with and to change. Everything that proceeded is just ego trying to turn me to stone, to nothing because it knows I am too strong, too good, too powerful to not. It rages because it knows I'm close to breaking through. The summit near, can I give it the final push? Can I prove my ego wrong? Can I pick up the pen? Can I open my mouth? Can I lean on myself? Can I let my true self be my strongest self? Do it baby. Do it for yourself.

And then I proceeded to ask myself a series of questions:

- *What does success look like?*
- *What am I avoiding?*
- *What am I grieving?*
- *What am I scared of?*
- *What am I grateful for?*
- *What brings joy and meaning to me?*
- *Why can't I finish what I start?*
- *Why do I push relationships away?*
- *Am I creating this hell for myself or have I just opened up my eyes to the reality?*
- *At what point is it too much? At what point is the work detrimental?*
- *How does the knowing know?*

- *Where does the flow come from?*
- *What are the answers?*

I don't understand this phase — I can be depressed, I know how to be angry, I know how to avoid, but this feels empty. Void of emotion. Swimming in the ether without gravity. It's ungrounding. What does it mean? What do I do? How do I stand and be and exist? I'm winning but what does that mean when it feels like this? This doesn't feel good. This is existential. This is a burden. This is yucky. How do the people do this?

I want there to be more.
I want it to mean more.
I want it to be worth more.
More. The thing we're taught is bad.
But to settle is worse.
To not hope.
Wish.
Dream.
To be constantly disappointed.
Or to be constantly surprised.
To live in fear.
To live in dull.

Equal. Balance. Even. The light, the dark. The good, the evil.

- *You cannot have one without the other and what happens when you can't find your way back?*
- *Is he what I want or is it the fear?*

- *Did I ever really love him?*
- *What does love mean?*
- *How am I supposed to know what is true?*
- *Do I really know myself?*
- *Who am I?*
- *What do I want?*

I think I'm avoiding myself. I think I have been for thirty-three years. I think there have been moments where she came through but then, I hid. I ran. I avoided. I did what I do best. What does this mean? What do I do with this knowledge? I sit with it. I see it. I see her. I see me.

In the days following my spiral and surrender, the rain gradually changed from a methodic torturous drumming sensation to a pleasant background beat — without trying I just stopped resisting it. I started listening more closely, not just to the storm outside, but to the subtle cues within. My journal became my mirror, my anchor more than ever. My newly purchased tarot cards allowed me to keep going deeper. I wasn't searching for clarity as much as I was reaching for presence — anything that could root me back into the now, into myself.

November 9, 2024
SANTA TERESA, COSTA RICA

How can I continue to do for myself? To use the time, to be the time? To not waste it? This now becomes the question and will lead to the answers. Will lead to the holding and self-love I'm so deeply desiring. I can be my own companion and love and soul and heart. Let it be.

I wrote that after getting my quad stuck on the opposite side of the river that separated my jungle casita from the main road. With no other option, I had to rely on three young Tico boys who wordlessly guided me along a steep, slippery ravine to a narrow footbridge suspended above the roaring current. Barefoot, mud up to my knees, I laughed at the absurdity — at the symbolism. The jungle, wild and unapologetic, didn't care that I was heartbroken. It just kept going. Growing. Dripping. Rebuilding.

And I realized, maybe I could do the same.

I think I'm more secure in my romantic attachment style and capacity to love than I give myself credit for — than he gave me credit for and that annoys me.

That realization stung. It wasn't just about McDreamy not seeing my strength — it was about all the ways I had downplayed it myself. All the times I let someone else's vision of me become my own. But I was still here. Still growing. Still asking the questions.

November 10, 2024
SANTA TERESA, COSTA RICA

"Pay attention to how you cope when you're hurting today."

I underlined that phrase three times.

What does it look like?
What does strength look like?
What do you want?
What do you really want?

*Pay attention. Notice the synchronicities. The angel
numbers. The small things. See what pops up. What
happens.*

That day, I observed myself with the quiet curiosity of a
researcher. I didn't scroll through my phone to escape the ache.
I didn't call anyone to fill the silence. I let the discomfort rise
and settle, wave by wave. I sat in my little casita, flickering with
candlelight, the rain tata-tat-tatting against the tin roof. To my
right, a stack of oracle and tarot decks waited patiently. To my
left, Lu's warm, steady breath grounded me. I sipped my coffee
slowly, letting each moment unfold without distraction.

I was beginning to understand that this too was a form of
strength — not rushing to heal, but choosing to stay present.
To notice. To allow. I paid attention to the small signs — the
angel numbers that blinked on clocks and receipts, the butterfly that landed softly on my balcony in a rare moment of sunshine. The breath that kept moving in and out of my body, even
when it felt heavy.

Grief had shattered me, but it hadn't emptied me. There
was still life inside. There was still desire. And in the stillness
— in the quiet moments I once ran from — those desires began to softly, bravely, rise to the surface.

The jungle didn't stop for me, and maybe I didn't need to
stop for grief either. Maybe I just needed to walk with it. Barefoot and muddied. Still choosing forward.

TWENTY-SEVEN
THE TIDE INSIDE

There's a moment when grief and healing begin to co-exist — not in harmony, not yet, but in constant dialogue. That's where I found myself as I settled into Santa Teresa. A space that had once held so many memories of McDreamy and I, now stripped bare. Now mine to fill. Or at least, try.

I was living in duality. On one hand, I held the promise of rebuilding. In the other, the fragments of what had just fallen apart. There was no illusion of balance. Just the day-to-day work of becoming someone new, someone more true. I was still crying often, still questioning everything, still waking up unsure of where the strength to keep going would come from. But I was showing up. That counted.

Luckily, I had a friend walking the path alongside me. Just days after McDreamy had broken up with me, I received a voice note from Fernanda — a woman I'd met at the Wild Woman retreat in Mexico. Born in Brazil, raised in Venezuela and the United States, she carried an effortless calm, a grounded grace. Her voice always felt like truth wrapped in warmth

— eloquent, steady, thoughtful. She seemed like someone who already knew what she needed to do, she just had to believe she was ready to do it.

Intuitively, I had a feeling she was going through a break-up too. Unfortunately, I was right. I immediately invited her to join me in Costa Rica. A few days later, her flight was booked.

She arrived like a mirror and a balm — deeply in touch with her intuition, able to sense and name the things I was only beginning to feel. Her presence softened my hard edges while also reminding me of my strength. She showed me how to slow down and be with what is, how to trust myself again.

Each morning, we lit palo santo, made coffee, pulled cards and sat. With ourselves. With the rain. With the ache and the hope. We didn't try to fix anything — we just let it be. This was no longer the liminal space. This was the reckoning. The rebuilding. The reclamation.

My girls had shown up so fiercely for me while I was in Denver and now I was receiving that same support in Santa Teresa. It was the silver lining in the darkest of storms — soft, steady and exactly what I needed to remember who I was.

Santa Teresa was pushing me deeper — into myself, into my shadows, into the duality of healing and heartbreak. Some days felt expansive, like I could see the whole world from where I stood. Other days, I could barely make it out of bed, the weight of everything I was moving through too heavy to carry. But even in that weight, I kept showing up. For myself. For my healing. For the version of me that I knew was waiting on the other side of this storm.

November 11, 2024
SANTA TERESA, COSTA RICA

*I want it to be shiny and good and big and beautiful,
even through the sorrow and pain and uncertainty — the
ability to see the rainbow at the end of the storm. And
to build from that because the world is inherently good.
We have our different versions of good and so thus the
tolerance should be. The peace should be. The love should
be. I have been able to transcend so many lifetimes through
these thirty-three years, I've had the ability to see so much
in such a short amount of time that my perspective is wide.
The scope is there. How can that be conveyed in order to
alchemize? To help heal? I see so much pain and hurt, and
it's justified, and it must be healed. How can we heal?*

Even as I wrote those words, McDreamy found his way
into my dreams. My subconscious wasn't done with him, not
even close. The ache still lived in my body.

November 12, 2024
SANTA TERESA, COSTA RICA

*Sensual dreams about McDreamy — he brought out the
joy and fun and he erased my insecurities. How can I find
that in myself? Make that my normal energy? Yes I'm deep
and serious and transformational but I need to be pulled
out of that too.*

It was an honest reckoning — not just with the loss of him,
but with the parts of me that felt easier to access when I was

with him. I missed how he made me feel. But what if I could make me feel that way too?

Two days later, the spiral hit again. My mind unraveled in the middle of the night, looping on things I couldn't control — sex, power, purpose, identity. All the things that had been tied to him. And to every man before him.

November 14, 2024

SANTA TERESA, COSTA RICA

A fitful night of sleep looping about:

- *McDreamy.*
- *Power.*
- *Work.*
- *Sex.*
- *Inability to control.*

What does that tell you?

When I "lose" sight of things, I spiral. How can I honor that and allow myself space to release and relax?

I still have expectations and those need to be honored and released.

And then later that night after a meditation and breathwork session:

I forged my own path tonight — it was so uncomfortable and it happened. And it will continue to blossom. The manifestation is already starting to come through.

And

I miss the beard stroke. My God, the feeling that hit my stomach watching that. The ache. *Cry face emoji.*

The duality. The balance. Thus is life. The beauty of life.

Because that's what Costa Rica was teaching me — how to hold it all. The expansion and the contraction. The growth and the grief. The ache and the aliveness. All of it was welcome here. And all of it was part of the becoming.

And as the becoming became more — as the days unfolded with grief and strength sitting side by side — I felt a deeper call echo through my chest: it was time to cut the cord.

The full moon rose high and wide over the jungle, reflecting off the ocean, illuminating everything it touched — even the parts of me I hadn't yet been ready to let go of. I gathered my journal, sage, palo santo, two crystals McDreamy had gifted me and a handful of tissues. Dressed in a loose, pale linen set, I settled atop my bed, the fabric cool against my skin. The sliding glass door was open to the elements — the rain had finally stopped and the humid air drifted in, thick with the scent of earth. Outside, the monkeys rustled in the tree behind my apartment, their calls mingling with distant waves and the occasional chirp of crickets. My heart knew it was time. My body knew it too.

November 15, 2024
SANTA TERESA, COSTA RICA

Full moon cord cutting ritual —

On this day, I cut energetic ties with McDreamy. This includes any past anger, resentment or expectations and any current hopes or expectations and any future hopes and expectations. I release it all. So that whatever is meant to be, to manifest, to create, can be so. With or without him. I cut this energetic cord and leave behind only love, light, happiness, peace and gratitude. May this act grant me the peace and healing I need and provide him with the freedom he needs. May we both move forward in love, strength, integrity and vulnerability. May we both forgive and heal and open up to whatever the Universe has in store for us, whether that is together in partnership or alone in dignity. May we both receive what we need. And want. And deserve.

McDreamy, I love you. I would have chosen you every second of every day for the rest of our lives. I would have worshipped you as my king. I would have given you light and love and support and protection and joy and adventure and honesty. Instead, I give that to myself. I release you and all promises and expectations. I honor you and the time we had. Be free, both of us. I cut this energetic cord between us and allow a beam of light to connect us instead. To be left as a reminder of all that we shared and as a path should we choose to make it concrete and stable in the future.

I love you. I love you. I love you.
I release you. I release you. I release you.

And then, in the stillness that followed, I breathed. It wasn't final. But it was another beginning. A sacred step in the direction of myself. Of trusting that even though I couldn't see what was ahead, I could still move forward.

Two days later, the ache returned with vengeance.

November 17, 2024
SANTA TERESA, COSTA RICA

I miss him so bad that it hurts. Physically and truly hurts. Who am I without him? I don't want to be without him. I thought cutting the cord would feel better, really I just feel worse. And hopeless. And aimless. And so lonely. I literally yearn for him. I don't know how to do this.

A breakup, a really truly heartbreaking breakup is the ultimate fake it until you make it.

And why do I feel like it's just now hitting me all over again? The depth and brevity of it. The realness of it.

It was as if the cord I had cut tried to reattach itself overnight — not from him, but from the part of me that was still clinging, still longing, still not ready to say goodbye. The feelings I had hoped would eventually catch up to McDreamy were instead bouncing off his silence and landing squarely in my chest. The Universe demanded, "Are you sure you're ready for this? Is this what you really want?"

I knew what my friends wanted for me — closure, clarity, a clean break. I even knew what my higher self wanted — freedom, space, peace. But I wasn't there yet. And I wasn't going to pretend I was. I made a vow to myself that I wouldn't bypass this grief. I wouldn't put a bow on it and call it healed. I would stay, even if it meant being in it longer than I wanted to be. Because this was the work. The real work. The kind of grief that carves new space inside of you so more light can eventually get in.

Two days later, a new wave hit — not one of pain, but of yearning for recognition. For someone to see the mountain I'd been climbing.

The morning light slipped through the shade, slanting across the tile floor. The air was thick with jungle damp — warm, still, the kind that clung to your skin before you even moved. I sat cross-legged on the bed, Lu curled beside me, her breath soft and steady against my leg. A blanket was pooled in my lap, my journal resting open atop it, waiting.

I stared at the page.

I didn't know what I wanted to write — only that something inside me felt tight and unspoken. I closed my eyes and took a deep breath, letting it drop low into my belly. One Mississippi. Two. And then the words came.

I've just wanted to be seen, to be understood, to be told "Wow, that's a lot and look how far you've come."

My pen hovered for a second. And then, something clicked.

It was subtle, like fog parting on a trail, revealing just enough of the next step to keep going. My chest lifted. I looked out the window toward the palm trees swaying in the breeze and felt it land — not just in my mind, but in my body.

This was the book.

Not the version I'd been trying to write — the one about travel, adventure and reinvention, dotted with heartbreak. That wasn't the heart of it. This was about the *becoming*. The breaking. The quiet work of reassembling myself — not as the world wanted me, but as I truly was.

I looked down at the journal and kept writing, the words rushing now like water finding its path: The false identities I'd shed. The grief that had hollowed me out and somehow made space for something softer. The healing that wasn't tidy or cinematic — just honest. Cyclical. Sometimes unhinged.

It wasn't about the places I'd been. It was about the woman I'd become in the process.

I reached down and scratched behind Lu's ear. She stirred, then settled again. I took another deep breath. The tightness in my chest hadn't fully lifted, but something inside had shifted.

Not everything needed to be figured out right now.

This was enough.

This moment. This page. This truth.

And maybe that was the whole point: that healing isn't a finish line — it's a daily practice. A thousand tiny choices to come back to yourself, again and again.

I smiled. Picked up my pen. And kept going.

The clarity didn't last forever. It never does. But it was a start — a thread I could follow. Two days later, I found myself back on the page, reaching for something deeper.

November 21, 2024
SANTA TERESA, COSTA RICA

This deep knowing of reaching another dimension. That I had it all figured out. That my being and healing had evolved. That something has shifted. I was inherently different. I am different. And that at the same time, I can't quite put my finger on why.

Sex came up a lot. That I hid it and refused to give it out of fear and avoidance. The regret, deep in my belly knowing I withheld just as much as McDreamy had. That I was the downfall. That I wasted my own time not fully in. How can one love without restriction? Without fear? With their whole human essence? There is so much I wanted to say to McDreamy last night, that I wanted to apologize for, to take responsibility for so that it can be new and fresh. We talked about it all, except the sex. That it wasn't enough because that is where I repressed myself, withheld, avoided, until I felt safe and whole and complete, which never happened. And so it crumbled. It crumbled because we both couldn't be secure. And now I'm here. Sad, alone, yearning. Trying to grow and be the most authentic and vulnerable version of myself so that a partnership can be exactly what I want and need it to be and deserve it to be.

That journal entry hit me like a wave. I read it again and again, as if the answers I was searching for were between the lines. I hadn't just been grieving McDreamy — I had been grieving the version of myself I never let exist in that relationship. The one who wasn't afraid to be fully seen, fully felt, fully loved. The one who gave without holding back. The one who didn't wait for safety to show up before showing up herself.

This wasn't just about loss anymore. This was a deep invitation to return to myself. To stop waiting to be chosen and choose me.

As the days passed, I let it all move through me — waves of clarity, anger, grief and reflection. I began to see the ways I'd been complicit in my own pain. How I had been emotionally guarded while telling myself I was open. How I withheld the full force of my truth in moments that asked for surrender. And how, in protecting myself, I had also limited our connection.

It wasn't just with McDreamy.

I had already forgiven my parents in the temazcal — I had felt that moment of release, of truth — but living that forgiveness was something else entirely. It had been nearly two years since we'd spoken, and while the silence gave me space to heal, it had also calcified parts of me.

Now, I was learning how to soften. Not to re-engage or re-enter old patterns, but to let go of the resentment that still lived in my body. I didn't need to rehash the past — I needed to free myself from it.

This wasn't about blame anymore — it was about responsibility. About making peace with my part and choosing not to shame myself for it. Because when I could look at the ugly parts — really look — I didn't spiral. I softened. I forgave.

And in that softness, I took a step toward becoming someone new.

November 23, 2024
SANTA TERESA, COSTA RICA

There's so much in me but it doesn't always know how to get out, how to speak the right words. There's a story to be told but it doesn't have the outline, the direction, the motivation. So where does that leave things? When one wants to write but doesn't know how or what? I say that and yet it's there. It's trying. It's raw and vulnerable and scared. And yet it can. It can do it all. Everything I have is here. Everything I need is inside of me. I am the medicine. I'm so proud of you. So proud — look at where you are right now, living out your worst case scenario and yet still finding positives and growth in it. That's the magic. You are the magic, the light. Don't let life dim it.

That dance — between holding on and letting go — was relentless. Some days I moved with grace. Other days I stumbled. But I stayed in it. I showed up — barefoot, tender, messy. I danced. Not just emotionally, but physically.

Each morning, I moved my body like a prayer. Sometimes in silence. Sometimes to pulsing beats that cracked something open. I danced alone on tile floors slick with sweat. I danced under jungle canopies, on crowded dancefloors where strangers became mirrors.

And on this particular evening, in the middle of an ecstatic dance, I heard the music swell and a voice rise through the speakers:

"Are you ready for change to come?"

My breath caught. Was I?

Was I ready to release who I had been — the partner, the planner, the one who tried so hard to hold it all together?

"Are you ready for miracles?"

What if the miracle wasn't McDreamy coming back, but me coming back to myself?

"If it all came down to love?"

Could I let that be enough? Not the timeline, not the outcome — just love. Raw and unconditional. Love for him. Love for me.

"Would you let down your walls?"

Could I finally stop guarding my heart like a fortress? Could I be soft and safe?

"Are you ready to face the fear?"

I felt it rise — the fear of being alone, of being too much, of being forgotten. I let it move through my limbs. I let it sweat out of me.

"Are you ready to rise above?"

Yes. God, yes. I was tired of circling the same grief, tired of shrinking. I was ready to rise.

The beat pulsed. My feet hit the ground like a drumbeat. I was alive inside the question.

"Well, it all comes down… it all comes down to love."

And there it was — the truth I couldn't dance around.

I placed my hands on my womb, the music still echoing through the space, and the question that had been quietly waiting finally emerged: "Do I want to be a mother? Not someday. Not hypothetically. But truly."

And deeper still: "Was it him? Was it McDreamy who awakened that desire? Or was it simply that being with him gave me a glimpse — a safe enough place for the dream to come to the surface?"

Was that part of what I was grieving, too?

The music faded, but the questions remained, reverberating in my chest like aftershocks. And in that stillness, I heard the quiet voice again — the one I always hear when I finally stop searching outside of myself: "The story doesn't have to be perfect to be powerful."

It wasn't about getting it right.

It was about showing up — one messy, honest movement at a time. And I was finally doing that — on the dance floor, on the page, in the mirror.

Like all seasons, my time in Santa Teresa began to wind down. The rain softened. My journal pages grew fuller. My breath came easier. I had come here to heal. To grieve. To remember who I was without McDreamy — and to slowly become someone new. And while the questions hadn't all been answered, something had undeniably shifted.

The ache was still there, but it no longer consumed me. I could carry it and still move. I could miss him and still choose myself.

And so, with a full heart and steady feet, I began my journey back to another reality — ready to breathe in the air at higher altitudes once more.

TWENTY-EIGHT
A DANCE A DAY KEEPS
THE SPIRALING AWAY

I LANDED IN DENVER beneath a soft gray sky, the kind that made everything feel still, like the city itself was holding its breath. It had been two months since I left. Nearly four months since the night McDreamy broke the silence with those words in the van. Since I had packed up what was left of my dignity and boarded a flight back here — heart shattered, mind spiraling, body buzzing with grief.

Now I was back, but I wasn't the same.

I had been reshaped in Costa Rica. Held by the jungle, stripped by the rain. I had felt the ache of absence and the quiet miracle of surviving it. And now, here I was — home, or at least a version of it — stepping back into my Denver condo with different eyes, a stronger spine, a wider heart.

The silence of the space greeted me like an old friend. I moved slowly, reacquainting myself with the shiny appliances, the light that filtered through the windows and the stillness of a place that once felt like a prison but now felt like a mirror — reflecting back all the places I'd been, all the versions of me

I'd traveled with. The gray couch sat where I left it, softened by time. The deep green velvet kitchen chairs and rich caramel leather bar stools added warmth against the sleek white counters. My yoga certificate rested on the shelf above the desk, nestled between incense sticks and statues from Bali. A giant ten-foot macramé I made with my own hands adorned the master bedroom wall. Photos of Lu peeked out from various corners, anchoring the space with her familiar presence. Even the sarcastic candle above the toilet — "Don't do drugs in the bathroom… without me" — remained untouched. It wasn't just a condo. It was a collage of a life I had built — piece by piece, trip by trip, memory by memory. And now, I was home again.

December 16, 2024

DENVER, COLORADO, UNITED STATES

The last time I sat in this condo, I wasn't sure I wanted to leave, to move forward, to see what was on the other side. Now I sit here and I see a stronger version of myself. A version that knows the hard is there but is willing to face it so that she can grow rather than continue to repeat the same old patterns. This new version feels just that, new. Like a baby deer on unsteady legs, except this version wants that so there can be growth. So there can be joy and magic and light. What a change. And I almost didn't do it out of fear. And what would that have resulted in besides being stuck and sad? You're doing it my love and I am so proud of you.

It was surreal, coming back to the physical place where so much had burned to the ground — the place I returned to when I needed space from my parents, where I took the call that ended my employment, where I battled myself, where my partnership had blown up, where the version of me that had been so unsure, so consumed by grief, had last stood. But now, that woman had evolved. She had walked herself through the fire and didn't come out unscathed — but she had come out *true.*

And then it was Christmas Eve. I was in the Midwest, not Florida. I wasn't spending the holiday wrapped in the warmth of McDreamy's family, but instead curled on the couch beside Jacqueline's tree while she spent the evening with her family, watching the enchanting twinkle of lights while the quiet ache inside me pulsed like a second heartbeat.

The contrast was jarring — last year, love had been abundant and present. This year, I was grasping for closure, for comfort, for something to make the silence feel less deafening. And yet, I found myself doing what I always do: ritualizing the moment. I pulled out small scraps of paper and began a sacred end-of-year tradition — writing thirteen wishes, each holding a thread of hope. One to keep, twelve to burn, sending each one into the sky for the Universe to work its quiet magic while I focused on the thirteenth, the one I'd carry with me.

December 24, 2024
CHICAGO, ILLINOIS, UNITED STATES

This is never where I thought this year would end. This is never how I anticipated this year to go. And I can't change it. I can only see it, reflect on it and move forward. So I shall.

Good that was found —

- *Strength.*
- *Girl gang.*
- *Santa clarity.*
- *Routine.*
- *Confrontation of the past.*
- *Inner child healing.*
- *Therapy.*
- *Work contracts when I needed them most.*

I stared at those words in my journal, blinking back unexpected tears. Because they were true. Despite the pain, the chaos, the heartbreak — I had found good. I had found me. Not the version of me that shrank to be palatable or performed for love. Not the one who blurred her edges to fit someone else's vision. But the one who sat in the discomfort and stayed. The one who chose healing over habit, truth over illusion, growth over the easy way out.

This wasn't the ending I had envisioned. But maybe — in some way I couldn't yet understand — it was the exact one I needed. The ending that could finally clear space for a beginning. A soft start. A steadier step forward.

But the first day of the new year hit me like a brick.

January 1, 2025
ST. LOUIS, MISSOURI, UNITED STATES

Everything happened so abruptly that I'm not sure I had the adequate space to realize I was going into a new year without the love of my life — I could only now process the immediate grief and emptiness. But when the clock struck midnight, the overwhelming and daunting feeling that I was taking on a whole new year without him, struck home.

The stack of moments I wish I got to experience with him were getting bigger, clouding the time I got with him. They say grief takes at least a year to process, but what happens when you reach year two, and three, then four and suddenly the time without them is longer than you ever had with them? How light is that weight of grief in your pocket? Do they feel the weight? I always said no matter what time McDreamy and I shared together, would be just perfect because that was meant to be — now I wonder if that was "growth" or my intuition knew it wouldn't last? Then it's like, why does it hurt so much? Why is it so constantly raw? How can I shift my energy to myself, to be magnetic when he's in my dreams, my waking thoughts, the empty space next to me? The weight of emptiness is heavier than any kettlebell I've tried to swing. When does it get lighter?

That morning, I wrapped my hands around a cup of coffee and looked at Kelly, at Lu playing with her toys — the same scene I'd seen a hundred times before. But something about it felt different. Or maybe I was. Maybe I had finally stepped into the version of myself who could feel everything and still not fall apart. Maybe this was where the real work began.

Because the grief didn't end at midnight. It wasn't swept away with the fireworks and champagne. It followed me — quieter now, more spacious, but still very much alive.

And still, I had made it here. To a new year. A new page. A new possibility.

That was the phrase I clung to like a life raft. The idea that something different — something lighter — might eventually find me, even if I couldn't see it yet. I had spent so many days trying to dodge the sharpest edges of my grief, but now I was confronting it head-on. Letting it hit me. Letting it move me.

In one of my therapy sessions, my therapist asked how I got out of the loops in my head. The answer was clear: Physical movement.

"Okay," she said, "but what can you do easily? Every day? You can't live in a yogilates class."

And that's when it hit me: dance.

Starting on January 1, I committed to *A Dance A Day*. One song, every day. I'd choose it intuitively, add it to a growing Spotify playlist and post a clip of myself dancing on Instagram. No rules, no pressure, just movement — messy, joyful, emotional, honest.

It became my anchor and my reminder that even in grief, I could still take up space in a positive way. I could still feel good. I could still come home to myself.

My classic mantra became a steady pulse: "The only way out is through." So I went through. One step, one song, one dance at a time.

As I walked home from my neighborhood pilates studio, I looked around the shop fronts and the bars that were opening for the night, young couples and the painfully obvious first dates dotting the sidewalk, and I thought to myself:

"Denver was my safe haven — where I came to start over after the divorce. To claim back my power. To do what I wanted when I wanted. And then I invited someone in. When I wasn't fully ready, when I was trying to be on my own. And then he was in it, all of it was him. I opened my safe haven, I let McDreamy in. And at some point, it was him, and not the place that was my safe haven. The one I could unapologetically be myself around, who knew all my secrets, who I trusted, who I wanted to be more with, do more with, achieve more with. And even though I chose him, he stopped choosing me. My safe haven was no more. And then I came back to Denver and it was tainted fully with him. I can't go anywhere or do anything without thinking of him. And then having to go through the pain of him not choosing me all over again. I never get a break from the pain of not being chosen. And what's worse is I still choose him. There's nothing more that I want than for him to choose me.

It's officially been three months since we broke up and I don't understand why I'm still choosing someone who isn't choosing me — what is wrong with me that I'm torturing my-self in this way? Why is my self worth so nonexistent that I'm doing this to myself? How does one choose themselves? How does one choose themselves and still honor the love they have for another? What is real and what is my hurt ego? Am I nor-mal? What even is normal?

The thing is, I don't even mind going through this process, I welcome it as I level up, the thing I want most is though, is someone next to me through it all — to read my journal to, to hold me when I cry, to sit in ski traffic with me, to cook with, to dance with, to say goodnight to. I'm realizing I need to learn how to be on my own and I also don't think that means always and forever because I hate that learning — I know how to be alone, I'm an only child whose parents don't want a relation-ship with, for fucks sake. It simply comes down to not wanting to be alone. I want a partner. I want McDreamy but he doesn't want me so how can I heal the best I can so when someone chooses me and I choose them, it works? I feel like I've failed so many relationships and I just want one that lasts. That values the commitment at the same level that I do."

I slowly climbed the three flights of stairs to my condo, admiring the twinkling lights and snow sparkling as it fell. I opened the door to my hallway and keyed in the code to my door. My jaw tightened as I thought:

"I want this.
I deserve this.
I accept this."

And that was the shift — maybe small, maybe seismic —
but it was there. I was beginning to release McDreamy inch
by inch, not because the love wasn't real, but because I had to
make space for something *more*. Something aligned. Something that also chose me back.

That night, I let myself dream again — not of him, but of
the man who could come next. I began shaping him: his energy,
his depth, his joy. The way I wanted to feel beside someone.
And most importantly, how I wanted to feel within myself.

The ding of a text woke me as the soft light was filtering
through the shades, bringing me back to reality — it was Mc-
Dreamy: "See you tomorrow. Let's meet up to exchange the
last of our stuff."

I shot upright, startling Lu from her place at my feet. Heart
pounding, I rushed to the mirror, searching my reflection for
some kind of answer. Four months. It had been four months
since we'd last seen each other, since we unstitched our lives.
And now, we were about to share space again — not by accident or coincidence, but by design.

Still groggy, I reached for my phone to check my inbox. A
flight confirmation email sat at the top, reminding me I was
headed back to Costa Rica in just a few weeks. I opened it without thinking, ready to daydream about sunshine and surf —
but then I saw it: his name. McDreamy. On the same itinerary.

My breath caught. I had totally forgotten we'd booked the
same flight months ago, back when everything still felt possible.

He hadn't suggested canceling our flights. Neither had I.

I crumpled to the floor, my face in my hands: How was I

supposed to endure being so close to him 30,000 feet in the air?

I wasn't sure what scared me more — seeing him again or seeing who I would become in his presence. Could I stay grounded in my healing, my wholeness, with him beside me again? Could I show up as the woman I'd worked so hard to become?

I didn't know. So I did the only thing I could think to do — I reached for my journal, the question already circling like a storm cloud overhead:

How does one choose themselves?

- *Making choices based on my stability and safety.*
- *Flowing with creativity.*
- *Only allowing those that fully honor me into my sexual presence.*
- *Using sexuality for good.*
- *Releasing control and not being guided by fear, anxiety or lack.*
- *Living in love, for oneself and others.*
- *Respectfully sharing my piece and peace.*
- *Tuning into my intuition, listening and following its guidance.*
- *Working with spirit and asking for help.*

It's a mind-body-soul choice, always.

I stared at the words on the page, knowing these were all things I was fully capable of, if I allowed myself to be.

I recited them to myself as I got ready to meet up with McDreamy — wearing just enough makeup that it accentuated the tan glow from Costa Rica. I recited them to myself as I texted my best friend two pictures of outfits, asking her advice on what to wear. I recited them to myself as I drove the 20 minutes to the meeting spot McDreamy and I had agreed on the previous day. I recited them as I pulled up to the empty parking lot of the brewery, the sky gray.

When he finally pulled up and walked into my field of vision, he quite literally took my breath away. The ache in my chest, the familiar swell of everything I had been trying to release — it was all there. But so was this strange, grounded knowing.

We quickly shuffled bags and boxes between our vehicles, returning each other's things to their rightful owner. The time felt too short, the questions in my heart about us still lingered. "Do you want to grab a drink?" I asked.

He looked down at his phone uncertainly, "Um... yeah, I guess I can make that work."

We walked inside, awkwardly ordered and paid for our own drinks and then sat across from each other at a high-top.

"So, how have you been... considering, you know, everything?" He timidly asked, as if he was too scared to allude to our relationship. Like it would be poking a bear.

I laughed, "It's had its ups and downs, but being back in Costa Rica was really great. And then I spent time with Jac and Kelly over the holidays."

We continued like this, just barely brushing the surface of each other's lives. After an hour, we both got up, not quite sure how to end the evening. We hugged then I got back in my car and drove away. When I was sure I was clear of his presence, I pulled off to the side of the road and punched up a text:

ME: I just left him. We kept it very light — talked

about work and skiing and surfing and Santa. I'm really proud of how I handled myself — I showed up strong and light and love, just like I wanted to. I don't think there was any indication of a future, but neither of us brought it up, which sucks, and I know literally anything can happen. I'm happy I saw him and also now, in this after-moment, it's hard. So it's a little confusing and I'm still trying to wrangle all the mixed feels.

ME: But you know what? As I say this, I just remembered something — he was sketching this vision for his life about a year ago, like drawing all the things he wanted. I leaned over, smiling, expecting to see us there. But I wasn't.

ME: There was no version of me in his dream. No hint of our life together.

PIPPA: Oh babe ☺

ME: I knew then, you know? On some level, I always knew he wasn't fully choosing me.

ME: Maybe he thought he was. Maybe in his own way, he was. But it wasn't how I wanted to be chosen. Not all in. Not the kind of choosing I needed.

PIPPA: That's such a brutal realization.

ME: And the worst part is I let it happen. I kept

showing up for someone who didn't show up the way I needed. I've been doing that for years. Even before him.

ME: I thought I loved myself — and I did, to a point — but clearly not enough to demand the love I actually want.

ME: And I'm mad at myself for that. Like, truly mad.

PIPPA: Be gentle with yourself.

ME: I want to be. But I've wasted so many years in relationships that were fine... just not right.

ME: I know it's all hindsight. And I couldn't have known then what I know now. But it still stings.

PIPPA: Of course it does.

ME: I want to forgive myself. I really do. But I'm not there yet. I need to sit in this a bit longer. Let it work its way through me before I can fully let it go.

PIPPA: That's fair. You're doing the work. And I'm so proud of you for seeing all of this with clear eyes 🖤

ME: Thanks. I just needed to get it out 📖

As the moments ticked by in the hours and days after our

meetup, I remembered — letting go isn't a one-time decision. It's a choice I have to make again and again, in the quiet moments, in the stillness, in the echoes of what once was. I can still hold my truth gently in the palm of my hand, but the weight of it can't keep me from taking the next step forward.

The truth was, I still missed him. Desperately. He was staying in Denver — he signed a year-long lease. I was leaving — my condo was going on the market in just a few weeks. It felt like the ultimate test of trust — trusting the space, the timing, the unfolding. Trusting myself.

I closed my eyes and whispered to the Universe: "I send him out with love. And if it's meant to be, I trust he'll come back."

And then I experienced a micro moment of relief as my emotions shifted. From grief to grace. From blame to forgiveness.

As always, I made a date with my therapist and then I curled up in the corner of my couch with my journal and let it all pour out — the things I had buried deep inside, the regrets I had carried for too long, the shame I hadn't dared speak aloud. And I gave myself permission to forgive. To lay them down and finally set myself free.

I am worthy of love, success and abundance. As I trust in life's flow, I effortlessly receive more than I could have ever imagined.

My dream life is:

- *Flowy.*
- *Balanced.*
- *Inspirational.*

- *Experiential.*
- *Love.*
- *Light.*
- *Strength.*
- *Creative.*
- *Abundant.*
- *Stable.*
- *Reflective.*
- *Fulfilling.*
- *Easeful.*

I'm ready to forgive myself, for all of the unspeakable things that have flooded me, for the choices I made because I was too scared of what I should have done, to release the shame and guilt and grief.

- *Stealing my friend's necklace in third grade.*
- *Stealing in high school.*
- *Abandoning my high school best friends.*
- *Cheating on GI Joe.*
- *Everyone I've ever shit talked.*
- *Not breaking up with the Man in Finance in college.*
- *Getting back together with the Man in Finance.*
- *The fights and rage with the Man in Finance.*
- *Manipulating GI Joe.*
- *Marrying GI Joe.*
- *Resenting GI Joe for my own choices.*
- *Allowing McDreamy to call the shots.*
- *Not speaking up for what I wanted with McDreamy.*
- *Fights with my parents.*
- *Not being who my parents wanted me to be.*

• *Wreaking so much havoc on my journey to find myself and hurting people along the way of discarding them like they didn't matter.*

Connie, I forgive you. I forgive you. I forgive you. Please release yourself from this torment. You deserve to be happy, healthy and loved. You deserve everything you wish for and more. You are worthy of love, belonging and your dreams. They, and even more goodness you can't even think of, is waiting for you. You only need to step into it — your power, your magnetism, your light. It's there when you're ready. It's your choice, just like everything is. You get to choose happiness. So choose it.

I forgive myself for these circumstances I have created. I forgive myself. I forgive myself. I forgive myself.

And when I melted into that forgiveness — into the lightness I thought might come with it — the weight of depression came crashing back down like a tide I couldn't outrun. So I didn't fight it. I let it wash over me.

I curled into the corner of my gray couch, wrapped in my weighted blanket, navy blue against my skin. Candles flickered on every surface, their soft glow dancing across the walls. The fake fire crackled on the TV screen, casting a warm light that tried to fill the quiet. Lu snored gently at my feet.

Because this was part of it, too.

And with that came peace.

It didn't arrive like fireworks or some grand revelation. It came in a quiet moment — the kind that usually goes unnoticed — when I realized I was no longer fighting the tide. I had finally stopped resisting what was. I wasn't through the grief, but I had learned how to sit beside it. How to witness it. How to hold it without letting it consume me.

And from that peace, clarity began to bloom.

Not all at once, but in flickers — realizations that illuminated what I had previously been too tangled in hope and heartbreak to fully see. That loving someone deeply doesn't always mean they're meant for you. That choosing yourself sometimes looks like letting go of someone you wanted so badly to choose you.

And with clarity, came the rarest and perhaps most sacred thing of all: presence. The ability to simply be.

And because I did the work — because I chose to stay, to breathe, to face it all — the Universe offered me a glimpse of what healing can bring.

January 21, 2025
DENVER, COLORADO, UNITED STATES

In my dream, I was bigger than McDreamy. More vibrant.

A symbol. A message. A reflection. I wasn't shrinking anymore.

And in order to keep expanding, I knew I needed some help. On recommendation from my astrologer, I reached out to a medium named Mindy that would focus on advising and on what's to come — someone I had never spoken to before, who knew absolutely nothing about me. And yet, within minutes, she was speaking truths that left my jaw on the floor.

She started by sharing channeled messages from my guides. Everything she said felt like a direct line from my soul to her lips. There was no way she could have known these things —

and still, she knew. I was stunned with how specific it was. I felt so seen.

When it came time for my questions, I asked about two things weighing heavily on my heart: my career and McDreamy.

On work, she didn't hesitate. "You're never going to do just one thing," she said. "You thrive in the chaos. That's your magic." Photography came up repeatedly — not once, not twice, but more than ten times. "You have an eye," she insisted. "It's part of your story, part of your expression." She told me I was already an expert in the things I wanted to teach — I just needed to believe it. To trust it. To share it. And then, with the kind of humor only spirit guides can deliver, she added, "If you don't start being more diligent with your book, it's going to take you years to finish it." I laughed — a deep, soul-cleansing laugh. They weren't wrong.

She reminded me to have more fun. That I hadn't truly let myself play in a long time. That lightness wasn't frivolous — it was sacred.

And then, of course, we got to McDreamy. She said, "It's going to be there until it's not," about the way he still lingered in my thoughts. I asked if we were meant to be together. My guides shrugged. Literally shrugged. They said he has a lot of work to do — that he hasn't done it yet and he's not ready.

Then came the part that made my chest cave in. The baby I saw during my Ayahuasca journey? The one with his eyes and my skin? "He's real," Mindy said. "He was your child in another lifetime. It was a glimpse, not a promise. It's one possibility for this lifetime, not meant to be a source of pressure or a prediction."

She explained our soul connection ran deep — we'd been together in many lifetimes, which is why this breakup felt so tangled and intense. And most importantly, she confirmed what I already knew deep down but had been too scared to fully believe: "The love between you two was real. For both of you."

I sobbed. Because sometimes even when you know, you need to hear it.

She closed by telling me something that felt like a lifeline: "You're doing so well. Keep going. Focus on yourself. Focus on your female friendships. That's where your magic is blooming right now. Everything is okay. We promise we aren't trying to hurt you — your soul loves to grow and expand. Sometimes it takes pain to do so."

And I could feel it — the truth of that. That no matter what happened next, I was on the right path. That I didn't have to figure everything out, I just had to keep choosing myself.

Every day. Every step. Every word I wrote. The rest would come.

And then, what felt like the final piece of an ever-growing puzzle slid into place. I was ready — not because the pain was gone, but because I had met it. Held it. Let it teach me.

January 31, 2024
DENVER, COLORADO, UNITED STATES

Healing — I am in control of my pain. I am in control of my healing.

Those words echoed through me like a quiet drumbeat. I no longer needed to run. I didn't need someone else to make it better. My healing was mine now. And because of that, I could finally face what came next.

It was time to board a plane back to Costa Rica.

It was also time to say goodbye to Denver. My condo —

the one I bought when I believed in permanence, in foundations, in forever — was officially on the market. I was releasing yet another chapter, another version of me.

And in that release, something unexpected happened — my mom reached out. A quiet text, a gentle nudge, to soften and see where the magic could bring us. It was the beginning of a bridge being rebuilt. The space I had created by letting go of my home also created room for a reconnection I wasn't sure would ever come.

February 1, 2025

DENVER, COLORADO, UNITED STATES

If these are my final moments in the condo — thank you. For the home, the safety, the stability, the abundance, the service, for everything. What an honor it has been to be the owner of such a beautiful space. May you make the next owners incredibly happy. Thank you. Thank you. Thank you.

I walked through the space slowly, letting my fingertips graze the walls, the way you might run your hands over a memory. I said goodbye to the light through the massive windows, the beautiful kitchen, the seat in the shower, the corner where Lu always curled up after walks. I said goodbye to the version of me who had moved in — full of hope, exhausted by the journey, still believing that maybe if I just tried hard enough, I could hold it all together.

But holding it all together wasn't the goal anymore.

The goal was truth. And trust. And flow.

It was walking away not because I failed, but because I was ready for something new.

And as I stepped out the door, suitcases in hand, a deep knowing rose in my chest: I had outgrown this chapter.

And the next one was waiting — somewhere between the crashing waves of Santa Teresa and the stillness of a heart that had been broken wide open and was still beating anyway.

TWENTY-NINE
LU TRIES TO COMMIT SUICIDE

THE WHEELS TOUCHED down on the warm, familiar tarmac of Costa Rica and with it came a wash of emotion I wasn't prepared to swallow. A lump formed in my throat as the Spanish welcome message came over the intercom. It had been four years since I first arrived here, sun-drenched and full of possibility, wrapped in the glow of a love I thought would carry me through. Now, I returned feeling more like a melted ice cream cone, sticky and unformed — a different woman entirely.

I grabbed my carry on, straightened my shoulders and tried not to squish too hard against McDreamy's firm body as we disembarked from the tiny plane. His closeness and smell enveloped me one final time and I held my breath against the onslaught of urges to grab him, rest my tired head on his shoulders. None of that would do. This was another chapter. This was the return to the land that had first shown me what freedom felt like. And now, I had to see if it could hold me through the ache. McDreamy and I did an awkward "Okay, well see you around town," and half wave as we bid each other goodbye at the small airport entrance, each getting into our separate taxis. I had no idea what the next months would hold.

Just then I heard a ping from my phone and a message popped up from Fernanda: "How'd the flight go babe?"

So I settled into the cab's hot pleather seat, made sure Lu was happy and panting out the window next to me, and sent a voice note:

"Just got in the cab and saw your message pop up. Short answer? I made it through without being a complete psycho. No sobbing, no meltdown, no weird sniffing him mid-flight — which honestly feels like a small miracle.

Now we're both here. In this tiny town of 3,000 people — where everything might remind me of us. It's like being on the same university campus. I'm trying not to spiral, but I can already feel it. Like, I'm bracing for it. Seeing him at the café, our favorite beach spot, even that stupid grocery store where we used to pile too many maracuyas into the cart — it's all just waiting for me.

It's not even him I'm worried about running into. It's the ghost. Not him as a ghost, I mean like... the ghost of our relationship."

I knew I sounded a bit crazy, but I also knew she would get it so I continued, not worried about what the cab driver would think of my WhatsApp monologue:

"I've been thinking how romantic relationships have their

own energy signatures and independent gravity fields —
they become a separate Universe that only the two people
weaving it can access. But that's bad news for me because
there's a version of life that thinks our relationship is
still alive and kicking — the ghost of us is just hanging
around, riding quads and sipping coconut water like
nothing ever ended. It's dead. But it doesn't know it yet.

So yeah… it's gonna be a ride. I'll keep you posted, my
love."

I settled into my one-bedroom apartment atop the hill and
promised myself this: I would keep walking forward — even
when it was hard. Especially when it was hard. I had left behind the weight of Denver — my home, my relationship, my
old patterns — and arrived here unsure but willing. Willing to
choose a new way. Willing to meet myself fully.

So I did what I always do — I lit a candle, pulled an oracle
card and opened up to a fresh journal page, asking the land to
speak to me, to hold me, to guide me through the unknown.
But this time, I didn't stop there. I built an altar in the empty
corner of my bedroom — a sacred space stitched together with
the symbols of everything I was calling into my life.

As soft music echoed from my speaker, I placed flowers
for beauty and grounding. A crisp $100 bill to anchor finan-
cial stability and abundance. An amethyst crystal etched with
the moon phases, a reminder to ride the waves and trust my
intuition. Candles to honor the intensity and love burning inside me. Headphones for the music and movement that kept
my spirit awake. A photo of me hugging myself, a testament to
self-love and trust. And another — a photo of me in lingerie
— to embody my confidence, my sensuality, my unapologetic

feminine power. Finally, I placed my journal at the center, a vessel for truth and creation.

This wasn't a restart. It was a continuation. A deeper dive. A soft, firm promise to trust the magic even when I couldn't yet see it. To remember who I was — and who I was still becoming — even when the road ahead was wrapped in mist.

February 2, 2025
SANTA TERESA, COSTA RICA

The feeling hasn't faded — and what will that bring as these days go by? What magic will come forth? Where can I continue to loosen my grip and let it all flow? Mama, I ask for your direct help and guidance as I move through. Please provide obvious signs so that I can move with my greatest good in mind and allow space so magic is the only option and the roadblocks dissipate like fog in the sun. Bring clarity and strength and love and light. Thank you, thank you, thank you.

That morning, sitting on the beach with coffee in one hand and green juice in the other, I made another promise: I wouldn't let his presence derail me. I wouldn't let the chance of running into him — or hearing his name — dim my light. I wouldn't give my power away again.

I would walk through Santa Teresa as the woman I was becoming — grounded, kind, full of grace. Especially when it was uncomfortable. Especially when it hurt.

This chapter, I decided, wasn't about getting over him. It was about returning to the pieces of myself I'd lost. Choosing me — again and again. A homecoming in the truest sense.

At least, that's what I told myself — until the bravado faded.

One of my favorite DJs, Le Youth, was playing a private villa party that weekend. Determined to show up in a new way — not all or nothing, just present — I got dressed in my psychedelic skirt, dusted glitter across my collarbones and sipped slowly on an espresso martini. Not to numb or escape, just to enjoy — a small act of balance I was learning to claim for myself. I was surrounded by girlfriends, laughter bubbling between us as we walked through the villa gates, the bass pulsing through the air like a heartbeat.

To the left: a dance floor already buzzing with movement. To the right: an open lawn and a bar glowing under string lights. I scanned the crowd out of habit — and there he was. McDreamy. Of course. I had felt his energy the second I stepped inside.

"I need a drink. Now," I said sharply, grabbing my friend's hand and beelining toward the bar.

We exchanged pleasantries when we inevitably crossed paths — a quick hug, a smile that didn't quite reach either of our eyes, a "You look great." He tried to linger, hovering near the edge of my group like he might be invited in. But we subtly boxed him out, circling tighter, lifting each other with eye rolls and belly laughs.

Eventually, McDreamy and I found our rhythm on the dance floor. Separate circles. Separate lives. But the air between us still sparked — stolen glances, eyes locking in the strobe light.

Then he tried to dance with me. Drifting closer, reaching toward me. I felt the heat of his hand and the weight of the past pressing in. Before he could close the distance, my friend caught the moment and spun me away — graceful, deliberate — twirling me right out of his reach.

That was the moment he got the hint.

I didn't look back. I left with my girls that night — glitter smeared, heart intact, dancing my way forward.

When I woke the next morning, I rolled over in bed, reaching for my journal and I wrote:

February 9, 2025

SANTA TERESA, COSTA RICA

Underneath it all, is the sad, lonely child who just wants to be loved and spend her life with someone. This young girl who didn't feel good enough for anyone, who was scared and sad and alone. McDreamy made her feel safe and wanted, then discarded her like a used tissue. He confirmed her worst fears. He ruined her. She's so scared to admit how much he ruined her. She's scared she'll never make it back. That she'll be lost forever. The power she gave to him, the power he still has. She doesn't know how to do it alone, how to move. And worse, she doesn't want to because she's hoping he comes back to save the day. What's worse — waiting or moving on? Losing her life or her second chance with him? Why is the obvious choice the former yet she chooses the latter?

I didn't try to run from the ache. I let it rise and spill — the voice of my inner child, small and trembling, begging for someone to come back and make it all better.

And this time, someone did. Me.

Little Connie, I'm so sorry. I wish I could give you McDreamy, I do. I wish I could give you the healed, perfect man you are asking for in him, the one you know exists somewhere inside of him, but my love, he doesn't exist right here and now. Right now he can't give you what you want and deserve. But you can give yourself what you need — everything is already inside of you. And I'm here. The version of you that is healed and strong and love and light and peace and joy. This version is you. You are it all, my love. And I'm so sorry this is how you had to learn this. That this heartbreak had to be so debilitating. That you felt worthless and unlovable and used. Because you are worth it all, you are so loved, and so needed. Little Connie, I love you and I am so proud of you. Little Connie, you can do this, and I am right here with you.

Grief and heartache doesn't end. But neither does love.

And as I continued to walk this ever-winding path, I began to understand that healing was never about erasing the love — it was about remembering the parts of myself I'd once handed away. Loving myself back into wholeness meant returning to Little Connie, the one who only wanted to be held, seen, chosen. It meant holding her with tenderness. Sitting beside her in her sadness. Offering her the very safety I had once looked to others for.

And as I did that — really did that — something shifted. She softened. And in her softening, I let go just a little more of the fantasy, of the denial, of the need to be chosen by him to feel good enough.

February 10, 2025
SANTA TERESA, COSTA RICA

McDreamy —

I realize that you may have differing emotions than me so I ask that you meet me with grace, patience and understanding. And also respect, out of our time together and the significance that played in both of our lives. I have been reading, and recently completed the book Conscious Uncoupling — it's a process to end a relationship in a mindful, respectful and compassionate manner. It's focused on personal growth rather than blaming and negative talk. Through this, I sat with and held my inner Little Connie, I examined and accepted my shadow self, and I allowed my present self to be hurt and angry and depressed. My journey on this healing path is not over and yet I'm at a place where I don't think I can move forward without more closure from you. This closure comes in the form of release, a release of all the spoken and unspoken agreements you and I made. The following list is not comprehensive so any that have not been spoken, are also released:

- *My person.*
- *My safe space.*
- *My hero.*
- *The love of my life.*
- *Lu's dad.*
- *The only man I've ever wanted to have children with.*
- *My life partner.*
- *My adventure buddy.*
- *Boo-boo.*
- *My best friend.*
- *My emergency contact.*
- *My soulmate.*
- *My home.*

They say that the most loving thing you can do for a person is letting them go so let this be covered in all the things you love — waking up in a tent along a river, salty crunchy snacks, feeling the wave's energy, a cold plunge, spotting an animal in the wild, the post-lift endorphins, a fried chicken sandwich, your freedom.

They also say that letting someone go is the most loving thing you can do for yourself so here I am choosing myself.

I will always love you but I will no longer be waiting for you because now I know what I deserve. Not a half-hearted maybe. Not a love that comes with caveats. But a full-bodied, hell-yes kind of love. A love that chooses me back. I'm closing the door. I truly wish you nothing but happiness.

I closed my journal with trembling fingers and laid back on the pillow on my bed. My heart cracked like a chipped quartz crystal — not shattered, but cracked in that deliberate way healing requires. I hadn't just written those words for him. I'd written them for me. For the version of me that kept clinging to the fantasy, that waited by the door of possibility just in case he came back with a different ending.

I walked to the ocean at sunset and breathed the words again to the waves: "I release you. I release you. I release you."

The tide pulled them away. And I stood a little taller.

As fate would have it, the Universe and the ghost of our relationship wasn't quite done with me yet.

Driving home from the sunset, golden light still painting the treetops, I was deep in reflection and feeling as sensitive as a newly emerged butterfly — it was as if my heart had no skin, every emotion touching bone. Lu sat content in her box at the front of my quad, her ears flapping in the wind, as always.

Until suddenly, she wasn't.

In a flash, she leapt forward, launching out of her seat and landing directly in front of my wheels. I was going full speed. There was no time to brake.

The world stopped. My breath caught as I slowed down and pulled to the side.

Panic seized me. I couldn't look. "Is she... gone? Did I just kill my dog?" My chest tightened, tears instant. Then the thought automatically came that I wish wouldn't. "I wish Mc-Dreamy was here."

Slowly, I twisted my torso, afraid to fully turn around. My mind filled with images I couldn't unsee, dread pooling in my gut. "If he was here, I could handle any outcome," I thought.

But then — there she was. On the side of the road, belly to the ground, tail wagging like absolutely nothing had happened.

I collapsed onto the ground and wept in an ugly gasping sort of cry that had become all too familiar in the wake of my breakup.

Lu ran over, tongue out, licking my face as I crouched down to pick her up. She had puffed out her chest and acted proud, like she had just pulled off the greatest stunt of her life. I clung to her, sobbing and laughing all at once, shaking with adrenaline and disbelief. My miracle dog. My heartbeat outside my body. "You're okay. You're okay. You're okay! I need to tell Mc-Dreamy what just happened, he's not going to believe this," I thought. Another part of me was exclaiming, "You sneaky girl. You knew exactly what would happen."

I poked and prodded her little frame, searching for pain, for a wince, anything. Nothing. She was fine.

Then I pulled my cell phone out of my shoulder bag and before I could overthink it, I did the unthinkable, I dialed his number on WhatsApp. It felt like life had just screamed at me: "Life is short. Don't waste it."

The adrenaline rushed through my temples as the phone rang once, twice, three times, then his warm deep voice: "Hey Connie, what's up?"

"Lu... Lu was the ultimate dingus, she jumped out of the moving quad. I ran her over but I didn't actually hit her. I think she's okay." I stumbled through my words.

"Oh my God. Is she okay? Are you okay? Where are you? I can make a seatbelt for her." He replied, instantly making me feel at ease.

We hung up after a few more reassurances, the kind you give when neither of you knows what else to say. "I'll see you tomorrow," I said, setting the phone down, heart still pounding and pulled Lu a little closer into my sweaty body. I didn't expect him to actually show up — but he did.

THIRTY

BACKFLIPPED AND MADE MAGIC

T HE NEXT AFTERNOON I paced my apartment, Lu curled up and content, completely unaware of the storm she'd set in motion. I caught my reflection in the mirror — sun-kissed skin, windblown hair, the same eyes that had seen too much and still wanted more, the red thong bikini I knew drove McDreamy crazy. I told myself I was calm, unattached. But my heart betrayed me — thudding louder with every passing minute.

Then, I heard the gate open. The crunch of the gravel under shoes.

I opened the sliding door and there he was — that familiar crooked grin, a spool of rope and clips in hand.

"I brought supplies," he said. "Let's make her a seatbelt."

We bent over the quad, threading rope, testing buckles and adjustments. Our fingers brushed once. Then again. We laughed — a sound that felt like an echo from another life. When we finished, he looked at me and said, "Beach walk?"

We walked for three hours — two miles down, two back — the tide low, the sky bruised with late afternoon light. Our voices meandered just like our feet, skipping from light to heavy, past to present.

He said he was happy being single. That the quiet had taught him things.

Then, almost casually, like it meant nothing and everything at once, he said, "I don't want to have to tell someone I love them every day."

I nodded, then stopped walking — almost regretting that I let him speak first, given what I was about to admit. "I'm at a crossroads," I said, steady and clear. "I can go either way. But if you choose me — fully — I'm yours. If you can't... I walk away."

He didn't say much. Just looked at me with that unreadable face and nodded once. We turned back toward the apartment.

At the door, it was awkward. Not quite goodbye. Not quite invitation. I tried to fill the silence.

"Well," I said with a crooked smile, "I guess this red bathing suit wasn't enough to convince you..." remembering the look on his face when I tried it on just the year prior. Feeling the heat work its way from the center of my core up to my cheeks.

He raised a brow. "It definitely has me on edge."

He took a step toward the bed. Then another. Slow, measured. His eyes locked on mine, waiting.

When he reached the edge, he sat — shoulders tense, hands on his thighs like he wasn't sure what would happen next.

The air thickened.

I moved.

I pulled the shade closed in one swift motion, the music from the pool still drifting through the window like a distant echo. Then I turned, crossed the room in a few deliberate steps and placed my hands on his chest.

Then shoved him back.

He landed with a thud, and I climbed onto his lap, strad-
dling him — anger, desire and something unspoken coursing
through me like wildfire.

It was as if nothing — and everything — had changed.

His body was familiar. The rhythm. The collapse. The
reach.

But this time, I didn't disappear inside it.

When it was over, I leaned back into his arms. But I didn't
cling like I used to. Instead of searching for his promise, I
swung my legs off the bed and planted my feet on the floor.

We stepped into the shower together, wordless. He soaped
my back like he always did. But there were no giggles, no grasping. Just quiet water and quiet knowing.

When we dried off, he kissed my cheek, patted Lu on the
head and walked out the door.

An electric shiver surged through me, sending me pacing
the room — hands on hips, breath tight, heart pounding. I
walked back and forth, barefoot on cool tile, adrenaline buzzing beneath my skin like static. Lu watched from the couch,
eyes steady, head tilted, sensing the shift.

I had made this choice from power. Not from longing. Not
from fear.

But from the deep well of worth I had spent years digging.

And I knew.

He wasn't it.

He never would be.

And it was time to let him go.

And the Universe wanted to hammer home the point —
the next time I saw McDreamy was just a few days later. It was
a late night and the beach club was closing. I was heading to my
quad when I spotted his — parked just a few down from mine.

But it wasn't empty.

There was a girl clinging to him from behind, her arms wrapped tightly around his middle. She was tiny, with dark hair slicked back in a high ponytail and a tight black dress that barely covered anything. Her legs dangled off the side of the seat like she didn't weigh a thing. She looked young. Carefree. Like someone who hadn't yet been asked to hold the weight of a man's uncertainty.

He reversed slowly out of the parking spot, and as he shifted into drive, he turned over his shoulder — and his eyes met mine.

A direct hit.

My spine straightened, stomach lurching like I'd been socked in the gut. But I didn't look away. I forced my face into stillness, holding his gaze like it was a dare.

And in that split second, the thoughts came rushing in — sharp, involuntary, a flash of fire in my chest.

"I'm better than her.

I hope he sees my face when he cums tonight.

I hope he remembers what I feel like when he touches her.

I hope she knows she's a placeholder."

The quad pulled away in a cloud of dust, taillights shrinking into the darkness. And I just stood there, the cool salt air clinging to my skin, pretending like I wasn't unraveling.

The next week, I passed him on the beach. And again, he wasn't alone.

A different girl walked beside him, her board tucked under one arm, long sandy-blonde hair falling in effortless waves down her back. She wore a tiny bikini, the kind that says "I know you're looking," and laughed at something he said, tossing her head back like they were the only two people on the sand.

They were barefoot and tanned, dripping in that surf-glow

energy, heading toward the waves like they belonged to each other. Like they'd done this a hundred times before.

My stomach clenched.

"Really? Another girl already? How long until she's in your bed too? Did I ever look that carefree next to you?"

I kept walking, eyes fixed on the path in front of me, pulse pounding in my ears. I didn't stop. Didn't flinch. But inside, it hit like a wave I didn't see coming — crashing into the fragile scaffolding I was building around my healing.

Another week later, he walked into the same restaurant where I was having dinner with a girlfriend.

I noticed him before he noticed me — or maybe he did and just pretended not to. Either way, I stayed still, quiet, pretending to be absorbed in the conversation as I tracked him out of the corner of my eye.

Minutes later, she walked in.

Another girl.

She floated through the doorway with the kind of ease that made you look twice. Her hair was pulled back into a delicate flower claw clip, petals catching the glow of the hanging lights. She wore a clinging silk dress — the kind that whispers when it moves and makes everyone wonder who she's there to meet.

She didn't hesitate.

She glided around the table, bent down and kissed him on the cheek before slipping into the seat across from him — like she belonged there. Like this was a regular thing.

"I've had it with him," I scowled to my friend, stabbing the tiramisu with a fork and taking an angry bite, trying not to let the sweetness dissolve my rage.

"He's pathetic. He's nothing. Don't pay him any mind, sweetie." My friend coaxed patting the top of my hand, trying to bring my eyes back to hers instead of sending daggers Mc-Dreamy's way.

But I couldn't help it — the bitterness climbed my throat like bile, the anger churned in my stomach, threatening to erupt and make a volcanic mess of my life all over again.

But the volcano did erupt. I got home and let it — the debris, the magma, the hot ash. It all came pouring out. I stayed in bed for two days with the shades drawn, swallowed by silence. No playlists. No distractions. Just me and Lu, buried under the covers. Fernanda knocked. I didn't answer. The texts piled up. I ignored them all.

When I finally emerged, I looked like someone who had gone through hell and come back changed. My eyes were swollen, my hair a tangled mess, my skin dull from too much crying and not enough light. But there was something else too — a steadiness in my spine. A quiet resolve. I looked like a woman who had survived herself.

The grief was still there, but it no longer had power over me. I had betrayed myself — again — by settling for less, by confusing scraps for a feast, by pretending I was okay with being chosen halfway. But now I saw it clearly. I saw *me* clearly.

A few mornings later, I walked the beach at dawn with a friend, the sky painted in soft pastels, the tide gently retreating at our feet. She had wavy brown hair pulled into a loose braid and eyes that were both supportive and questioning — the kind that held space but didn't let you hide. We picked up shells and bits of sea glass, small treasures left behind by the night.

As we wandered, I dared to say it aloud — the truths that had been blooming inside me.

"If this were a movie," I said, the wind tugging at my hair, "this wouldn't be a story about heartbreak anymore."

She looked over, waiting.

"This is a story about wholeness," I said, smiling at the words as they left my lips. "About coming home — not to a person, not to a place, but to myself."

And this time, I meant it.

She encouraged me to see things differently.

Like, maybe the Universe wasn't cruel.

Maybe it was meticulous — carving lessons so precisely into my life that they didn't just land in my mind, but etched themselves into the marrow of my being. So I would never again confuse almost-love for the real thing. So I would never again trick myself into betrayal or self-abandonment. So I would finally, fully choose me.

This was never just about love lost — it was about the sacred return to myself.

As we continued walking, I opened up about more than just McDreamy. I told her about the rift with my family — how the fractures had reopened old wounds and stirred up the familiar ache of feeling alone in the world. I shared how the unexpected work stress had pulled the rug out from under my financial security, how my mental health had buckled under the weight of it all. And then, on top of it, the heartbreak — gut-wrenching and disorienting — that shattered not only a relationship, but my sense of safety.

Everything I thought I had figured out had crumbled.

It felt good to speak it aloud — not just to my journal, not just to my therapist — but to someone witnessing me in real time. Someone who didn't flinch or try to fix it.

So we sat in the sand as the orange and pink sun began to warm our faces. I sifted shells and stones through my fingers and said quietly, "The breakup cleared me. Wiped the slate clean. And now I'm holding the pieces of myself — not to figure out what to fix, but to choose, intentionally, which ones I want to carry forward. Which ones I love enough to keep."

In the weeks that followed, every quiet morning ritual that stretched into the afternoon, every moon ceremony with my girlfriends, every ocean wave I paddled into — they were all stitching me back together. I had already done the heavy lifting, scraping off the old graffiti scrawled across my inner walls. Now it was about rewriting the truth — letting my soul speak freely, clearly, unmistakably.

The altar. The breathwork. The jungle. The cards. They weren't just tools. They were mirrors, reminding me of the woman I've always been beneath the programming and pain. Of the truth I carried long before I let anyone else rewrite it. I wasn't lost. I wasn't broken. I was remembering.

Piece by piece, day by day — ritual by ritual, conversation by conversation — I rebuilt myself. Through tear-soaked journal pages and long walks filled with hard truths. Through therapy, tarot and Earth's medicine. Through the laughter and loyalty of the women who showed up when I didn't even know how to ask.

Jacqueline and Kelly and Stef and Pippa and Fernanda and Lisa and Kelsey — my girl gang. The family I was building in Santa Teresa. They held me when I couldn't hold myself, they reminded me who I was when I forgot.

I uncovered a new foundation. One not built on performance or perfection, but on presence. On truth. On radical self-love.

There was no sudden light switch. No clean, cinematic resolution. But there was peace. A quiet steadiness in my body. A rootedness I hadn't felt before. One I'd earned.

All the little realizations started to stitch together — the ones that happened in real time, when I caught myself spiraling and paused. When I asked: "What would a secure version of me do right now?" And then I acted from that place. Not from panic or fear but from groundedness. From the woman I was becoming.

Because that's the real work — not avoiding the triggers, but learning how to meet them with grace.

That was the shift. This whole time, I had been *trying* to trust — to trust people, the path, the purpose, the pain. Now I *do* trust. I trust that there is a higher purpose. That even when it looks messy and feels impossible, the Universe is conspiring in my favor. I trust that I can be scared and tired and still keep going. That I can fall off track and still return to myself.

This story continues as long as I keep moving forward. As long as I keep riding the waves and hiking the mountains. As long as I keep dancing. As long as I meet the ugly — the heartache and grief, the triggers, the shadow — with truth and compassion. As long as I remember that the real magic, that was always me. As long as I remember that my capacity for grief is only a mirror of my capacity for love — boundless. For if I feel it this deeply, it means I also loved that beautifully.

This isn't about perfection. It's about choosing again. Choosing trust. Choosing healing. Choosing love. Choosing to be the magic. Not just once — but every single day.

I looked at Lu and said, "I want more, so I'm choosing more."

And with that, I took one final breath into the girl who once begged for someone to choose her and exhaled into the woman who finally chose herself.

I put on my new anthem, cranked it all the way up and

started to move — letting the lyrics coat my skin in shivers as
the rhythm carried me somewhere new:

"When heaven takes you home,
And you're untouchable,
Tell 'em how you backflip through tragic,
Show 'em how the struggle made magic."
— HEAVEN TAKES YOU HOME, BY CONNIE
CONSTANCE AND SWEDISH HOUSE MAFIA

AFTERWORD

FOR MY THIRTIETH birthday, I finally allowed myself to feed both sides of my persona — the ones I had spent most of my life compartmentalizing. The wanderer and the wild child. The deep feeler and the disco queen. Up until then, I didn't know how to accommodate these so-called "multiple personalities" that lived inside of me — my range of interests, my contradictory thoughts, my craving for both stillness and spectacle.

So I honored them both.

One weekend I was in Las Vegas, dancing like a stripper on top of tables, covered in glitter and tequila, my body electric with movement and freedom. The next weekend, I got lost in Glacier National Park, my feet blistered and soul cracked open under the weight of endless miles of hiking and the silence only nature can offer.

It was on a 17-mile hike, somewhere between the sound of my breath and the crunch of earth beneath my boots, that Varun turned to me and asked, "What do you want to be known for when you die?"

I paused — not just from the question, but from the weight of it. From the recognition that, for so long, I had been afraid to even ask myself that. I'd been so busy performing, achieving, running, building, proving. Afraid that if I stopped, I'd find nothing underneath. Afraid of the quiet.

Pema Chödrön wrote, "To be fully alive, fully human, and completely awake is to be continually thrown out of the nest. To live fully is to always be in no-man's-land, to experience each moment as completely new and fresh. To live is to be willing to die over and over again."

And in that moment, high in the Montana air with the sun painting the peaks gold, I exhaled and let a part of me die. The part that thought I had to be one thing. The part that believed I needed to shrink myself to be digestible. The part that couldn't see how contradiction was simply another name for wholeness.

After a few deep breaths and some careful consideration, I answered, softly but clearly: "A light."

Not perfect. Not always certain. But bright. Warm. True. Something to help others find their way — just as I have finally begun to find mine.

And that's what I want this book to be. Not a manual. Not a map. But a lantern.

A reminder that you are not broken. That healing is not a destination but a returning. To your softness. To your strength. To your truth. That grief and joy can sit beside each other. That heartbreak can be an opening. That choosing yourself is never the wrong choice — even when it's the hardest one.

This book is for the one sitting alone on their couch, wondering if they'll ever feel okay again. It's for the dreamer who's lost their way, the lover who wasn't chosen, the seeker who's trying to remember who they really are.

It's for anyone walking through their own fire, wondering if the other side is even real.

I'm here to tell you: it is.

And it's even better than you imagined. Not because it's perfect — but because it's yours.

ACKNOWLEDGEMENTS

To each of you who held me — whether in arms' reach or from across the globe — thank you.

Words will never fully capture what your presence has meant to me, even in the moments I'm sure you wanted to knock some sense into me. Your patience, your belief, your unwavering love — it was the lifeline I didn't always know how to ask for but always, somehow, found wrapped around me.

You witnessed me at my most lost and still reminded me of my light. You celebrated my messy steps forward. You stayed when it would have been easier to step away. You allowed me the space to stumble, to rage, to cry, to dream — and still, you held the vision of who I was becoming even when I couldn't always see her myself.

You taught me that real love doesn't demand perfection — it holds space for the becoming. You taught me that healing isn't linear — it's a dance, a messy, clumsy, beautiful dance. You showed me that even in my deepest loneliness, I was never truly alone.

This story, this homecoming, is not just mine. It's ours. It's stitched together with every conversation, every long hug, every teary-eyed laugh, every late-night text and call, every whispered prayer you sent out into the Universe on my behalf.

I love you — to the cosmos and back, and then some.

Thank you for being part of this story. Thank you for helping me find my way home.

Alex — Thank you for always having the champagne ready.

Andrew, Jeremy, Kendall, Marisa — Thank you for lending me your laptops when mine was stolen — true tech heroes — and for stepping in so I could keep this dream alive (and hit my deadlines).

Emily — My book doula, editor and publisher. You taught me how to write a novel, how to tell my truth, how to share it authentically. Thank you, for holding my hand every step of the way in this beautiful writing journey.

Energy healers — Lauren, Mindy, Pavan — thank you for showing me my inner truth. For sharing it in a way that wasn't too heavy for me to hold but enough that it created momentum for change.

Fernanda — A path in which I wish we didn't have to walk in parallel along, but am so thankful I had you by my side. You carried me into this next evolution of self.

Jacqueline — Our lives have taken such different shapes, and yet, you always meet me exactly where I am. You are my anchor and my mirror. You'll forever be my favorite late-night phone call.

Kelly — Your spirit is a breath of fresh air and being around you makes it impossible not to laugh, to sing, to dream bigger. Thank you for always bringing me back to myself.

Lisa — My soul knew you before we even met and I'm so honored that we get to spend real time together in this lifetime. You beautiful, creative, spunky human, you.

Samantha — Thank you for the brilliant title idea. I owe you.

Scharn — You love big and selflessly, always placing others

before yourself. Thank you for seeing me through so many versions of who I've been — and loving each one.

Stef — An expander in so many ways. Your grounded spirit and no-nonsense love have kept me sane more times than I can count.

McDreamy's parents — You filled a space I didn't even know I was still trying to patch. I thought I just needed to hide the hurt, but you gently reminded me that love doesn't have to be earned or proven — it can simply be given. Thank you for loving me like a daughter.

Mom and dad — We've had our fair share of clashes and growing pains. Some of it's been messy, some of it heartbreaking, but I wouldn't change a thing. Everything I've shared in this book is a reflection of my experience, never a critique of your character. I love and respect you deeply. Let's close this chapter and write a new one together — one defined not by expectations, but by mutual love and understanding.

Therapists — Lynne, Julie — thank you for helping me to find my stability, for straightening the spirals in my mind, for walking this path with me.

Varun — Thank you for your perspective shifts, big and small. And of course, your very important questions.

Ariel, Caroline, Catrina, Dani, Danielle, Gina, Harriet, Jane, Jen, Jordan, Julie, Kelsey, Lindsay, Mariel, Marisa, Melissa, Morgan, Nicole, Rachel, Sahmaya, Shelby, Sloane, my entire Santa Teresa family — You've each played a role in stitching me back together. Whether it was a quick check-in, a shared adventure or a long, wine-filled night of unfiltered truth, you reminded me what it means to be seen and loved. Thank you. For everything.

A LETTER TO THE READER

DEAR READER,
If you've made it this far, thank you — not just for reading, but for witnessing. Not just the soaring highs or the gut-wrenching heartbreaks, but the quiet, messy, complicated, gloriously human middle. Thank you for wading through it all with me.

But I want to tell you something important: this isn't the whole story.

When I wrote the final chapters of this book, I believed I had crossed some kind of finish line — that I had chosen myself fully and could finally exhale. And in so many ways, I had. I was softer, steadier, more rooted in myself than I'd ever been.

But life, in its infinite wisdom, keeps offering new invitations. New mirrors. New truths.

Since finishing the manuscript, I've been challenged all over again — by longing I thought I had already let go of. By the ache of watching someone I once loved move on, again. By the realization that I still have a pattern of holding on when something feels *almost* right... even when I know, deep down, it's not.

And still, I keep choosing the work.

I extended my stay in Costa Rica, grounding in one place

longer than I had in years. After nearly a decade of movement, I paused. I stayed still. I rooted.

And in that stillness, I finally met myself. Not the curated version. Not the one built for performance or survival. But the truest one — wild, worthy, whole.

I stopped running.

I stopped performing.

I stopped waiting for someone else to choose me.

And I chose me.

Fully. Softly. Fiercely.

I've realized that my love of travel was never just about the places — it was about the permission it gave me to become. In new cities with new people, I could be whoever I wanted. Reinvention became my safety net. I was chasing versions of myself, trying to find the one that finally felt like home.

This book became a map — not to a destination, but to myself. It reminded me that healing doesn't come with a gold star or final exhale. It arrives in quiet nudges, in moments of truth, in the willingness to meet myself again and again.

After I turned in the first draft, more chapters unfolded. I sold my condo in Denver — the one I once thought I'd build a life in — and with it, officially released a chapter of my story I had outgrown. Then, just weeks later, my grandma passed away. I flew to Arkansas to celebrate her life and wish her peace and a pain-free afterlife. And in doing so, I was reunited with my parents for the first time in nearly three years. It was terrifying. And it was beautiful. A reunion layered in tenderness, boundaries and grace. One I wasn't sure would ever happen — and one that cracked my heart open in an entirely new way.

And still, I keep choosing the work.

Because healing, I've learned, isn't a straight line — it's a spiral.

It's one dance a day — sometimes literal — through grief, hope and becoming.

It's asking the hard questions.

It's softening when it would be easier to harden.

It's coming home to yourself, over and over again.

If you're in it right now — the swirl, the ache, the letting go — I want you to know that you're not alone. I created a companion journal, *The Only Way Out is Through*, for exactly those moments. It's filled with prompts and practices that held me — and continue to hold me — through the darkest nights. You can find it (with a discount) by scanning the QR code in the back of this book.

So if you're here, wondering when the pain will stop or the doubt will fade — I can't promise it ever fully will. But I can promise this:

Your capacity will grow.

Your clarity will sharpen.

Your peace will deepen.

You will remember your power. Again and again.

This story doesn't end with a wedding or a perfect job or a bow-tied version of success. It ends — and begins — with truth. With presence. With the courage to keep becoming.

Thank you for walking beside me, I'll keep walking too.

— Connie Kulczycki

THE ONLY WAY OUT
IS THROUGH

IF THIS BOOK met you in a season of heartbreak, grief or letting go — please know that you don't have to navigate it alone.

Scan the QR code below to access *The Only Way Out Is Through*, a guided journal I created to help you move through the emotions, not around them. Think of it like your own at-home retreat experience.

Filled with prompts, practices, quotes and space to feel, this journal is the companion I wish I had when my world was falling apart.

You've already taken the first step by turning these pages. Let's keep walking.

MOVE WITH ME

MUSIC CARRIED ME through the hardest moments of this story — it reminded me who I was when I forgot and helped me come home to my body when words weren't enough.

Scan the QR codes below to listen to the playlists that shaped this journey:

♫ **No Longer Her(e):** Each of the songs documented throughout this memoir, plus a few extras.

🎭 **A Dance A Day:** One song, one dance, every day. What started as a simple therapy prompt became a ritual of joy, embodiment and release.

Let them move you, the way they moved me.

AUTHOR BIO

CONNIE KULCZYCKI IS a writer and digital nomad who has spent the last eight years traveling the world in search of truth, healing and home. With a background in marketing and a passion for storytelling, she weaves personal growth, spiritual insight and emotional depth into everything she creates. Her work centers on helping women reclaim their voice, worth and desires through raw self-inquiry and embodied transformation.

When she's not writing, Connie can be found guiding women through major life transitions, teaching yoga or chasing sunsets with her dog, Lu. *No Longer Her(e)* is her debut memoir.

Learn more at **www.mindbodyworld.co** or follow her journey on TikTok at @conniekulczycki and on Instagram @ckulll.

Published by BOSS (Being of Sacred Service) Books. Toronto ✦ Tulum

Cover photography by Lisa Brester.
Illustrations by Connie Kulczycki.
Interior Design by Emily Snyder.

Made in the United Kingdom

www.ingramcontent.com/pod-product-compliance
Lightning Source LLC
Chambersburg PA
CBHW021213130626
46554CB00004B/1197

* 9 7 8 1 9 9 7 7 6 5 0 2 8 *